SWEDISH PERSPECTIVES ON PRIVATE LAW EUROPEANISATION

As part of the European integration, an ambitious programme of harmonisation of European private law is taking place. This new edition in the *Swedish Studies in European Law* series, the work of both legal scholars and politicians, aims to create a modern codification in the tradition of the great continental codifications such as the BGB and the Code Civil. A significant step towards this development was taken in 2009 with the creation of the Draft Common Frame of Reference which contains model rules for a large part of central private law. The process raises a number of questions. What are the advantages and disadvantages of such an intensive process of harmonisation? Are there lessons to be learnt from the Europeanisation of private law through history? Are there any further steps which have been taken in order to create a European private law? What is the future of European private law? These crucial questions were discussed at a conference in Stockholm, sponsored by the Swedish Network of European Legal Studies. This important volume includes the answers offered by leading scholars in the field.

Swedish Perspectives on Private Law Europeanisation

Swedish Studies in European Law

Volume 9

Edited by

Annina H Persson and Eleonor Kristoffersson

·HART·

OXFORD · LONDON · NEW YORK · NEW DELHI · SYDNEY

HART PUBLISHING

Bloomsbury Publishing Plc

Kemp House, Chawley Park, Cumnor Hill, Oxford, OX2 9PH, UK

HART PUBLISHING, the Hart/Stag logo, BLOOMSBURY and the Diana logo are
trademarks of Bloomsbury Publishing Plc

First published in Great Britain 2017

First published in hardback, 2017
Paperback edition, 2019

A catalogue record for this book is available from the British Library.

Library of Congress Cataloging-in-Publication Data

Names: Persson, Annina H., 1963– editor. | Kristoffersson, Eleonor, editor.

Title: Swedish perspectives on private law Europeanisation / Edited by Annina H. Persson and
Eleonor Kristoffersson.

Description: Portland, Oregon : Hart Publishing, 2017. | Series: Swedish studies in european law ;
volume 9 | Includes bibliographical references and index.

Identifiers: LCCN 2016048079 (print) | LCCN 2016048396 (ebook) | ISBN 9781849466974
(hardback) | ISBN 9781509900961 (Epub)

Subjects: LCSH: Civil law—European Union countries—International unification. |
Civil law—Sweden. | International and municipal law—Sweden.

Classification: LCC KJE995 .S94 2017 (print) | LCC KJE995 (ebook) | DDC 346.24—dc23

LC record available at https://lccn.loc.gov/2016048079

ISBN: HB: 978-1-84946-697-4
PB: 978-1-50992-975-7
ePDF: 978-1-50990-095-4
ePub: 978-1-50990-096-1

Typeset by Compuscript Ltd, Shannon

To find out more about our authors and books visit www.hartpublishing.co.uk. Here you will find
extracts, author information, details of forthcoming events and the option to sign up for our
newsletters.

Preface

This volume, *Swedish Perspectives on Private Law Europeanisation*, deals with an area of law that has grown in importance. European private law is undergoing a major harmonization process as part of European integration. Many legal scholars and politicians have worked towards setting up a modern codified system of European law, which resembles the great continental codifications such as the BGB (Bürgerliches Gesetzbuch or German Civil Code), the French Code Civil and others. A significant step towards this development was taken in 2009 with the creation of the Draft Common Frame of Reference (DCFR), which contains model rules for a large part of European private law. What are the advantages and disadvantages of this intensive harmonization process? Are there lessons to be learnt from the Europeanization of private law throughout history? What further steps, in addition to the DCFR, have been taken in order to create a system of European private law? What will be the future of European private law?

These important questions were discussed at a conference in Stockholm, Sweden, on 22–23 April 2013. The conference was sponsored by the Swedish Network of European Legal Studies. The speakers were a mixture of well-known experts and a selection of younger scholars in the field. The topic of the conference was the harmonization of private law in the European Union. Despite this, there seemed to be a consensus at the conference that a full harmonization of private law was not the right path to follow. Instead, a partial harmonization was suggested. The development of private law since the conference has also shown that the system of private law is unlikely to be fully harmonized in a near future.

This important volume offers an insight into the interesting discussions that took place at the conference and developments since the conference. The volume contains a selection of chapters all written after the conference, but based on the discussions at the conference. Hence, the chapters are up to date. The chapters focus on the following themes. Firstly, the Europeanization of private law throughout history. Secondly, the European initiatives working towards a system of European private law, and thirdly, the future of European private law—problems and perspectives. The objective of the Swedish Network for European Legal Studies is to establish an independent forum that allows researchers to meet and discuss legal issues at both a national and an international level within the field of European law. We would like to thank the Network and the co-organizer of the conference, Professor Joakim Nergelius, Professor of Law at Örebro University, Sweden, for their support regarding this project.

Annina H Persson,
Professor of Private Law at Örebro University

Eleonor Kristoffersson,
Professor of Tax Law at Örebro University

Table of Contents

Part IV: The Future of European Private Law

Table of Cases

Table of Legislative and Quasi-Legislative Instruments

Italy

Roman Law

Part I

Introduction

1

A Plea for True Harmonization in Europe

J MICHAEL RAINER

S PEAKING ABOUT EUROPEAN legal culture implies knowledge of what Europe is and what we should understand by the term legal culture. Notwithstanding the difficulty of finding even a geographical definition of Europe, as far as its legal culture is concerned, I do not wish to limit Europe to the borders of the European Union (EU). A look at Norway and Switzerland should be sufficient proof of my reluctance. Undoubtedly, the EU has added interesting and considerable aspects to the European legal culture, for example, the purpose of the directives and their transposition into the national legal systems, the European Court of Justice and the increasing influence of its jurisdiction on national jurisdictions. However, it is now universally recognized that the idea of unifying the law on the basis of the directives and regulations, and of the creation of a common court could never have become a reality without the existence of substantial common roots.

These roots are manifold and can be summarized as our common legacy consisting of ancient philosophy, Roman law, Judaism, Christianity, the Renaissance, the Enlightenment, the American and French Revolutions, liberalism and constitutionalism. These elements led to the creation and the development of general rules, which form the fundamental basis of our existence: human rights and democracy. This common foundation is the result of a continuous struggle in order to achieve the above-mentioned aims and it was by no means an easy and uncontested evolution from Ancient Athens and Rome to today. To my mind, the law played an essential role in forging the European mind and intellect in exactly the way we know it.

Let us start with the past—we are deeply indebted to the Roman lawyers who insisted on creating a secular legal system, while excluding the influence of the different religions and their officials. From this time on—and this represents a crucial difference with many other civilizations—it was the law that dominated religion and not vice versa. We owe the fundamental concepts of individual rights—the rights of the person—to our Roman ancestors and we owe a scientific legal understanding and thinking to them, as they applied the rules of the Greek scientific thinking to the law. Finally, at the centre, were their reflections on the idea of justice. The Roman lawyers based their legal system on case law, which unlike English case law, was continuously developed with the aid of scientific methodology until the end of the Roman Empire. Roman law only survived the fall of the Empire as the law of the Latin-speaking population. A longlasting change was initiated during the 12th century, a century which must be considered as a true Renaissance period in Europe from a multitude of points of view. Historians tell us, for instance, about an economic boom—probably due to climatic changes—of enormous dimensions. Lawyers in Bologna rediscovered the true Roman law books, above all the Digest of the Emperor Justinian and proposed to the public authorities to introduce it as the basis for legal teaching. Teaching not just a practical education, and teaching based on a scientific legal system could only develop in the direction of scientific teaching.

The 12th century is the cradle of university life. Its birthplace was indeed Bologna and the public secular teaching was organized and financed by the state in order to form young lawyers. The secular law of the Roman State became the frame of modern secular statehood. By the end of the century, students from all over Europe moved to Northern Italy to study the law in the Roman law books, while professors moved abroad, first to France, then to the rest of Europe. One of them, Vacarius, reached Oxford. The professors' teaching was structured and they wrote down or dictated what they taught. It was the beginning of modern legal writing, starting with the commentaries. It is known that people from Scandinavia went to Italy and so Roman legal thinking and Roman legal principles smoothly made their way northwards.* The foundation of the universities of Copenhagen and Uppsala strengthened the influence of Roman law over Scandinavia.

If we were to glance at Europe in the year 1500, we would indeed find a well-established legal unity based on legal teaching (in Latin naturally), the commentaries written by the Italian professors called glosses and the institutional books written by Bartolus and Baldus, who were considered to be the most outstanding lawyers and who were very popular all over Europe. Above all we would notice the common legal terminology, a conceptualization due to these common presuppositions. However, despite and notwithstanding this apparent common basis, the concrete reception of Roman law in legal practice led to very different results depending on the different political realities and the various regions of Europe.

Contrary to what many scholars assert, common European law never existed as far as concrete application was concerned, but instead there were

---

* See Anners, E, *Den europeiska rättens historia 1*, (Norstedts Förlag, Stockholm, 1974) p 181.

many different legal systems in which Roman law played different roles. These differences were reinforced by the historical process following the French Revolution, which saw a new period of codification, the writing and publication of law books called codes regulating different fields and branches of the law, in particular, civil law, commercial law, criminal law and procedural law. The first codification to be completed was the French one; its most prominent book the Civil Code 1804, which is still in force today.

For the first time in European history, an entire legal system was put down in a normative and, moreover, national language understood by the people. For more than a millennium, law had been taught and often also administered in a language known only to the experts and not understood by the people. As opposed to, for example, Italy, Spain and above all Germany, France had a longer tradition of using the national idiom. This is also the case in Sweden. In France, not only was the law in the northern part of the country normally administered and applied on the basis of regional customs (coutumes) written in the local language but, since the end of the 17th century, scientific writing generally had moved towards the modern French language. One of the most prominent and important works for European legal thinking is Jean Domat's book, *The Civil Law in its Natural Order (Les Lois Civiles dans leur Ordre Naturel)*. Domat (1625–696) was a very learned judge from the Auvergne region who spent many years in Paris on a royal pension. If Roman law still forms a part of our common heritage, we owe it to a large extent to Domat. From the sources of the Digest of Justinian, he drew a system in which the legal institutes were presented in a structured way. He freed the Roman legacy from the heavy ballast of hundreds of years of interpretation and judicial decisions, and underlined its importance by writing in the national language accessible to all. The fathers of the Code Civil and above all the leader of the commission composed of only four lawyers who drafted the Code Civil had the wherewithal to follow Domat's systematic lessons.

Jean Etienne Marie Portalis (1746–1807) also followed the debate on the first French Constitution where we can read that a Civil Code should be 'clair et simple'. Today, we can admire the result of the commissioners' work—a near-perfect law book written in a comprehensive structured way following Domat's principles and full of solutions deriving from the Roman legal tradition. The actual content was to a large extent taken from the treatises of Joseph Robert Pothier (1699–1772), a judge and professor in Orléans, who in comparing the manifold expressions of the customary law of northern France to the applied Roman law of southern France, invented the methodology of legal comparison. Why was the Code Civil such a success? The French Civil Code was adopted by many countries and in Sweden, the introduction of a code was fiercely debated in the years before and after the fall of Napoleon. Sweden finally decided not to codify, but the intellectual influence of the French laws even in 19th century Sweden cannot be denied.

When we speak about the importance of the Roman legal culture within the European legal culture, it is due as much to Domat and Portalis as it is to the German legal tradition bearing in mind the legal writings of Friedrich Carl von Savigny (1779–1861), an exceptional lawyer and intellectual. He insisted again, just as Domat had done before him, on the importance of the Justinian sources and even excluded any other references. German legal culture was deeply affected by his teaching and the BGB, the German Civil Code from 1900, is the codified version of Savigny's and his pupils' research and writings. On the basis of the Roman sources and above all Digest of Justinian, the adepts of the German Historical School (Historische Schule), founded by Savigny, created the modern conceptualism of the law (Begriffs-jurisprudenz). As opposed to the French Civil Code, the German Code was not adopted as such by other countries, but the scientific efforts of Savigny and his pupils were for a very short period of time accepted in all German-speaking countries and still today German conceptualism is considered to be one of the most important methods in the field of legal thinking and legal application.

The most important aspects of European legal culture should be understood as inviolable general principles and a common general legal understanding and thinking on the basis of the laws of the Romans as they have been read and interpreted in modern times. These assertions do not only concern the narrower field of private law but are also based on our knowledge regarding public law. Montesquieu's *De l'esprit des lois* (1730) found a model for the modern division of powers and the fundamental idea of checks and balances in the Constitution of the Roman Republic. There can be no doubt that the fathers of the American Constitution, among them Adams, Jefferson, Madison and Hamilton, were deeply indebted to Montesquieu. A few generations earlier, Hugo Grotius had explained the foundations of international public law in his *De iure belli ac pacis*, a work deeply indebted to classical antiquity and full of citations from the Roman laws. While a substantial uniformity of legal thinking, legal methodology and application continued throughout continental Europe until the end of the 18th century due to university teaching on the basis of the most important Roman law books and their medieval interpretation, a very particular development took place in England. English Law, based on very particular terminology and above all with a very particular legal contents in public and private law, often remains a mystery to a continental lawyer. However, despite its singularity, English law is also one of the major streams of law deriving from Roman law. To begin with, with the Norman conquest in 1066, it was shaped by continental law—the law of Northern France. The law was further influenced by the continent through its Lord Chancellors who proposed new solutions based on notions of equity, derived from their former functions as clergymen of the Roman Catholic Church whose laws were based on Roman law or when already, in the middle of the 12th century, a professor from Bologna had started teaching Roman law in Oxford and, finally, when the United Kingdom introduced the Sale of Goods Act in 1893 based on the French model. However, English law remained a very special legal system due to a proud national development. Above all the law was written in the national language and it was therefore made for the people.

Although English law is the best known example of a unique legal system, it is not the only one; many systems have developed their own particular sets of rules even if their common roots may be considered deeper and stronger. I have already mentioned France and Germany with their common Roman heritage, which have each evolved very different legal systems. Even if, as far as the basic terminology is concerned, the mutual understanding between German and French lawyers is easier than between lawyers from the continent and the British Isles (UK and the Republic of Ireland), it definitely does not lack difficulties. To understand the French legal system, a German lawyer must study it and eat and breathe it and vice versa. The same applies if we think about Italy, Spain and Sweden. It is thus safe to say that there are many different legal systems on the European continent, which have evolved differently after centuries of particular circumstances and after the decline of the Latin language throughout Europe while local languages were developing. We can count many differences in the approach to the law; in legislation, jurisdictions, legal education, legal science, in the way a law is written down, in the way a court makes a decision. We are aware of the decisive importance of our national languages for the development of each legal system and above all of the inviolable right of all citizens to understand and access he law as a central aspect of our democracy. I shall not describe the manifold advantages of each of our legal systems here, but I would like to underline the particularities of Swedish law as proof of the importance of a national language during the course of legal history, the well-known Sveriges rikes lag of the year 1734 and King Charles XII, the legal teaching at prominent universities of, above all, Roman law which was taught and discussed also in Sweden. We have to mention the renowned Swedish King Gustav Adolf Vasa who created the courts of Stockholm and Gothenburg and insisted that only learned judges, ie judges who had studied law at a university—and studying law at a university meant studying Roman law—could sit in these courts. Finally, the Swedish model may also throw light on very modern developments like the discussion on codification and the excellent specific laws that were created as an essential contribution to European legal culture during the 20th century, the development of family law and the law of succession, and finally the invention of consumer protection. Sweden has been a forerunner in all these fields, a model for the other European countries and not only for Europe, but also for countries outside Europe We could in fact highlight the singularity of any of our European legal systems and thus admit that a centralized legal system is alien to European legal culture. This is why the harmonization of certain aspects of the law should be prepared and adopted with enormous legal sensibility and a deep knowledge not only of the different laws but also of the different legal systems of Europe. To my mind, EU legislation, through its directives, can sometimes be described as weak and poor; poor in its content and in its language. A thoroughly considered systematization is completely lacking. The jurisdiction of the European Court of Justice appears in a better light even if we need to review the way judges are appointed through political decisions.

Should we harmonize, maybe even codify our laws? Can we do so? Should we do so? Should we introduce a Civil Code for Europe? There have been a number of attempts at harmonizing civil laws and two well-known groups, the Academy of Private Lawyers in Pavia under the direction of Giuseppe Gandolfi and The Study Group on a European Civil Code headed by Christian von Bar have worked very hard in order to propose a civil code, at least in part. I have worked enthusiastically in both groups. However, my experiences of the last 16 years have led me to the conclusion that I am no longer in favour of such artificial and premature reforms. To my mind, certain questions must be raised and certain problems should be resolved. To begin with:

— We must start a debate on how to legislate and how to codify. This debate must include the structure, content and style of the laws. Should the laws be more descriptive or abstract? Should they be written for lawyers or for the people?
— The use of the English language as the only working language. This weakness has proved to be fatal in the past. The texts that have been drafted up to now by different groups and different persons do not use a common and unique English legal terminology. Nobody thought of discussing which English terminology should be used. We have at our disposal, for example, the English legal terminology, the legal terminology of Scotland and that of the common people, or should we expressly create a new English legal terminology, a terminology for Europe, for the new code? As far as legal terminology is concerned, the results will remain poor without consensus on this matter. This inconsistency of terminology must have had deep repercussions on the contents of the texts produced thus far. The main reason is that the English language is normally used in a practical rather than a legal way; it is after all the only language understood by everybody in the different groups and circumstances. Above all, we should develop a system that accommodates the drafting of legislation in more than one language, a sort of bi- or even trilingual system of legislation. Here, we should be open and look beyond the borders of the EU and there we will discover two prominent examples of bilingual codification: Louisiana and Quebec have developed a legal English terminology on the continental concepts and both are known to be excellent legal systems. In Canada, the

juridical bilingualism is the essence and the basis of modern legislation. In this sense, the need to create substantial legal dictionaries containing exhaustive descriptions of the different legal concepts and their exact meanings in different circumstances will become evident. A methodology to elaborate such dictionaries with the contribution of legal science and legal practice seems to be essential. This methodology should also take into consideration a multilingual approach and the support offered by translations.

— A systematic and deep structural collaboration between legal theoreticians, namely professors, and practitioners, namely judges, is essential for the future of harmonization. Both legal professions working closely together should give answers to the questions raised and try to develop a new and truly European methodology of harmonization.

Friedrich Carl von Savigny, whom I have already mentioned as one of the greatest scholars and jurists of all times, was fiercely opposed to any codification in Germany. In 1814, writing his renowned pamphlet, 'Of the vocation of our age for legislation and jurisprudence (legal science)', he stressed that his historical period was not mature for the undertaking that a common codification for Germany would have entailed. Even in a country where a common language was spoken, Savigny criticized the lack of a common legal language, a common legal terminology and of a common legal culture. He was right. When Germany achieved those aims, when lawyers finally spoke the same legal language because a common legal science had created a remarkable unitarian legal culture, the codification process could start.

If we look at the presuppositions of codification in Europe, it is more than evident that we have to take into consideration the huge variety of very different but well-functioning and well-established legal cultures and systems, in which many different languages are spoken. We cannot destroy our heritage, which lies in its variety nor can we ever be allowed to substitute it with an inconsistent, inapplicable and anti-democratic common codification. All our legal cultures form a part of Europe; each of them can contribute in a fair and positive way to the progress of laws in Europe. The Swedish example teaches us, in such an outstanding manner, how just one legal system has contributed to the benefit of all the other European legal systems. The time is not yet ripe for unification but it is possible for us to support a slower path towards harmonization. Today, the task at hand is to get to know each other, to study the different legal systems, their history and where they stand at this point in time. Our task is to shape a new open-minded European lawyer who knows and understands more than one legal system and more than one legal language. Our generation has the task of changing the legal education system in a truly European way, of sending our students to all the EU countries not just a few. Our task is to start a profound discussion on a new methodology in the fields of law, encouraging co-operation between universities, the legislative systems and the jurisdictions. However, let us not forget that Europe is a unity built on diversities and that our strength lies and will always lie in this unity that is a consequence of the diversities.

With these ideas and this methodology, we should proceed naturally and not artificially on the path towards harmonization. This harmonization will always be the result and product of the depth of the discussions on the different legal systems and cultures. Politically, economically and culturally, we will get closer and closer, and perhaps in the future Savigny's prophecies will become a reality also for our beloved Europe.

Part II

Europeanisation of Private
Law Throughout History

2

The Historical Roman Roots of 'Continental' Law Systems

DANIELE MATTIANGELI[*] AND LISA KATHARINA PROMOK[**]

I. INTRODUCTION

ONE OF THE most important professors of Roman law, Peter Stein, a Cambridge emeritus, said: 'When we think of the legacy of classical antiquity, we think first of Greek art, Greek Drama and Greek Philosophy; when we turn to what we owe to Rome what comes to mind are probably Roman roads and Roman law.'[1] The Greeks speculated about the nature of law, about its place in society, about its deep justice and about its philosophical roots. The Romans, on the other hand, did not pay much attention to the theory of law. Instead, they were deeply interested in the rules governing the individual's property, the different rights of the individual, the legal proceedings and various aspects of 'everyday' private law.[2]

The aim of this chapter is to describe the roman roots of the continental legal systems, such as the French, German, Austrian and Italian legal system. This is done by giving a brief overview of the developments that led to the codifications of private law.

[*] Senior Scientist, Faculty of Law, University of Salzburg, Austria.
[**] PhD student, University of Salzburg, Austria.
[1] P G Stein, *Il diritto romano nella storia europea* (Milano, Raffaello Cortina Editore, 2001). Translated from: *Roman law in European history* (Cambridge, Cambridge University Press, 1999) 1.
[2] Stein, *Storia* (2001) 1.

II. HISTORICAL OVERVIEW OF THE ROMAN LAW EXPERIENCE
FROM THE BEGINNINGS UNTIL ITS RECEPTION IN THE
EUROPEAN NATIONAL LEGAL SYSTEMS

A. Roman Law and its Development until *Corpus Iuris Civilis*

The ancient Roman law *(ius quiritium)* began to develop in the fifth or sixth century BC with the *pontifices* and this first phase ended with the so-called first Roman codification: The Twelve Tables. From the fifth century until the second century BC, Roman private law *(ius civile)* was developed by professional jurists and became highly sophisticated. It was a sophisticated case law system with a technical superiority of reasoning, but not readily accessible to the layman.[3]

The civil procedural law was based on the old systems of the *actiones*. The *actiones* were a number of claims that the plaintiff could use to protect his rights. At the same time, from the third to second century BC, the Roman *praetor (peregrinus and urbanus)* began to create new rules under the *ius honorum*. The rules of the *praetor peregrinus* were opened to all the people, and for the first time also to foreigners. The *praetor's* rules were created to integrate, to extend and to renew the jurisprudential law of the *ius civile*. During this time, the so-called *Republican* period, the Roman civil law (a genuine case law system) was comparable with today's common law, and the *ius honorum* was comparable with the current principles of equity.[4]

The proceedings of the *ius honorum* were originally based on the judicial procedure of the *iudicia bonae fidei*. Those were proceedings in front of the *praetor,* based on equity. They transformed into a new procedure in front of the *praetor*: the proceeding *per formulas*.[5] This new proceeding was accessible to all citizens and to all foreigners *(peregrini)*.[6]

The professional jurists and the *praetor* continued to interpret and to renew the civil law and the *ius honorum* until the third to fourth century AD. In 133 AD, Salvius Julianus codified the so–called *edictum perpetuum*, which consisted of all the praetor's rules that had existed up until then. The emperor Augustus, for his part, attributed an official 'power' to the most important jurists, the *ius respondendi*. The different interpretations of civil law given by these jurists were binding precedents.[7]

After the fourth century AD, the Roman law continued its expansion through the Oriental province of the Empire and was spread all over the new

---

[3] ibid 5.
[4] ibid 11.
[5] M Kaser, *Römisches Privatrecht* (München, Beck Verlag, 2005) 372.
[6] R Zimmermann, *The Law of Obligations: Roman Foundations of the Civil Traditions* (Oxford, Clarendon Press, 1996) 140.
[7] Stein, *Storia* (2001) (n 1) 21.

populations that were established in the territory of the Empire. Roman law reached its peak in the sixth century at the time of the Byzantine emperor Justinian. Justinian managed to create the first major law codification in human history: the *corpus iuris civilis*.[8] The *corpus iuris civilis* contained three fundamental parts: the code or *codex* (a collection of law statutes), the *digesta* (a collection of legal cases and comments relating to the praetor's rules) and the institutes or *institutiones* (a study book for the jurists). The fourth part is the part of the *novellae*.[9]

The *novellae* was a collection of imperial statutes that entered into force after the promulgation of the code. The *corpus iuris civilis* consisted of all the most important Roman cases and of all existing imperial statutes of that time. It was a special compilation of legal materials made to summarize he entire Roman law during the eighth century. After the death of Justinian, his text vanished for about six hundred years until it was rediscovered by the school of Bologna in the twelfth[10] century under the leadership of the famous jurists *Irnerius* and *Pepo*.[11]

B. Roman Law in the Middle Ages until Modern Time

Six hundred years after its compilation, Justinian's digest came to use in Western Europe as a source of rules and arguments. No doubt there had been manuscripts lurking in Italian libraries, but their bulk and the difficulty of understanding them had hitherto deterred potential readers. All surviving manuscripts of the digest today derive ultimately from a sixth century *codex* in Pisa, which was seized as war loot by the victorious Florentines in 1406 and is now part of the Laurentian Library in Florence.[12]

The relationship is not direct, but can be traced to a lost, amended, copy made in the eleventh century and known as *Codex Secundus*. This version was the source of the *vulgata* or *litera bononiensis*,[13] which was studied in the twelfth-century schools. The recovery of the entire *corpus iuris civilis* was a slow process, extended over much of the twelfth century, due to difficult work of the glossators.[14] The digest is available in three parts, known as *vetus, infortiatum,* and *novum.* The division bears little relation to the

---

[8] H Schlosser, *Grundzüge der Neueren Privatrechtsgeschichte* (Heidelberg, CF Müller Verlag, 2005) 29 et seq.
[9] Stein, *Storia* (2001) (n 1) 34,41 et seq; Zimmermann, *Law of Obligations* (n 6) 18, 26 et seq.
[10] Schlosser, *Grundzüge* (n 5) 37 et seq.
[11] Stein, *Storia* (n 1) 43.
[12] Stein, *Storia* (n 1) 53 et seq.
[13] J M Rainer, *Das römische Recht in Europa* (Wien, Manz Verlag, 2012) 78.
[14] Rainer, *Römische Recht* (n 13) 82 et seq.

original structure, *vetus* being books 1 to 24.2, *infortiatum* books 24.3 to 38 and *novum* books 39 to 50.[15]

With the teaching of Irnerius at the University of Bologna, the Roman law of Justinian began to have a new life and to spread all over Italy and Europe. At that time, the University of Bologna had many students from Italy (the so-called *intramontani*) and from all Europe (the so-called *ultramontani*). The revival of the Roman law started in Italy with Irnerius, Pepo and the school of the *glossatori*. Pepo was a consultant judge, his teaching was based on the citations of the texts of the code and of the institutes. He was also in the position to cite the digest in his forensic arguments. Irnerius was maybe the most important person for the rediscovery and the renewal of the Roman law. He marked the separation between the science of law and the practice of law. He reinvented a new jurisprudential science and proceedings to solve legal problems. The study of Roman law and the development of the Roman law school was rooted in Italy throughout the later Middle Ages due to the school of the *commentatori* (*Bartolus* was the most important professor).[16]

In France, there was another important school of Roman law influenced by Guido de Cumis and Pierre de Belleperche. They formed the so-called school of Orléans.[17] The school of Orléans takes the name from the University of Orléans. In the sixteenth century, with the advent of humanism, France took over the leading role with the *école de l'exégèse,* or *mos gallicus,*[18] through the work of jurists Alciatus and Cujas.[19] In the seventeenth century, it was the turn of the Netherlands to give the discipline a new impulse, as a result of the teachings of Grotius.[20]

In the sixteenth and seventeenth century, the so-called reception of Roman law in the different national systems in Europe, began through the teaching of Roman law in the different European universities. Throughout Europe, each country felt the need to develop a legal system inspired by Justinian's texts and that each evolved its own set of rules shaped by local circumstances. In Scotland, for example, the reception began in 1583 with an official act of parliament which refers to a civil law rule as "the disposition of the common law", by which the so-called *ius commune* was meant and not the English common law.[21]

At that time, three important universities, Aberdeen, St Andrews and Glasgow introduced the teaching of canon and civil law. In England, the situation in the sixteenth century was more complex. England did not

---

[15] Stein, *Storia* (n 1) 54.
[16] Stein, *Storia* (n 1) 56 et seq.
[17] Rainer, *Römische Recht* (n 13) 95 et seq.
[18] Schlosser, *Grundzüge* (n 5) 45.
[19] Rainer, *Römische Recht* (n 13) 155 et seq.
[20] Stein, *Storia* (n 1) 83.
[21] Stein, *Storia* (n 1) 106 et seq.

adopt a civil law (Roman and canon law) system, even though the English common law and the principles of equity were strongly influenced by that legal system.[22] For example, the most important institution of equity is the trust, and it derives from the Roman *fiducia*. At that time, the universities of Cambridge and Oxford began to teach Roman civil law as well.[23]

The reception of the Roman law in France began in the thirteenth century with the school of Orléans, and continued with the *mos gallicus* and with the introduction of the Roman procedural law in the seventeenth century. It finally ended in the nineteenth century with Napoleon's *Code Civil* (1804). The intellectual fathers of Napoleon's *Code Civil* were Pothier, a magistrate, and Domat, a Roman law professor. But the code was written by a remarkable jurist, Portalis.[24]

Portalis managed to write the code in a unique way, with general and yet comprehensible rules. The *Code Civil* written by Portalis was a great legal work, understandable by all people and not only by jurists. The French Civil Code is still the base of many modern codes such as the Italian, the Spanish, and many Latin American codes. The reception of Roman law in Germany began quietly in the fourteenth century with the introduction of the study of Roman law in different German-speaking universities: Prague (1348), Vienna (1365), Heidelberg (1385) and Cologne (1388).[25]

In the last decades of the fifteenth century, certain *Schöffen* courts, such as that in the free city of Frankfurt am Main, allowed the use of a form of Roman-canonical procedure, with written pleadings drafted by trained advocates. It was the first step for the reception of Roman law in the Holy Roman Empire (the old German/Continental Europe Kingdom). The ease and speed with which Roman law was received in Germany in the early sixteenth century were surprising.[26] During this period, the Supreme Court of the Holy Roman Empire (*Reichskammergericht*) adopted the Roman procedure and had to decide according to the common law (*gemeines Recht—ius commune*) of the Empire, which was based on the Roman rules.[27]

In the seventeenth century, the reception of Roman law in Germany increased massively, and even after the end of the Holy Roman Empire, the Roman rules were adopted by the new Prussian Kingdom. In the eighteenth century, the Roman rules were the common law of Central Europe, and they were used in Germany, Poland, Czech Republic, Austria, Hungary, Bavaria, and in the entire territory of the Austrian Empire.[28]

[22] Rainer, *Römische Recht* (n 13) 129 et seq.
[23] Stein, *Storia* (n 1) 108 et seq.
[24] Stein, *Storia* (n 1) 111 et seq, 139 et seq.
[25] Stein, *Storia* (n 1) 109 et seq.
[26] Schlosser, *Grundzüge* (n 5) 76 et seq.
[27] Stein, *Storia* (n 1) 109–113.
[28] Stein, *Storia* (n 1) 111 et seq.

III. THE CODIFICATION MOVEMENT OF PRIVATE LAW
IN CENTRAL EUROPE

At the end of the seventeenth and during the eighteenth century, a new codification movement began in Central Europe, in order to translate Roman law into German. The first attempts of these 'national codification movements' were the Bavarian Civil Code (1756 AD), the Prussian *Allgemeines Landesrecht* (ALR 1794),[29] and the Austrian codification (the first draft was the *Codex Theresianus* 1766, the second was the ABGB (*Allgemeines Bürgerliches Gesetzbuch*), which finally came into force in 1812.[30]

The Bavarian Code was a practical Roman case law text, written in clear German and without any trace of general legal theories. The Prussian ALR was another example of Roman case law with 19,000 articles, written in German. The *Codex Theresianus* (8,397 articles) did not come into force and it was a mixture of Roman law, natural law and *ius commune* of the Middle Ages. Its 'father' was Karl Anton von Martini. In this Code, he introduced a general legal theory, influenced by Roman law and natural law.[31]

The ABGB was the product of a famous Austrian jurist, Franz von Zeiller, who produced a code of 1,502 articles, which came into force in 1812.[32] The Austrian ABGB was strongly influenced by the institutes of Gaius, a Roman jurist, by Roman law of course, by natural law regarding legal theory and finally, by Immanuel Kant regarding philosophy.[33] At the end of the eighteenth century, and during the nineteenth century, following the French revolution, during German romanticism and under the influence of the new philosophical ideas of this century, a new school of Romanists started in Germany: The historical school. The school was founded by the famous Romanist, Friedrich Karl von Savigny. He reinvented the Roman law and created the modern science of the *Pandektistic*.[34]

The German science of the *Pandektistic*[35] transformed and renewed the subject yet again. They purified Roman law from its medieval influences and were thus able to 'rebuild' the ancient Roman law into its original state, without the 'filter' of Justinian. They not only reinvented the Roman legal theory (*Die Systematisierung*) but also renewed the modern legal theory (*die moderne Rechtswissenschaft*).[36]

---

[29] Rainer, *Römische Recht* (n 13) 203 et seq.
[30] Zimmermann, *Law of Obligations* (n 6) 21.
[31] Stein, *Storia* (n 1) 137 et seq.
[32] Rainer, *Römische Recht* (n 13) 238 et seq.
[33] Stein, *Storia* (n 1) 139.
[34] Stein, *Storia* (n1) 140; Zimmermann, *Law of Obligations* (n 6) 29, 1130.
[35] Schlosser, *Grundzüge* (n 5) 151 et seq.
[36] Stein, *Storia* (n 1) 141 et seq.

The two most famous Romanists of this school were Rudolf von Jhering,[37] who wrote *Der Geist des römischen Rechts,* and Bernhard Windscheid's *Lehrbuch des Pandektenrechts.*[38] This school and the pandect-based science were the fathers of the German BGB (*Bürgerliches Gesetzbuch* 1900, still in force, with modifications). The influence of this Roman-German legal science was immense, even outside of Germany.[39]

Another important codification was the Italian Civil Code of 1942,[40] which remains in force today (with modifications). The Italian Civil Code is a French-based civil code, with a strong influence of the German pandect-based science.[41]

IV. CONCLUSIONS AND FINAL REMARKS

Fundamental to an understanding of the different modern legal systems in Europe, from both a theoretical and practical perspective, is an understanding of its roots and the roots of the legal systems from which it has evolved. In this chapter, we have shown that there are mainly two different methods of reception of Roman law which have been significant for the development of the civil codes of continental Europe: the reception based on the commentaries of the *Corpus Iuris Civilis* of Justinian and the reception based on the German Pandectistic School. The reception based on the commentaries of the *Corpus Iuris Civilis* of Justinian is founded on Roman law as it was understood at the time of the sixth century during the Byzantine Empire. The reception based on the German Pandectistic School is a modern phenomenon dating to the eighteenth and nineteenth century, but with the aim of rebuilding the ancient Roman law from before the time of the emperor Justinian. Hence the Pandectistic School relies on older Roman law. The Roman law roots of the French Civil Code are Justinian, the roots of the German BGB are Pandectistic, whereas the Italian Civil Code is strongly influenced by both schools. When EU harmonization measures such as the Draft Common Frame of Reference, are taken, the similarities of European Private Law may easily be over-estimated. There are apparent differences across the various European legal systems, from the British common law system to the various continental systems of Germany, France or Austria, or the mixed legal systems of Scotland and the Nordic countries. Hence, harmonization of European Private Law is a challenging project.

---

[37] Rainer, *Römische Recht* (n 13) 345 et seq.
[38] Rainer, *Römische Recht* (n 13) 332 et seq.
[39] Stein, *Storia* (n 1) 149 et seq.
[40] Schlosser, *Grundzüge* (n 5) 217 et seq.
[41] Stein, *Storia* (n 1) 152 et seq.

Part III

Harmonisation of Private Law in the EU: Comparative and Global Perspectives

3

The Influence of European Initiatives in National Courts—The Case of the Spanish Supreme Court

YOLANDA BERGEL SAINZ DE BARANDA*

I. THE INFLUENCE OF EUROPEAN INITIATIVES IN NATIONAL COURTS**

THE DIFFERENT NON-BINDING initiatives promoted by several working groups to modernize the law of obligations and contract law in Europe, have had a major influence in EU countries.

In this chapter, we focus on three of those initiatives: The Principles of European Contract Law (hereinafter, 'PECL'),[1] the Principles of European Tort Law (hereinafter, 'PETL'),[2] and the Draft Common Frame of Reference (hereinafter, 'DCFR').[3] We are aware of the importance of other initiatives to harmonize private law in Europe and their major impact cannot be disregarded (eg, the Principles of European Insurance Law), but we focus our attention on these three texts due to their broader scope and the key role that they have played in this harmonization process.

* Professor of Civil Law at Universidad Carlos III de Madrid, Spain
** This chapter is the result of my participation at the International Spring Conference organized by the Swedish Network for European Legal Studies that took place in Stockholm on April 22 and 23, 2013.
[1] The Commission on European Contract Law (Lando Commission), Principles of European Contract Law Parts I and II, 1999, Part III, 2002 at www.frontpage.cbs.dk/law/commission_on_european_contract_law/
[2] European Group on Tort Law, European Principles of Tort Law, 2005 and 2009 at www.egtl.org/
[3] Study Group for a European Civil Code, outline edition 2009 at www.sgecc.net/

Scholars have often commented on the influence of such non-binding texts on national legislators and arbitration,[4] but little has been said about their influence on the judiciary. It is true that the impact on legislation has been considerable, as national laws have been amended or in the process of being amended taking into account all these European soft-law initiatives. We might, for instance, just mention their impact on the reform of the German BGB or modern Dutch law,[5] and in the future modernization of the French[6] and Spanish[7] Civil Codes.[8] However, apart from the influence on law-making, we cannot disregard the enormous effect that these non-binding texts have on the national courts. The power to achieve harmonization does not only lie with national legislators, but also with the national courts. We might even say that the harmonization of European private law through the judiciary might be a better way to achieve harmonization as it is slower, less radical and more adapted to the legal traditions and necessities of the different European countries.

In this chapter, we will not discuss whether harmonization is a good or a bad thing, although it is being questioned these days. We will describe how these texts have affected the European legal system and how they have influenced the judiciary, in particular the Spanish Supreme Court.[9] We are aware of the impact of these texts in other jurisdictions; the fast and profound influence of the DCFR on the Swedish Supreme Court is well

[4] However, the influence of these European initiatives on arbitration proceedings is smaller than on national courts. Other initiatives, such as the UNIDROIT Principles, have been more influential in arbitration. It has been pointed out that this is probably due to their scope; the UNIDROIT Principles being applicable to international commercial contracts; the liberty that the parties have in arbitration proceedings and the fact that arbitrators tend to use comparative law in their decisions and are not bound by the application of a particular national law (Perales, P, 'Principios de UNIDROIT y PDCE en el arbitraje internacional', in *Principios de Derecho Contractual Europeo y Principios de UNIDROIT sobre Contratos Comerciales Internacionales* (Madrid, Dykinson, 2009), p 163.

[5] See, eg, Busch, D, Hondius, EH, Van Kooten, HJ, Schelhaas, HN, Schrama, WM (eds.), *The Principles of European Contract Law and Dutch Law. A Commentary* (Nijmegen/The Hague/London/Boston, Ars Aequi Libri/Kluwer Law International 2002); and, with regard to their influence in the judiciary, Busch, D, 'The Principles of European Contract Law before the Supreme Court of the Netherlands. On the Influence of the PECL in Dutch Legal Practice', ZEuP, 3/2008, pp 549–562.

[6] There are several ongoing projects in France and the aim is to reform French contract law. Among them, the Proposals for Reform of the Law of Obligations and the Law of Prescription (this is the official translation of the Catala report), led by Professor Catalá from 2005 (the 'Avant-projet Catalá'); the Proposal for the Reform of the Law of Contract of the Académie des Sciences Morales et Politiques led by Professor Terré in 2008, and the group of the Cour de Cassation set up to work on the Avant-projet Catalá led by Pierre Sargos of 2007, stand out.

[7] Spanish Proposal for the Modification of the Law of Obligations and Contract Law (hereinafter, the 'Spanish Proposal') by the General Commission of Codification, Ministry of Justice, 2009.

[8] The Spanish Civil Code is also referred to in this chapter by the abbreviation 'Cc'

[9] Spanish Supreme Court judgments are referred to by the abbreviation 'STS'.

known,[10] but we shall focus on the Spanish High Court because it has been extremely active in receiving, studying, assuming and using these European texts.

The texts did not really foresee the influence that they were going to have on the judiciary. Article 1:101 (4) PECL only states that: 'these Principles may provide a solution to the issue raised where the system or rules of law applicable do not do so'.[11] The PETL were even more timid. Under Goals and Objectives, after pointing out the differences in the foundations of Tort Law in the European legal systems, it says that the PETL 'have an important academic as well as practical value'. The DCFR is more explicit. Among its Purposes (Purpose 8), it considers itself 'a possible source of inspiration' for national legislators and for the judiciary, continuing the trend started by the PECL. Thus, 'it will have repercussions for reform projects within the European Union at both national and Community Law levels, and beyond the EU. If the content of the DCFR is convincing, it may contribute to harmonious and informal Europeanisation of private law'.

As we have mentioned, the Spanish Supreme Court has been open to the incorporation of these texts in its judgments. And not just open but deeply affected by them. These European initiatives have been quoted by the Spanish Supreme Court many times for a variety of reasons. The figures speak for themselves. It all started with a very active assumption with regard to the PECL that continues today. In 2008, the Spanish Supreme Court mentioned the PECL twice, a further two times in 2009, once in 2010, once in 2011 and seven times in 2012. The lower courts have followed suit, quoting the PECL at least 260 times between 2006 and 2012.[12] It continued with the deep impact of the PETL, which were mentioned four times by the Spanish Supreme Court in 2010, once in 2011 and twice in 2012. The lower courts have mentioned the PETL at least 79 times between 2006 and 2012. Finally, the DCFR had an immediate influence on the Spanish Supreme Court. It was mentioned no less than ten times in 2010, twice in 2011 and three times

---

[10] For example, the first judgment quoting the DCFR on 3 November 2009 (commented by Grochowski, M, 'The practical potential of the DCFR judgment of the Swedish Supreme Court of 3 November 2009, Case T 3-08', ECLR (2013); 9 (1), 96–104).

[11] The Preamble of the UNIDROIT Principles, in their 2004 version, is bolder. It provides that the UNIDROIT Principles may be 'used to interpret or supplement domestic law'. Explaining how such use shall be effectuated, the Preamble states that 'in applying a particular domestic law, courts and arbitral tribunals may be faced with doubts as to the proper solution to be adopted under that law, either because different alternatives are available or because there seem to be no specific solutions at all', the Principles should be a 'source of inspiration'. And thus, 'the domestic law in question would be interpreted in accordance with internationally accepted standards...'

[12] Incredible figure, although we have to admit that mostly, lower courts refer to them by quoting what the Supreme Court has said about a particular matter. However, this is not always the case, and lower courts sometimes use the European texts on their own initiative.

in 2012. The lower courts have quoted the DCFR at least 19 times between 2010 and 2012.

It would be unfair if we did not point out that these initiatives which we are considering have had other companions in the mind of the Spanish Supreme Court. The United Nations Convention on Contracts for the International Sale of Goods (hereinafter, the 'CISG'), which has been part of the Spanish legal system since 1 August 1991[13] and the UNIDROIT Principles of International Commercial Contracts (hereinafter, 'UNIDROIT Principles')[14] have also been an important tool in the hands of the judiciary for the modernization of the Spanish law of contract and law of obligations.[15] In fact, the UNIDROIT Principles and the CISG had a strong influence on the PECL. Articles from these two texts are quoted in many judgments alongside the corresponding article dealing with the same subject in the European initiatives that we are referring to here.

That said, there are three basic questions that we intend to answer in the remainder of this chapter. For what purpose does the Spanish Supreme Court use the non-binding European initiatives? In what matters has it used them? And, the most important question with regard to the necessary legal support of the decisions, what is the legal basis for their use?

II. PURPOSE PURSUED AND SUBJECT MATTERS INFLUENCED BY THE EUROPEAN INITIATIVES

A. The Principles of European Contract Law

The Spanish Supreme Court has made reference to the PECL for three different reasons: (i) to confirm legal principles or rules of the Spanish legal system; (ii) to confirm previous interpretations or previous principles set by the Spanish Courts; and (iii) to interpret national law in accordance with the PECL, arriving at solutions very close to those provided for in the PECL, but adapted to the particularities of the Spanish legal system.

---

[13] The adhesion instrument is dated 17 July 1990, but was not published in the Spanish Official Bulletin until 30 January 1991 (BOE n° 26; rect BOE 22 November 1996, n° 282).

[14] UNIDROIT Principles (Rome, 1994, 2004, 2010) at www.unidroit.org.

[15] In this regard, see, Perales, P, 'La aplicación jurisprudencial en España de la Convención de Viena de 1980 sobre compraventa internacional, los principios UNIDROIT y los Principios del Derecho Contractual Europeo: de la mera referencia a la integración de lagunas', *La Ley*, año XXVIII, n° 6725 (2007). The web page www.uc3m.es/cisg contains a list and a summary of all the decisions of the Spanish courts and courts in other Spanish-speaking countries that mention the CISG.

With these three different aims, the Supreme Court has touched upon the following areas:

— The confirmation of legal principles or rules: good faith and fair dealing (1:201);[16] excuse due to an impediment (8:108);[17] the right to damages and the measure of damages (9:501, 9:502, 9:505).[18]

— The confirmation of interpretations or principles set by the Spanish courts: the sufficient agreement and determination of price (2:103/6:104);[19] the legal interpretation of silence when there is duty to disclose (2:204 and 4:107);[20] primacy of the common intention of the parties in the interpretation of contracts (5:501);[21] preliminary acts relevant for the interpretation of contracts (5:502 [a]);[22] change of circumstances (6:111);[23] requirements for the termination of contracts (8:103, 9:303);[24] the right to withhold performance (9:201);[25] the possibility of extra-judicial termination (9:303);[26] the effects of termination (9:305 to 9:308);[27] future losses which are reasonably likely to occur (9:501 (2)[b]);[28] the right to damages and extension (9:503);[29] the presumption of the solidarity of obligations (10:102).[30]

— The interpretation of national law: the refusal of early performance (7:103);[31] fundamental breaches (8:103 [c]);[32] the compensation of debts through a court decision (13:102).[33]

Commenting on all the matters where the Supreme Court has referred to the PECL goes beyond the scope of this chapter. From this list, we would like to highlight those that have had the greatest impact on the modernization of the Spanish law of obligations.[34]

---

[16] SSTS 6080/2006, July 4; and 4977/2006, July 11.

[17] STS 822/2012, January 18.

[18] STS 532/2012, July 30.

[19] STS 362/2011, June 7.

[20] STS 242/2012, April 24.

[21] STS 285/2012, May 8.

[22] STS 285/2012, May 8.

[23] SSTS 822/2012, January 18, and 820/2013, January 17.

[24] SSTS 305/2012, May 16; 485/2012, July 18; STS 532/2012, July 30; and, 526/2012, September 5.

[25] STS 30/2013, February 12.

[26] STS 485/2012, July 18.

[27] STS 532/2012, July 30.

[28] STS 799/2009, December 16.

[29] STS 532/2012, July 30.

[30] SSTS 7351/2005, October 31; and 4977/2006, July 11.

[31] STS 924/2006, September 27.

[32] SSTS 705/2005, October 10; 305/2012, May 16; STS 532/2012, July 30.

[33] STS 321/2007, January 5, which has had great influence on posterior judgments (eg, STS 805/2009, December 10).

[34] With regard to the modernization of the law of obligations by the Spanish Supreme Court see, Roca Trías, E and Fernandez Gregorachi, B, 'The Modern Law of Obligations in the Spanish High Court', ERCL, 1/2009, pp 45–59; Díez-Picazo, L, 'Tribunal Supremo y

Firstly, there is the question of whether there is sufficient agreement for the conclusion of a contract and how the price should be determined (2:103/6:104). Article 1.445 Cc provides that 'by the contract of sale one of the parties binds himself to deliver a specific thing and the other to pay for it a specific price, in money or something representing money'. The wording of this article has been criticized for several reasons. One of them is that in practice the initial determination of the price in the contract is not necessary. In this regard, the decision of the Supreme Court of 7 June 2011 concerning the determination of the price of fuel in long-term contracts, provides that the indetermination of some of the elements of the contract is not an impediment for its perfection, as long as there is consent with regard to elements which are sufficient for the contract to be performed. From this, the Supreme Court understands that Articles 2:101 and 2:103 PECL (a contract is concluded if the parties intend to be bound and they reach sufficient agreement; and, there is sufficient agreement if the terms have been sufficiently defined so that the contract can be enforced) are 'illustrative'. With regard to the determination of the price, the Court refers to Articles 6:104 (determination of price), 6:105 (unilateral determination by a party), 6:106 (determination by a third person), and 6:107 (reference to a non-existent factor) of the PECL.[35]

Secondly, it is interesting to point out that the Supreme Court has mentioned Article 9:303 PECL which provides: 'a party's right to terminate the contract is to be exercised by notice to the other party'. This possibility of the extra-judicial termination of contracts is not foreseen in Spanish law and has been historically thought to be against Article 1.256 Cc, according to which, the validity and performance of contracts cannot be left to the will of one of the parties. However, the Supreme Court has lately affirmed that the right to terminate contracts can be exercised not only by starting judicial proceedings, but also through a declaration properly addressed to the other party, without prejudice to the courts to examine its validity if challenged. In this regard, the STS of 18 July 2012 is very interesting because it refers to previous Supreme Court decisions stating this possibility, and also makes a comparative study of law on the matter, quoting French and Italian law,

---

Principios Europeos', *Noticias de la Unión Europea*, 305, Junio 2010, 79–85; Vendrell, C. 'The application of the Principles of European Contract Law by Spanish Courts', ZEuP, 3/2008, pp 534–548; and, Perales, 'Principios de UNIDROIT' (n 4).

[35] The Court completes this illustration of the interpretation with a reference to Art 1.277 of the Spanish Proposal for the Modification of the Law of Obligations and Contract Law which provides: 'The perfection of the contract is not impeded by the fact that the parties have not expressed the price nor the way in which it should be determined, as long as the will to conclude it is unequivocal and a generally set price can be understood as implicitly agreed'.

the PECL and the Spanish Proposal which is written in a similar way in Articles 1.199 and 1.482.[36]

Another subject of interest is the joint and several character of obligations (Article 10:102 PECL). The Spanish Civil Code sets the general rule that obligations have to be presumed to be joint but not several in Article 1.137. For many years, the Spanish Supreme Court has interpreted Article 1.137 Cc in such a way that this general rule should not be applicable in certain (if not most) cases. It has said that solidarity is the rule in non-contractual liability, commercial obligations, and in most cases of consumer law, where the presumption of solidarity better protects the weaker party against the producers and providers of goods and services. Furthermore, the Court has established that solidarity can be inferred from the contract when it can be understood that the parties wished the obligation to be joint and several.[37] Since there is very little ground for this interpretation of art. 1.137 CC under Spanish Law, the Supreme Court has turned to Article 10:102 PECL for a helping hand.

The Supreme Court has also referred to the PECL with regard to the matter of good faith and refusal of early performance. Article 7:103 (1) PECL provides that a party may decline a tender of performance made before it is due except where acceptance of the tender would not unreasonably prejudice its interests. The case in which the Supreme Court referred to this article regards a contract concluded by a company, a producer of plastics, and a car seat manufacturer, the latter buying the plastics from the former. On a certain date, the car seat manufacturer communicated to the producer of plastics that a particular colour of plastic was going to be substituted with a different one, as requested by the actual car manufacturer. The problem arose because the producer of plastics, in order to be prepared for new orders, had already manufactured a large amount of plastic in the colour that was going to be abandoned. It, therefore, started a lawsuit against the car seat manufacturer asking for the price of that surplus. Article 1.125 Cc provides that when a certain date has been set for the performance of obligations, they can only be requested on that date; and Article 1.127 Cc provides that the terms established in the obligations shall be presumed to be set for the benefit of both, debtor and creditor. However, the claimant denounced a breach of Article 1.258 Cc, which states that the contracts 'not only oblige to their performance, but also to all the consequences thereof in conformity with good faith, the usages and the Law'. The Supreme Court

---

[36] Article 1.199 §2 of the Spanish Proposal reads: 'The right to terminate the contract has to be exercised through the notification to the other party.' Article 1.482 §1 states: 'In case of lack of conformity, the buyer can ask for performance, reduce the price or terminate the contract by his own declaration addressed to the seller.'

[37] For a clear explanation of the interpretation of Art 1.137 Cc by the Supreme Court, see Caffarena, J, Commentary relating to Art 1.137, *Comentario del Código Civil*, II, Ministry of Justice (1991) pp 119, 120.

decided in favour of the car seat manufacturer because the general rules (as could clearly be deduced from Article 7:103 PECL) allowed the buyer to decline an offer of performance made before the due date.[38]

Finally, we would like to highlight the reference made by the Spanish Supreme Court to the PECL with regard to the requirements for the termination of contracts and the concept of fundamental non-performance. This is probably the most important area of those we are focusing on and, in particular, it reflects the changes that Spanish law is undergoing and is likely to be subjected to in the future[39] regarding the concept of non-performance. The Spanish Civil Code contains the concept of non-performance based on the fault or intention of the debtor and, when that non-performance takes place, only a rigid system of remedies is available. However, in the last few years, either through the law,[40] or the interpretation that the Courts are making of Article 1.124 Cc[41] (with the invaluable help of scholars), a new concept of non-performance is being introduced alongside a battery of remedies in line with those foreseen in the CSIG and the PECL. With this in mind, the Spanish Supreme Court has, as we have already noted, interpreted Article 1.124 Cc and established requirements for the breach of a contract to give rise to termination (bilateral obligation, relevant breach, performance of the party who asks for termination, principal obligation and expiry). With regard to the concept of a relevant breach or fundamental non-performance, the Supreme Court has stated that there is no need for a persistent will of

---

[38] The Court expressly said: 'Certainly the criteria of good faith in the performance of contractual obligations is a principle that integrate contracts in accordance with art. 1.258 C.c. .... However, this criteria does not command the creditor the obligation to pay for whatever the debtor has produced in anticipation of future orders that have not yet been made. In this sense, the general rules allow the creditor to decline an offer of performance made before the agreed due date, as can be clearly deduced from Article 7:103 (1) of the European Principles of Contract Law.' This decision is commented by Vendrell, 'Principles of European Contract Law' (n 34) 540, and Roca Trías and Fernandez Gregorachi, 'The Modern Law of Obligations' (n 34) pp 57, 58.

[39] The Spanish Proposal for the Modification of the Law of Obligations and Contract Law tries to bring the Spanish law of contracts and obligations in line with a possible future European law of contracts. With that aim, it unifies the system of contractual liability by incorporating the concept of conformity. The lack of conformity of the thing with the contract constitutes a breach of the contract that entails the use of a battery of remedies established in Art 1.482 (performance, reduction of the price, termination, and, in any event, if appropriate, compensation for damages).

[40] We have to highlight the importance of the incorporation of Directive 1999/44/EC in Law 23/2003 on Guarantees in the Sale of Consumers Goods, today integrated in the Rehashed Law of Consumers of 16 November 2007, in Articles 114–127. In this regard, see, for eg, Díez-Picazo, L, 'Reforma de los Códigos y Derecho Europeo', *ADC*, Book LVI, IV, Oct-Dic. (2003) p 1.575; and Morales Moreno, AM, 'Adaptación del Código Civil al Derecho Europeo: La compraventa', *ADC*, Book LVI, IV, Oct-Dic. (2003) p 1.609.

[41] Article 1.124 Cc provides: 'The right to terminate an obligation is considered to be implied in reciprocal obligations, in case one of the parties does not perform what he was obliged to. The party prejudiced may choose between demanding performance of the obligation or its termination, with a compensation for damages in either case. He may also ask for termination even after choosing performance, when such performance becomes impossible ...'.

non-performance in order to terminate a contract; the debtor's fault is no longer necessary for the non-performance that leads to termination. In this sense, the Court has said that it is sufficient if the purpose of the contract is frustrated or the non-performance impedes the satisfaction of the creditor's interests, or the aggrieved party has had reason to believe that the other party's future performance shall not take place (in line with Articles 8:103 and 9:301 PECL).

A final remark in this context; there are certain matters, particularly related to the modernization of private law, where the PECL have rather surprisingly not yet been referred to by the Supreme Court. We are thinking about the question of prescription (Article 14:201 PECL sets a general period of three years). The Court is of course bound by the prescription periods established in Spanish law, but it is odd that it has not mentioned the trend in modern private law towards the adoption of uniform periods of prescription, at least in order to put such a sensible question in perspective.

B. Principles of European Tort Law

The PETL have not been as successful as the PECL, probably because it is a more difficult area in which to achieve harmonization due to the differences between the European legal systems in this field. From English tort law to the elaborated and systematic provisions of the German BGB, and the general clause systems, such as those that exist in France and Spain. Moreover, this is without taking into account the different ways in which non-contractual liability has been interpreted by national courts (eg, the creation in France of the strict liability rule for damages caused by things and for damages caused by persons under control).

Having said that, we also have to say that in Spain, the PETL have had quite an impact,[42] and the role of Professor Martín-Casals[43] in this success is remarkable. This impact is understandable taking into account that the Spanish Civil Code contains very few articles on non-contractual liability[44] and that it has been up to the courts to interpret them and develop (not to

---

[42] The following webpage contains a summary of the judgments of Spanish Courts quoting the PETL from 2005 to 2011 in Spanish and English: www.uc3m.es/portal/page/portal/dpto_dcho_privado/area_dcho_civil/home/research/research_groups/petl

[43] Professor Martín Casals participated in the elaboration of the PETL, has translated them into Spanish and has published many studies that have made the PETL known to Spanish Courts and scholars.

[44] Only nine articles. Article 1.902 Cc contains a general clause, whereas Arts 1.903 and 1.904 contain rules regarding liability for others. Articles 1.905 and 1.906 Cc regulate liability for damages caused by animals, and Arts 1.907 to 1.910 very briefly refer to particular cases (eg, explosion of devices, excessive smokes, fall of trees, emanations from sewers, construction defects, etc).

say create) a system of non-contractual liability. Therefore, the interpretation of the articles of the Civil Code has for many years produced a great deal of jurisprudence. From 2007 onwards, this jurisprudence has constantly referred to the PETL in different matters[45] and for different reasons (but mainly, we would say, to confirm previous Supreme Court interpretations of the Cc):

— The confirmation of legal principles and the interpretation of the Civil Code by the Spanish courts: the difference between causation in fact and causation in law (3:101/3:201);[46] causation in law (closeness between damaging activity and its consequence/purpose of the rule (3:201 (a) and (c));[47] the liability for auxiliaries and their need to act within the course and scope of functions (6:102);[48] recoverable pecuniary damage (10:201);[49] the concept of personal injury (10:202);[50] the concept of non-pecuniary damage (10:301).[51]

— The interpretation of national law: required standard of conduct (relation of proximity or special reliance/dangerousness of the activity (4:102.1)).[52]

---

[45] Lower courts have also referred to other matters. For example, proof of damage (estimation 2:105 PETL) SAP Barcelona 583/2009, November 18; damage caused by multiple activities (3:103(1) PETL) SAP Granada 70/2010, February 12; the general rule of fault liability (4:101 PETL) STSJ Galicia 280/2010, December 14; the concept of abnormally dangerous activity (5:501 PETL) SAP Zaragoza 436/2010, September 30, and SAP Zaragoza125/2011, March 17; the purpose of damages (10:101 PETL) SAP Barcelona 445/2008, September 10 and SAP Ciudad Real 210/2008, October 24; restoration in kind (10:104 PETL) SAP Barcelona 445/2008, September 10; and the measure of damage (10:203) SSAP Barcelona 138/2010, March 12, 645/210, December 9, and, 447/2010, July 13. All these latter cases concern vehicle damage. The Court took note of Art 10:203 PETL to find that if the cost of reparation exceeds the value of the vehicle, the compensation shall be the value of the vehicle at the time of the accident, adjusting slightly upwards because of expenses and inconvenience. The victim can only recover the higher cost if it is reasonable to do so.

[46] STS 102/2009, March 2.

[47] Ibid.

[48] SSTS 1446/2007, March 6; 1091/2007, October 10; and 269/2010, May 14.

[49] STS 383/2011, June 8.

[50] SSTS 366/2010, June 15; 786/2010, November 22; and 383/2011, June 8.

[51] STS 366/2010, November 3. Interesting because, surprisingly, it is not from the First (Civil) Chamber of the Supreme Court, but from the Military Chamber. The case was about a member of the military who was sanctioned by a higher official for a petty offence. The sanction was set aside by the lower courts but the sanctioned member of the army was asking for compensation for his non-pecuniary damages. This compensation was not granted by the Supreme Court because it was thought that the damage had already been compensated with the sanction being set aside. The Court found inspiration for the concept of non-pecuniary damage in Article 10:301 PETL as psychological or spiritual distress, not including aspects of the material damage.

[52] SSTS 831/2007, July 17, and, 144/2009, November 21, 2008. It is very interesting that the Supreme Court has taken into account Art 10:202 PETL in considering whether compensation for future medical costs for the damage should be allowed. According to the Court, medical costs brought on by the accident, since they have the purpose of restoring health and are intended to assure the victim a minimum quality of life, can be compensated as monetary losses.

As has been pointed out, the Supreme Court has not always used the PETL correctly.[53] On many occasions, it has used them to enrich previous Supreme Court decisions and even to provide new interpretations of the law that are more in accordance with the new trends at the European level.

As regards the latter reason, the best example is the reference made to Article 4:102.1 of the PETL, which is also the provision that has influenced the most and not only the Spanish Supreme Court but also the lower courts.[54] The Spanish Code does not contain non-contractual liability rules related to the required standard of conduct. Therefore, the rules established for contractual liability in Article 1.104 Cc are taken into account. Article 1.104 Cc only provides for the circumstances of the particular case, person, time and place as criteria to decide whether the required standard of care has been met. As opposed to Article 4:102.1 PETL, which sets various criteria[55] to determine whether the required standard of conduct has been met. The Supreme Court has found inspiration in Article 4:102.1 PETL to revise its previous trend towards the raising of the standard of the diligence required.[56] Since an early decision from 2007,[57] the Supreme Court has

---

[53] For example, it has referred to 'required standard of conduct in supervision' (wording of Art 6:101 PETL; the fault liability of the person in charge of minors or mentally disabled persons, with a reversal of the burden of proof) with regard to liability for auxiliaries and their need to act within the scope of their functions, regulated as a vicarious liability in Art 6:102 PETL. Also, in cases of uncertain causation for which Art 3:103 (1) PETL provides for proportional liability, the lower courts have found inspiration to establish 'necessarily' joint and several liability. In this regard, see, Martín-Casals, M, 'The impact of the Principles of European Tort Law (PETL) in Spanish Case Law, 1 *JETL* (2010) pp 308, 309, 321, 325.

[54] We have counted at least 35 decisions of the lower courts between 2007 and 2011 quoting Art 4:102.1 PETL.

[55] As Professor Martín Casals has pointed out, some of them where already used by the Spanish Supreme Court (the dangerousness of the activity; the expertise to be expected; the foreseeability of the damage), while others are more related to common law countries (the relation of proximity or special reliance between those involved). See, Martín-Casals, 'Principles of European Tort Law' (n 53) p 319.

[56] Under Spanish Law, the general rule is still that there is no liability without fault (Art 1.902 Cc). However, the Spanish Supreme Court interpreted the Civil Code with the intention of benefiting the person who suffers the damage. For that reason, it has reversed the burden of proof (it is up to the agent to prove his diligence) and raised the standard of diligence required (only extreme diligence exonerates from liability). See, Bergel, Y, *Handbook on Spanish Civil Patrimonial Law* (Tecnos, 2011) pp 185, 186. Lately, a new trend has been noticed in the decisions of the Supreme Court, going back to the general principle of fault liability and putting aside the reversal of the burden of proof which only applies in particular cases (eg, extraordinary risk).

[57] The facts of the case were that a couple went to a friend's house for dinner. Upon arrival, the visitor lady, who knew the house, went straight to see her friend who was in the kitchen. In the corridor (with a low light) on her way to the kitchen, she stepped on a toy, which had been left there by one of her friend's children. She fell and suffered injuries. She sued her friends (and of course their insurance company). The Supreme Court found that the care required of hosts who are parents of a small child cannot cover any danger, however remote, and that playing with toys at home is not an abnormally dangerous activity, so there was no reversal of the burden of proof. This case is considered by Salvador Coderch, P and Ramos González, S, 'Relaciones de complacencia y deberes para con los invitados', *InDret* (2/2008) 286–289; and, Martín Casals, 'Principles of European Tort Law' (n 53) p 310.

been more restrictive in the recognition of the existence of fault, rejecting[58] the existence of liability in cases where damages occurred due to 'ordinary life risks'. In the case of an ordinary life risk, the victim must assume the damage.

C. Draft Common Frame of Reference

Very soon after its publication, the DCFR had a major impact in Spain. Scholars have commented on it and analyzed Spanish law in the light of the DCFR, and the Supreme Court very soon started to quote it in its decisions. The role of the Supreme Court Judge Encarna Roca Trías, who was part of the Co-ordinating Group within the Study Group that prepared the DCFR,[59] has been of great importance. Taking into account the influence of the PECL in Spanish courts, as we have seen above, it is not surprising that the DCFR has also had quite an effect (the DCFR incorporates a revised version of the PECL in its second and third Books).

Having said that, it is true that the PECL have not lost their importance for the Spanish judiciary since publication of the DCFR. If, as we have seen, the DCFR received much attention from the Spanish Supreme Court immediately after its publication[60] (mentioned four times in 2010,[61] the year in which it only referred to the PECL once), its effect has diminished since (it was quoted three times in 2012, while the PECL were mentioned seven

---

From this judgment, fault and liability have been excluded in cases of distractions of the victim, normal obstacles or activities, trips, slips, falls, etc (eg, finger caught in the door of a bar by another client (SAP Cantabria 84/2010, February 4); a fall in a shower with a non-slip floor (SAP Lérida 202/2010, May 13); a hand smashed by a hydraulic door in good working order (SAP Pontevedra 905/2010, December 10); an injured toe upon hitting it at the entrance of a bank door (SAP Asturias 419/2010, December 10); a fall from truck scales due to the distraction of the victim (SAP Castellón 71/2011, March 4), etc.

[58] Article 4:102.1 has also been quoted to decide that the required standard of conduct was not met and, therefore, liability existed (eg, negligence in the maintenance of a building (SAP Granada 17/2011, January, 21); the lack of due care upon not warning of an obstacle in a transit area (SAP Pontevedra 314/2011, June 8); a fall caused by a protrusion in the pavement that was not signposted (SAP Madrid 486/2011, October 4); the absence of necessary precautions in carrying works in a ditch (SAP A Coruña 293/2011, November 4)].

[59] Encarna Roca Trías was also involved in the translation into Spanish of the Principles of European Contract Law alongside Professors Díez-Picazo, L and Morales Moreno, A.M, chairman and member respectively of the General Commission of Codification that prepared the Spanish Proposal for the Modification of the Law of Obligations and Contract Law. The translation of the PECL was published by Civitas in 2002.

[60] STS 870/2009, January 20, already quoted the presumption of the solidarity of obligations in the DCFR (III-4:103(2)) to reinforce the rules providing for solidarity in Spanish consumer law; and STS 366/2009, May 25, mentions the DCFR with regard to the preference for the interpretation of contracts which gives its terms' effect (II-8:106) alongside the Spanish Civil Code provision (Art 1.284) and the PECL (Art 5:106) in that sense.

[61] In 2009 and 2010 always by Judge Roca Trías.

times in that year). This is probably because Spanish judges are still more familiar with the PECL and more comfortable referring to them than to the provisions of the DCFR.[62] Also, as lower courts study and quote Supreme Court decisions in their judgments, it might be that we will see a scenario where more lower court's decisions mention the DCFR[63] in the not too distant future.

These are the matters regarding which the Spanish Supreme Court has referred to the DCFR:

— Showing how a matter is regulated in modern legal systems or the differences between the European systems: the preference for interpretation which gives terms effect (Art II-8:106);[64] the revocation of donations for gross ingratitude (Art IV.H-4:201);[65] unjust enrichment (Art VII-7:102).[66]
— Confirmation of interpretations or principles set by the Spanish courts: good faith and acts according to previous conduct (Art I-1:103.2);[67] the double effect of the termination of contracts (end of obligations (Art III-3:509) and the restitution of benefits (Art III-3:510));[68] and the solidarity of obligations (Art III-4:103).[69]

With regard to the subjects of the DCFR mentioned in these decisions, we have to admit that we find many more judgments where the Supreme Court quotes it without a great need to do so. In our view, in most of these decisions, the provisions of the DCFR do not add much to the legal reasoning, but just help the Court to 'decorate' them. For instance, with regard to the legal nature of unjust enrichment, the Supreme Court mentions the DCFR to show the difficulty of its legal nature taking into account that 'it has different meanings in the European legal systems as shown in the proposed regulation in the DCFR'.[70] With regard to the possibility of revoking

---

[62] The DCFR is being translated into Spanish and it is expected to be published soon. Many studies have been conducted looking at its different provisions (many published by InDret (www.indret.com), but a whole translation is not yet available in Spanish. The most complete study is probably the commentary to Books II and IV by Vaquer, A, Bosch, E, and Sanchez, M, *Derecho Europeo de los contraltos. Libros II y IV del Marco Común de Referencia, 2 volumes* (Atelier, 2012).

[63] In 2011 and 2012, the DCFR started to appear in lower court decisions (eg, AP Málaga, 198/2011, April 14 (III-4:103); AP Tarragona 75/2012, February 28 (I-1:103(2); AP Ourense 140/2012, March 23 (III-3:509/3:510); and AP Murcia 213/2012, April 20 (III-3:510(5)).

[64] STS 366/2009, May 25.

[65] STS 261/2010, May 13.

[66] STS 306/2011, May 6.

[67] SSTS 769/2010, December 3.

[68] SSTS 380/2010, June 22.

[69] SSTS 597/2010, October 8; and 198/2011, April 14, both to do with the rule of solidarity in consumer protection cases (joint and several liability of the travel agency and the organizer in the first case; joint and several liability of the seller and of the manufacturer of air conditioning devices in the second).

[70] STS 306/2011, May 6.

donations for gross ingratitude of the donee, it quotes Article IV.H.-4:201 just to add to the Spanish regulation thereof, because the real question in the judgment lay elsewhere.[71]

Probably the most interesting question as to why reference was made to the DCFR is the one dealt with in the judgment of 3 December 2010. The facts were that a company and two people acting as solidary surety had contracted a line of credit with a bank. On the expiry date in 1993, the principal of the credit was not paid and so the bank closed the account with a resulting credit in the debtor's favour. Between 1993 and 2005, the bank and the clients were involved in different extrajudicial proceedings regarding the said credit because the debtor was insolvent. In 2005, the bank started proceedings to recover the amount due as the client was in a better financial situation. The lower courts had declared the principal due, but said that the action to ask for the interest on the credit had expired. The bank went to the Supreme Court claiming a breach of Article 7 Cc ('all rights have to be exercised in accordance with good faith'). According to the Supreme Court, the bank acted properly and quoted the doctrine of scholars[72] and Article I-1:103 DCFR (good faith and fair dealing),[73] to declare that what Article 7 Cc sanctions is a contradictory conduct of the creditor which has made the other party confident in the appearance created by such conduct.

III. LEGAL BASIS

So far, we have looked at the kind of issues involved in cases where the courts have raised these European initiatives, and we have seen their reasons

---

[71] The case was about an assignment of property and a donation (in the form of a sale) by a couple to their daughter with an alimentary obligation on the part of the daughter. The father died violently and it was the mother who was condemned for the death of her husband after being accused by her daughter. The mother sued her daughter asking for the contracts of assignment and donation to be declared null for simulation and the donation to be revoked for ingratitude of the donee. Article 648.2 Cc provides that donations can be revoked: 'when the donee attributes the donor with a crime giving rise to official proceedings or public accusation, even though he proves such a crime, unless the crime was committed against the donee himself, his spouse or the children under his authority'. The Supreme Court mentioned the DCFR to show how this cause of revocation of donations has been more openly regulated in modern systems. As the particular accusation of the daughter had been annulled for being a close relative, the key issue of the decision was how the term 'attribution' of a crime in Art 648.2 Cc be interpreted.

[72] 'According to scholars, good faith entails that a right cannot be exercised when its holder has not only not worried for a long time to exercise it, but also when with his attitude he has given his adversary grounds to think that the right shall not be exercised'.

[73] Article I-1:103: (1) The expression 'good faith and fair dealing' refers to a standard of conduct characterized by honesty, openness and consideration for the interests of the other party to the transaction or relationship in question. (2) It is, in particular, contrary to good faith and fair dealing for a party to act inconsistently with that party's prior statements or conduct when the other party has reasonably relied on them to that other party's detriment.

for doing so. The aim of the courts is clearly to modernize the Spanish law of obligations and law of contract, and to confirm previous interpretations of the Supreme Court in order to show that they are adapting to the new legal trends. We now have to consider what the legal basis is to achieve these goals by taking this path.

All these European initiatives (PECL, PETL and DCFR) are non-binding texts, which cannot be applied by courts because they are not part of national law. In Spain, for rules to become part of the Spanish legal system, they have to follow a publication procedure. Only rules published in the Official Bulletin are binding rules applicable by the judiciary.

Therefore, Spanish courts cannot apply these European initiatives as ratio decidendi in their decisions. This entails that courts can only use the European initiatives as a source of inspiration and as a helping instrument in the application of Spanish law.

The legal base for courts to use these initiatives in their decisions is Article 1.6 of the Spanish Civil Code. It states that: 'case law complements the legal system with the doctrine repeatedly established by the Supreme Court when interpreting and applying the law, the usages and the general principles of law'. Therefore, case law is not a source of law in Spain (as it is in Sweden). Judges and courts have the obligation to solve the cases by referring to the established system of sources of law (Article 1.7 Cc). The decisions of the courts only add to the legal system through the interpretation of the law.

The courts have to be very careful when using the provisions of these European initiatives. Their application and the use made of them rely on the discretion of the courts. In a country like Spain, where the system of sources of law is limited and strict, the use of these initiatives in court decisions has to be well founded; that is, they have to be used alongside other legal grounds or other reasons. The danger of using them in a different way is that the judgment can be said to be arbitrary and against the system of sources of law.

The courts cannot incorporate the European initiatives into the legal system through their judgments, but they can use them to interpret the law in a modern way, with a modern perspective. This is allowed and encouraged by Article 3.1 Cc. It provides that, 'the legal rules shall be interpreted according to the meaning of their wording, in relation to the context, historical and legislative precedents, *and the social reality of the time in which they have to be applied, attending basically to the spirit and the goal thereof*' (emphasis added).[74]

---

[74] Our translation and our emphasis.

The Supreme Court has expressed its view on these initiatives several times, in particular with regard to the PECL. In a judgment of 31 October 2006, referring to the CISG and the PECL, it said that:

> 'the criteria stated in an international disposition of a conventional character which is part of our legal system *(CISG)*, also reflected in a document that legally formulates the principles (…) common to the different legal systems *(PECL)*, in as far as they reflect and try to order, with the purpose of elaborating uniform rules, the practice followed in relations that exceed the national scope, should serve to integrate Article 1.124 Cc following the mandate to interpret it in accordance with the social reality of the moment in which it is applied.'

In a 2009 judgment, the Supreme Court stated: 'the common origin of the rules in the European Principles of Contract Law allow their use for the interpretation of the existing legal rules on our Civil Code' (Spanish Supreme Court Decision, 17 December 2009). Recently, in 2012, it said: 'no matter if they *(PECL)* are not positive legal rules, they have an undeniable doctrinal value' (Spanish Supreme Court, 30 July 2012)

We understand that the Supreme Court has been very smart in the use of these European initiatives for its own purposes. It has sometimes used them to confirm legal principles or previous interpretations of the Supreme Court with regard to a certain matter; at other times, in order to show how a particular question is regulated in modern legal systems or to show how the regulation differs from one system to another. When it has used them with the aim of modernizing Spanish law, it has added to national law by interpreting it in a way that de facto arrives at a solution that coincides with the solution given in the European initiatives. The Supreme Court has been very clever in its use of the possibility granted to it by Article 3 Cc. The Spanish Supreme Court finds that it is its duty, in accordance with Article 3 Cc to interpret the law by using these European initiatives, which are an example of the modern reality of law.

IV. CONCLUSION

The European initiatives are no longer an academic instrument. This 'soft law' is 'softly' entering and inspiring the national legal systems.[75] They started the practice through the inspiration of the legislators in the update of the national law of contract and law of obligations and, as has been our concern in this chapter, through the practice of the judiciary.

---

[75] Of course not all European legal systems are 'affected' in the same way and with the same intensity, but we have mentioned examples of great importance such as the case of Germany, the Netherlands, France and Spain. The different levels of impact probably depend on the difference of the Legal System concerned and on the judiciary of the different European countries being more or less open to external influences.

The Spanish Supreme Court has used the European initiatives with regard to a large number of diverging matters. Sometimes, the Court has relied on the prestige of the European initiatives to add to its decisions;[76] sometimes, they have been used as a firm legal resource to decide cases alongside Spanish sources of law or previous court interpretations; and, at others, in order to interpret the law of contract and the law of obligations and to adapt them to a new social, economic and political structure.

Discussions are currently focusing on how far we should go with regard to the harmonization of European private law. Our view is that the use of the European initiatives by national courts in order to interpret national laws in accordance with these initiatives is the proper way to achieve harmonization. It entails an 'informal' harmonization of European private law, but one which takes into account the cultural and social particularities of the different legal systems. Perhaps a smaller, but longer-lasting harmonization. At least for the time being.

---

[76] According to Professor Díez Picazo, this is (and should be) the only purpose of the Supreme Court when quoting the PECL (Díez-Picazo, L, 'Tribunal Supremo y principios europeos', *Noticias de la Unión Europea*, n° 305, June 2010, pp 79–85.

4

Unjust Enrichment in Swedish and EU Law

ELEONOR KRISTOFFERSSON*

I. INTRODUCTION

THIS CHAPTER DEALS with unjust enrichment in Swedish law under
the influence of EU law. In Sweden, there are certain problems regarding unjust enrichment. The principle of unjust enrichment is not codified in Swedish law. Hence, discussions have been ongoing for at least a
century as to whether unjust enrichment exists in Swedish law or not. In
the case law of the Supreme Court the principle of unjust enrichment seems
to have influenced the Court's decisions. In some cases, the principle even
seems to have been the sole legal ground for the Court's decision. However,
the fact that in those cases the Supreme Court has not clearly referred to the
principle is a problem, and it makes it unclear as to whether the Supreme
Court considers unjust enrichment as a non-codified general principle of
Swedish law and, as such, a part of Swedish law. Furthermore, the principle
has been debated by legal scholars of private law in a way that has made
it controversial—either you are in favour of or against unjust enrichment.
Most legal scholars in Sweden seem to have taken a position against the
principle, either by denying its appropriateness or by denying its existence
in Swedish law, or both. This is changing now. Under EU law, unjust enrichment is recognized as a general principle of private law, both by the Court
of Justice of the European Union (CJEU) and in the Draft Common Frame
of Reference (DCFR), the latter has, however, soft-law status.

The aim of this chapter is to discuss the impact of EU law on the principle
of unjust enrichment in Swedish law. The concept of 'EU law' is used in a
broad sense, including both 'hard' binding law and non-binding soft law.
The outline of the chapter is the following. First, a brief introduction to the
Swedish legal system. Thereafter, there is a section on unjust enrichment in
EU law. After that unjust enrichment in Swedish law is described followed

---

* Professor of Tax Law at Örebro University, Sweden.

by a section on the future of unjust enrichment in Sweden. The chapter ends with some concluding remarks.

II. THE SWEDISH LEGAL SYSTEM IN BRIEF

The Swedish legal system is a mixed legal system. It differs from the continental European legal systems insofar as the written law is not as extensive in Sweden, and the way of dealing with legal problems is not as dogmatic as in the continental systems, but rather characterized by a pragmatic approach. It differs from the common law systems insofar as the case law of the Supreme Court is not binding and the written law, in many cases followed by the preparatory works written while drafting the law, such as Governments Bills,[1] are the most important sources of law. The Swedish legal system is, however, not a mix between the continental and common law systems, but is a distinct legal system similar to the legal systems in Denmark, Finland, Norway and Iceland. These jurisdictions are part of the Nordic legal family.

Sweden is a large country with few inhabitants. Its surface area is approximately 1.5 times that of Germany, but there are only 9.5 million inhabitants. Despite the relatively small number of inhabitants, Sweden has many courts. For cases of administrative law dealing with the relationship between representatives of the public, such as public authorities, the state as well as the municipalities on the one hand and individuals and businesses on the other, there are three instances of administrative courts: 12 administrative courts of first instance,[2] four administrative courts of appeal[3] and one Supreme Administrative Court.[4] For private law cases and criminal law cases, there are ordinary courts: 48 district courts,[5] six courts of appeal[6] and one Supreme Court.[7] The large number of district courts can be explained by the fact that the procedure in the ordinary courts is oral and Sweden is such a big country. Since the procedure is mainly written in the administrative courts, Sweden has been able to reduce the number of administrative courts of first instance in order to increase the specialization and the competence of the courts.

Sweden has a constitution, but it does not have a constitutional court. Hence, there is no abstract standard control carried out by a court. The constitutional rights can only be efficient in relation to a specific case. They are subsequently tried by administrative or ordinary courts, depending on the case at hand.

---

[1] SW: *Propositioner.*
[2] SW: *Förvaltningsrätter.*
[3] SW: *Kammarrätter.*
[4] SW: *Högsta förvaltningsdomstolen.*
[5] SW: *Tingsrätter.*
[6] SW: *Hovrätter.*
[7] SW: *Högsta domstolen.*

In Sweden, it is common to talk about legal sources and a hierarchy of legal sources. The only formally binding legal source is the written law, but also the non-formal binding sources are called legal sources. There are two non-written kinds of sources that are very important as legal sources. These are customs and general principles. A well-recognized principle of Swedish private law is the principle of *conditio indebiti*—the right to reclaim money that has been paid by mistake.[8] As mentioned above, the preparatory works are an important source of Swedish law, together with the case law of the Supreme Administrative Court and the Supreme Court. Legal doctrine written by law professors and other legal scholars is often referred to by the courts. It is not, as in UK law, considered a problem that the courts in this respect are not completely independent from the universities.

Sweden does not have a complete codification of private law, such as, for example, the French Code Civil, the German BGB or the Austrian ABGB. Instead there are several smaller laws, such as, for example, the Contract Act, the Sales Act, the Consumer Sales Act and the Consumer Services Act. There is no special law for the sales of services in business-to-business (B2B) or consumer-to-business (C2B) transactions. For these kinds of transactions, other provisions have to be applied analogically. The scarce codification often results in there being no solution for a case in the written law. Consequently, the courts cannot apply the law in a very formal way (for example: 'there is no such right in the law, therefore no such right exists'), but have to find reasonable solutions where the law does not give enough guidance. In these situations, the court often uses a method of balancing the interests of both parties against each other in order to find which interest should prevail. This pragmatic way of settling disputes is characteristic of Swedish law.

To sum up this far, the Swedish legal system is neither a continental nor a common law legal system, but a mixed legal system of its own, belonging to the Nordic legal family. There is no constitutional court, and only somewhat fragmental private law legislation. Hence, the Swedish courts often settle disputes by weighing up the different interests of the parties against each other, rather than applying the law in a strict and formal manner.

III. UNJUST ENRICHMENT IN EU LAW

A. Unjust Enrichment in the Case law of the CJEU

In the *Messner* case, the principle of unjust enrichment is dealt with as a possible limitation of consumer protection.[9] The dispute before the national

---

[8] See, for example, the Swedish Supreme Court Cases NJA 1989 p 224 and NJA 2001 p 353.

[9] C-489/07 *Pia Messner v Firma Stefan Krüger* [2009] ECR 2009 I-07315.

court dealt with the implementation of Directive 97/7/EC of the European Parliament and of the Council of 20 May 1997 on the protection of consumers in respect of distance contracts.[10] This Directive has been replaced with the Directive on Consumer Rights (2011/83/EC).[11] Under Article 6(1) and (2) of Directive 97/7/EC, the consumer shall have a period of at least seven working days in which to withdraw from a distance contract without penalty and without giving any reason. The only charge that may be made to the consumer because of the exercise of his right of withdrawal is the direct cost of returning the goods. In the case of a withdrawal, the supplier shall be obliged to reimburse the sums paid by the consumer free of charge, except the direct cost of returning the goods. The Directive is a minimum directive, which means that the Member States may ensure a higher level of consumer protection than the level provided in the Directive.

In the case before the national court, the issue was whether the supplier had the right to compensation for the consumer's use of the goods during the withdrawal period. The CJEU stated that Article 6(1) and (2) of the Directive must be interpreted as precluding a provision of national law which provides in general that in the case of withdrawal by a consumer within the withdrawal period, a seller may claim compensation for the value of the use of the consumer of goods acquired under a distance contract.[12] Those provisions do not, however, according to the CJEU, prevent the consumer from being required to pay compensation for the use of the goods if he has made use of those goods in a manner incompatible with the principles of civil law, such as those of good faith or unjust enrichment, on condition that the purpose of that Directive and, in particular, the efficiency and effectiveness of the right of withdrawal are not adversely affected, this being a matter for the national court to determine.[13]

This case sets an interesting example regarding how the CJEU recognizes the principle of unjust enrichment as a principle of civil law, which can actually in certain cases delimit the scope of a minimum directive. Even though the Directive expressly states that the *only* charge that may be made in a withdrawal is the direct cost of returning the goods, there may also be a charge to compensate the supplier in order to prevent the buyer from being unjustly enriched. The principle of unjust enrichment is an additional unwritten legal ground to delimit the consumer protection provided for in the Directive.

[10] OJ 1997 L 144 p 19.
[11] Directive 2011/83/EU of the European Parliament and of the Council of 25 October 2011 on consumer rights, amending Council Directive 93/13/EEC and Directive 1999/44/EC of the European Parliament and of the Council and repealing Directive 85/577/EEC and Directive 97/7/EC of the European Parliament and of the Council. OJ 2011 L 304 p 64. The Directive should have been transposed into national law by 13 June 2014.
[12] C-489/07 *Pia Messner v Firma Stefan Krüger* [2009] ECR 2009 I-07315 p 29.
[13] Ibid.

In light of the case law of the CJEU in other areas of law, it is clear that that law may not be abused. In the case of an abuse, rights given by the strict wording of a directive may be recalled. For example, even though there is no provision in the VAT Directive limiting the right to deduct input value added tax (VAT) in the case of fraud, the CJEU refuses the right to deduct input VAT in such cases. In the joined cases *Italmoda et al*, the CJEU states:

'In this regard, it is appropriate to note that it follows from the case-law [of the CJEU] that the central function of the right of deduction provided for in Article 17(3) of the Sixth Directive, in the VAT mechanism designed to ensure complete neutrality of the tax, does not preclude that right from being refused to a taxable person in the event of participation in fraud'.[14]

This means that also in the case of the deduction of input VAT, when the person, who would enjoy the right of deduction, participates in VAT fraud, that person would have been enriched in an unjust way if the right of deduction was granted. Participating in fraud does not mean that the taxpayer who wishes to deduct input VAT has actually actively participated in the fraud. It is enough that the taxpayer knew or should have known about the actual fraud.

Furthermore, in the context of the repayment of charges levied in breach of EU law, when the so-called passing-on principle is applied, the CJEU sometimes refers to the principle of unjust enrichment.[15] When a Member State has levied a tax in conflict with EU law, the amounts paid by the taxpayers should be refunded to the taxpayers. In *Lady & Kid*, the CJEU ruled in its judgment that the rules of EU law on the recovery of sums wrongly paid must be interpreted to the effect that the recovery of sums wrongly paid may give rise to unjust enrichment only when the amounts wrongly paid by a taxpayer under a tax levied in a Member State in breach of EU law have been passed on directly to the purchaser.[16]

Consequently, the CJEU states that EU law precludes a Member State from refusing the reimbursement of a tax wrongfully levied on the ground that the amounts wrongly paid by the taxpayer have been set off by a saving made as a result of the concomitant abolition of other levies, since such a set off cannot be seen from the point of view of EU law, as an unjust enrichment as regards that tax.[17] This means that a Member State can refuse a recovery of the tax to a taxpayer, when the burden of tax is passed on to another

---

[14] Joined Cases C-131/13, C-163/13 and C-64/13 *Staatssecretaris van Financiën v Schoenimport 'Italmoda' Mariano Previti vof* (C-131/13), and *Turbu.com BV* (C-163/13), *Turbu.com Mobile Phone's BV* (C-164/13), and *Staatssecretaris van Financiën* [2014] not yet published.

[15] See Strand, M, *The Passing-On Problem in EU Law Damages and Restitution* (Uppsala, Uppsala University 2015) 233.

[16] C-398/09 *Lady & Kid A/S, Direct Nyt Aps, A/S Harald Nyborg Isenkram- og Sportforretning, Kid Holdning A/S v Skatteministeriet* [2011] ECR 2011 I-07375.

[17] Ibid.

person. This is often the case with indirect taxes, such as VAT. This refusal of repayment is based on the principle of unjust enrichment.

The principle of unjust enrichment seems to be part of the EU legal system, which can be applied in order to withdraw advantages given in the wording of EU law, when the strict application of the wording would lead to an unjust enrichment. The concept of unjust enrichment holds different meanings in different fields of EU law. In order to apply the principle of unjust enrichment correctly, the case law of the CJEU in the field at hand must be closely examined. The concept of unjust enrichment is broad and vague as such,[18] but the case law of the CJEU gives it specific and different meanings depending on the area of law.

B. Unjust Enrichment in the Draft Common Frame of Reference

The Draft Common Frame of Reference (DCFR) is an initiative on a draft civil code for the EU. It is non-binding soft law. Few scholars believe that it will result in hard-binding law.[19] In the DCFR, a number of general principles of European private law are identified. The protection of security by the law of unjust enrichment is principle number 35 of the DCFR. According to this principle, under DCFR, a wrongdoer is not permitted to profit from the exploitation of another's rights. Furthermore, a person, who confers an enrichment on another in circumstances where it is reasonable to expect a counter-benefit, is protected by being entitled to a reversal of the enrichment if the agreement on which reliance was placed turns out not to be valid. Consequently, the principle is both recognized and defined in the DCFR.

Book VII of the DCFR aims to deal with all liabilities arising out of the autonomous law of unjust enrichment. Under Article VII-1:101 paragraph 1, a person, who obtains an unjustified enrichment which is attributable to another's disadvantage, is obliged to reverse the enrichment to that other person. Paragraph 2 of the same article states that the following provisions specify the application of the general rule in paragraph 1. For example, it is specified under which circumstances the creditor has sustained a disadvantage and the benefit obtained by the debtor amounts to an unjustified enrichment attributable to the creditor's advantage.[20] Under Article VII-2:101, enrichment is unjustified unless the enriched person is entitled, as against the disadvantaged person, to the enrichment by virtue of a contract or other juridical act, a court order or a rule of law; or the disadvantaged person has consented freely without error to the disadvantage.

---

[18] Strand, *The Passing-On Problem* (n 16) 240.

[19] See, for example, Herre, J, 'DCFR och svensk rätt' *Svensk juristtidning* (2012) 935.

[20] See Monsen, E, 'DCFR and Restitution for Wrongs' *European Review of Private Law* (2010) 816.

Enrichment is also unjustified when the disadvantaged person has conferred it for a purpose that was not achieved with an expectation that was not realized. Enrichment has not been achieved by an increase in assets or a decrease in liabilities, receiving a service or having work done or use of another person's assets.[21] A disadvantage occurs in the opposite way to enrichment.[22] The specific rules on the principle of unjust enrichment in DCFR are in fact rather precise, and give the relatively vague principle much more substance.

IV. UNJUST ENRICHMENT IN SWEDISH LAW

As mentioned above, unjust enrichment is not codified in written law in Sweden. However, since the Swedish codification in civil law is incomplete, the principle could well exist in Swedish law anyway, as a general principle. In general terms, the concept of unjust enrichment can be said to consist of three criteria—the enrichment requirement, the loss requirement and the legal ground requirement:[23]

— One party is enriched (enrichment requirement)
— The other party suffers a loss due to this enrichment (loss requirement)
— The enrichment is without legal ground (legal ground requirement)

Unjust enrichment as a positive legal rule and in the shape of a general principle has been massively criticized in Sweden and the other Scandinavian countries.[24] Its main opponent was Hellner, who in his doctoral thesis from 1950 concluded that it is completely pointless to justify a provision with the principle of unjust enrichment and that there is no Swedish general principle of unjust enrichment. Since Hellner wrote his doctoral thesis on unjust enrichment and later on became a successful and well-recognized Professor of Law in Sweden, Hellner became the expert on unjust enrichment in Sweden. He kept his sceptical view of unjust enrichment until his death in 2002.[25] Until then, the non-existence of the principle of unjust enrichment in Swedish law was taken as a fact for most scholars and judges.[26]

After Hellner's death, the existence of the principle of unjust enrichment as a positive legal rule in the shape of a general principle in Swedish law has been the subject of academic discussions even though many Swedish

---

[21] Article VII 3:101 DCFR.

[22] Article VII 3:102 DCFR.

[23] Hellner, J, *Om obehörig vinst särskilt utanför kontraktsförhållanden* (Stockholm, Almqvist & Wiksell, 1950) 148, 187.

[24] See Schlechtriem, P, Coen, C, Hornung, R, 'Restitution and Unjust Enrichment in Europe', *European Review of Private Law* (2001) 378.

[25] See Schultz, M, 'Nya argumentationslinjer i förmögenhetsrätten. Obehörig vinst rediviva', *Svensk juristtidning* (2009) 948.

[26] See Martinsson, C, 'The Scandinavian Approach to Property Law. Described through Six Common Legal Concepts', *Juridica International Law Review, University of Tartu* (2014) 21.

legal scholars are not in favour of the principle. In an article from 2014, for example, three arguments against the principle of unjust enrichment were put forward.[27]

The first reason for stating that the principle of unjust enrichment is not suitable for Swedish law is that in Sweden, the 'transfer of ownership superstructure' is not applied.[28] The transfer of ownership is not a starting point when settling ownership issues.[29] Moreover, the question asked is not 'Has the ownership been transferred?'.[30] Instead, questions like 'Is the seller allowed to use the car until delivery?' or 'Does the buyer gain from the bankruptcy of the seller?' are asked.[31] The starting point is the real problem, not the abstract concept of ownership.[32] The second reason for stating that the principle of unjust enrichment is not considered to be appropriate for Swedish law is that it is not a good tool with which to direct behaviour. It is submitted that there are other methods and incentives that should be used instead of using other people's property.[33] The third reason put forward is that it is better to keep things separate from each other. Separate issues should be dealt with specifically in their own context. Unjustified enrichment is considered to be too broad and blunt, and hence risky.[34]

Scepticism towards the principle of unjust enrichment is nothing particularly Swedish. For example, the French Code Civil did not include a provision when it was introduced. It was up to the courts to deal with such cases where unjust results occurred. The French courts did so, and in the process developed a principle so far-reaching that had it been applied, it would have undermined many other principles of private law, such as contract law. Consequently, the notion of unjust enrichment as a shapeless beast that, if it were allowed free reign, would destroy all other principles, has evolved within the doctrine, together with the idea that the concept of unjust enrichment is a moral or natural matter and not a legal one.[35]

The main advocate for the principle of unjust enrichment in Sweden is Schultz. He considers unjust enrichment as a necessary line of reasoning in Swedish law, even though the principle is perhaps of a secondary nature in relation to more established principles such as the principles of *condictio*

---

[27] Ibid.
[28] Ibid.
[29] Ibid.
[30] Martinsson, Claes, 'Förhandlingarna vid det 39:e nordiska juristmötet i Stockholm den 18–19 augusti 2011' *Ejendomsrettens overgang—Norden contra verden, Foredrag av jur dr Claes Martinsson* (Stockholm 2012) 825, jura.ku.dk/njm/39/823-844-bilaga-1.pdf.
[31] Martinsson, *Ejendomsrettens overgang* (2012) 825.
[32] Martinsson, *Ejendomsrettens overgang* (2012) 826.
[33] Martinsson, 'The Scandinavian Approach' (2014) 21.
[34] Ibid.
[35] Gomes, Julio Manuel Vieira, 'Unjust enrichment: A few comparative remarks', *European Review of Private Law* (2001) 449, 450.

indebiti and *compensatio lucri cum damno*.[36] He explains the scepticism towards unjust enrichment in Sweden as a legacy from the Scandinavian realism period in the first half of the twentieth century.[37] Taking a legal dogmatic position, the concept unjust enrichment is obscure because the concept 'unjust' must necessarily have content. In that light, giving the concept 'unjust' content would almost be the opposite of Scandinavian realism where the written law should be applied strictly irrespective of possible 'unjust' results. Including a concept like unjust enrichment in the law undermines the fundamental ideas of Scandinavian realism.

The Swedish Supreme Court, as mentioned in the introduction, has not used the principle of unjust enrichment as the only legal reasoning when deciding a case. However, there are several examples of cases where the principle seems to have played an important role.

One early case is NJA 1925 p 184. In this case, a unit of land was sold with the reservation that the previous owner could fell trees for timber on the land. A timber prohibition was later issued based on a law that entered into force after the transfer of the property. The Swedish Supreme Court found that the seller was entitled to compensation based on the enrichment of the buyer, due to the increased value of his property.[38]

Another interesting case is NJA 1989 p 768 regarding illegal poker games. In this case, the organizer of the poker games was obliged to repay the betting sums he received to the poker players. The Swedish Supreme Court stated that if the sums had not been repaid, the betting company would have been enriched on entirely unjustified grounds.

Two cases where the Swedish Supreme Court has discussed the principle of unjust enrichment are NJA 1999 p 575 and NJA 2007 p 519. In the first case, the Swedish Supreme Court states that unjust enrichment is one of the main reasons for repayment due to the principle of *condictio indebiti*. In the second case, the Supreme Court refers to another case, NJA 1993 p. 13, which it holds was based on general principles of private law, such as the principle of unjust enrichment.[39]

As regards more recent case law from the Swedish Supreme Court, Case NJA 2014 p 1006 could be mentioned. The Supreme Court stated that the overcompensation that was sometimes the result of the application of the relevant provisions of the Interest Act (räntelagen 1975:635) could not be considered as unjust enrichment. Since the overcompensation in the

---

[36] Schultz, Mårten, 'Obehörig vinst-motiveringar', *Svensk juristtidning* (2012) 380, 383.

[37] Schultz, 'Nya argumentationslinjer' (n 25) 947.

[38] See also NJA 1924 p 372, NJA 1925 p 497 and NJA 1931 p 642, NJA 1924 p 372, NJA 1925 p 497 and NJA 1931 p 642; and, Schultz, M, 'Unjust enrichment—Sweden', (2000), at www.juridicum.su.se/user/masc/UNJUSTENRICHMENT.htm.

[39] Other cases where the principle of unjust enrichment could be traced are NJA 1999 p 793, NJA 2008 p 861 and NJA 2009 p 40, also in dissenting opinions before the SC: NJA 1999 p 793 (Håstad) and NJA 2009 p 41 (Lindskog).

shape of interest was stipulated under written law, the court could not apply the principle of unjust enrichment without being in conflict with the law. It is apparent that the Swedish Supreme Court does not reject unjust enrichment as a legal ground as such, but it is clear that the principle does not override written law.

V. THE FUTURE OF UNJUST ENRICHMENT IN SWEDISH LAW

Swedish legal scholars have in the past been influenced by, for example, German, French and Roman law, by studying foreign textbooks and visiting foreign universities. There are still professors in Sweden who are of the opinion that you cannot write a decent doctoral thesis in the field of private law without making a comparison with German law. From that perspective, it is not surprising that the concept of unjust enrichment has been present in the Swedish legal doctrine for a long time, even though it is neither codified in written law nor an established general principle of Swedish law.

Since Sweden does not have a more complete codification of private law, but rather a fragmental one, and there is no provision on unjust enrichment in Swedish private law, it could be submitted that unjust enrichment as a general principle could be useful in Swedish law, to fill a possible gap. Even though the Swedish Supreme Court has not relied on the principle of unjust enrichment as a sole legal ground for a decision, it has indirectly paved the way for the principle actually becoming part of Swedish law. In its judgments in NJA 2009 p 672, NJA 2010 p 629 and NJA 2011 p 600, the Swedish Supreme Court has stated that where other sources are lacking, Swedish courts may use the DCFR as a legal source. Hence, the principle could become a general principle of Swedish law due to the DCFR. DCFR has also had a great impact on Swedish legal literature.[40]

In the case law of the CJEU, it is almost expected that the principle of unjust enrichment is recognized in the national jurisdictions. In consumer protection cases, such as in *Messner*, too much consideration would be taken of the consumer's interests if consumer protection entailed that a consumer was unjustly enriched at the cost of a business. In Swedish law, however, the unjust result in distance sales is avoided by a specific provision stating that the consumer is liable to compensate the seller for depreciation if the consumer has used the goods more than what is necessary to examine the characteristics and functioning of the goods.[41] In this particular case, the principle of unjust enrichment is already implemented in Swedish law through a specific provision.

---

[40] See Herre, 'DCFR och svensk rätt' (n 19) 936.
[41] Section 15 Nr. 2 *lagen (2005:59) om distansavtal och avtal utanför affärslokaler* (the Swedish act on consumer distance sales).

In the case of the repayment of taxes and passing on the burden of taxes to other taxpayers, the principle of unjust enrichment is not covered in Swedish law. In my opinion, this is not necessary, since the CJEU does not refer to a domestic principle of unjust enrichment, but the principle of unjust enrichment seems to be part of EU law in this case. Hence, there is a principle of unjust enrichment that delimits another non codified principle of EU law, namely that taxes levied in conflict with EU law must be repaid to the taxpayer. In this respect, a judgment from the Swedish Supreme Administrative Court, however, indicates a certain reluctance with regard to this point of view. In its judgment RÅ 2002 ref 108, the Swedish Supreme Administrative Court found that inspection fees under the Swedish regulation 'alkoholförordningen' (1994:2046) were levied in conflict with EU law. The Court stated that the fact that the fees were actually passed on to other persons did not have any relevance in Swedish law, since there was no provision in written law that excluded repayment when the fee was passed on. This is a case from 2002. However, following recent Swedish doctrine, this case has been considered as meaning that the principle of unjust enrichment in relation to the passing on of taxes to other taxpayers does not have any relevance in Swedish law.[42] The line of reasoning behind this view, is that Member States have their procedural autonomy, and that passing on is part of this procedural autonomy. In my opinion, however, the principle of unjust enrichment is not a procedural issue but a material one. The procedural autonomy refers to how Member States proceed when they grant their taxpayers the right of repayment, whereas unjust enrichment in these situations relates to deciding the amount of money that should be repaid. Hence, in my view, the EU unjust enrichment principle with regard to the repayment of taxes levied in conflict with EU law should be directly applicable in Sweden.

VI. CONCLUDING REMARKS

When the Swedish Supreme Court states that the DCFR can be taken into consideration by Swedish courts in situations where there are no other sources of law available, it opens the door to the principle of unjust enrichment in Swedish law. The principle was heavily criticized in Sweden during the last century, although there are advocates of the principle today. The advantage of the DCFR is that it actually defines the principle in that a person, who confers an enrichment on another in circumstances where it is reasonable to expect a counter-benefit, is protected by the fact that that person is entitled to a reversal of the enrichment if the agreement on which

---

[42] Ståhl, K, Persson Österman, R, Hilling, M, Öberg, J, *EU-skatterätt* (Uppsala, Iustus förlag, 2011) 62 and Cejie, K, 'Skattenytt internationellt—direkt beskattning', *Skattenytt* (2011) 833.

reliance was placed turns out not to be valid. This definition gives the principle some content. The provisions in Book VII DCFR specify the different components of the principle of unjust enrichment such as 'enrichment' and 'unjust enrichment'. The fact that the principle is almost taken for granted by the CJEU lends further support for the principle in EU law.

For a long time now, Swedish courts have been able to decide cases without relying on this principle. This is a strong indication that there are many other ways of settling cases in Swedish law without applying the principle of unjust enrichment, for example, by applying the principle of *condictio indebiti*, but also by balancing the interests between the parties, thus finding a reasonable solution. Hence, my conclusion is that with the influence of EU law, the principle of unjust enrichment is likely to gain ground in Sweden.[43] However, since there is a strong well-established tradition of solving cases without applying this principle, the principle will probably be of secondary importance. Swedish courts may lend the principle more legitimacy by referring to the DCFR.

---

[43] See Schultz, 'Nya argumentationslinjer' (n 25) 949.

5

Comparative Property Law and the Profound Differences between Nordic Functionalism and Continental Substantialism— The (Ir)Relevance of Ownership

I. INTRODUCTION**

COMPARATIVE LAW CAN be both fascinating and frustrating. In some areas of law, significant preparatory work has already been undertaken—often as preparatory work underpinning different attempts to unify the law. The United Nations Convention on Contracts for the International Sale of Goods (hereinafter, the 'CISG') is one such example.

* Post doc, Faculty of Law, University of Stockholm, and former researcher in The Study Group on a European Civil Code in the Working Team on 'Extra-contractual obligations' (DCFR Books V–VII) at ELSI, Universität Osnabrück.
** The following literature is cited in abbreviated form: van Erp, S, 'Comparative Property Law', in Reimann, M and Zimmermann, R (eds), *The Oxford Handbook of Comparative Law*, (Oxford, OUP, 2006) pp 1043–1070; van Erp, S, 'European Property Law: a new and rapidly developing area of research and teaching', *EPLJ* 2012 pp 1–2; Faber, W, 'Scepticism about the Functional Approach from a Unitary Perspective', in Faber, W and Lurger, B (eds), *Rules for the Transfer of Movables: A Candidate for European Harmonisation or National Reforms?*, (Munich, European Law Publishers, 2008) pp 97–122; Füller, JT, 'The German Property Law and its Principles—Some Lessons for a European Property Law', in Faber, W and Lurger, B (eds), *Rules for the Transfer of Movables: A Candidate for European Harmonisation or National Reforms?*, (Munich, European Law Publishers, 2008) pp 197–215; Gretton, G, 'Book review', EdinLR 2009 pp 169–170; Hessler, H, *Allmän sakrätt: om det förmögenhetsrättsliga tredjemansskyddets principer*, (Stockholm 1973, Norstedts); Håstad, T, 'General Aspects of Transfer and Creation of Property Rights including Security Rights', in Drobnig, U, Snijders, HJ, Zippro, EJ (eds), *Divergences of Property Law, an Obstacle to the Internal Market*, (Munich, European Law Publishers, 2006) pp 37–44; Håstad, T, 'Derivative Acquisition of Ownership of Goods', ERPL 2009 pp 725–741; Lilja, M, 'Sweden', in Faber, W and Lurger, B (eds), *National Reports on the Transfer of Movables in Europe*, Vol 5, (Munich, European Law Publishers, 2011) pp 1–204; Martinson, C,

The work began as early as 1929. The comparisons quite frequently focus on the more visible aspects at the surface level of the law[1] seemingly reminiscent of common legal dogmatics—and are sometimes rather to be seen as *Legislation comparé* or *Fremdrechtskunde* than anything else.

Other areas of law have remained almost untouched, perhaps due to the lack of relevance for unification projects, or because basic assumptions in different legal systems are so radically different that to even find relevant criteria for comparison can be perceived as impossible. Such an area of law may have the potential to be both fascinating and frustrating, perhaps particularly the latter. Such an area may require you to dig deeper,[2] as well as more widely, and require a more interdisciplinary approach. The mainstream jurist may perceive such an approach as alienating and non-legal. Certain comparatists may also react with initial scepticism, however, on the other hand, the result may turn out to be fascinating and to contribute with genuinely new knowledge, which the comparatist at least would appreciate.

In more recent years, comparative property law has become the subject of research. The preparatory work on what later became the DCFR was a contributing factor. The PEL/Acq, the book on DCFR Book VIII, covers more than 1,700 pages.[3] Before that, property law could be described as *terra incognita* on the map of comparative law; it does not, for example, feature in the standard comparative law textbook by Zweigert and Kötz and property

---

'How Swedish Lawyers Think about "Ownership" and "Transfer of Ownership"—Are We Just Peculiar or Actually Ahead?', in Faber, W and Lurger, B (eds), *Rules for the Transfer of Movables: A Candidate for European Harmonisation or National Reforms?*, (Munich, European Law Publishers, 2008) pp 69–95; Martinson, C, 'Ejendomsrettens overgang—Norden kontra verden', NJM 2008 at www.law.gu.se/kontakt/personal/claes_martinson/Files/juridik/personal/Claes_Martinson/MartinsonEjendomsRF.pdf; Martinson, C, 'Johan Sandstedt, Sakrätten, Norden och Europeiseringen—Nordisk funktionalism möter kontinental substantialism', Jure förlag 2013, 571 s, SvJT 2014, pp 662–672; Martinson, C, 'Bridging the Gap, Review of "Property Law, the Nordic Legal Culture and the Europeanisation—Nordic Functionalism Meets Continental Substantialism", by Johan Sandstedt. Jure förlag 2013. 571 pages', *EPLJ* 2014 pp 280–284; Samuelsson, J, *Tolkning och utfyllning: Undersökningar kring ett förmögenhetsteoretiskt tema*, (Uppsala 2008, Iustus); Sandstedt, J, *Sakrätten, Norden och europeiseringen—Nordisk funktionalism möter kontinental substantialism*, (Stockholm, Jure förlag, 2013); van Vliet, L, 'Iusta Causa Traditionis and its History in European Private Law', *ERPL* 2003, pp 342–378; van Vliet, L, 'Transfer of movable property', in Smits, J (ed), *Elgar Encyclopedia of Comparative Law*, (Cheltenham, Northampton, 2006) pp 730–737; Wieling, HJ, Sachenrecht, Vol I, (Berlin, Heidelberg, 2006).

[1] On the levels of the law, eg, the surface level, see Tuori, K, *Critical Legal Positivism*, (Aldershot, Ashgate, 2002), Chapter 6.
[2] See, eg, van Hoecke, M, 'Deep Level Comparative Law', in van Hoecke, M (ed), *Epistemology and Methodology of Comparative Law*, (Oxford, Bloomsbury Publishing, 2004) pp 165–195.
[3] Lurger, B and Faber, W, *Principles of European Law/Acquisition and Loss of Ownership of Goods*, (Munich, European Law Publishers, 2011) referred to as 'PEL/Acq'. A recently published book needs to be mentioned too: von Bar, C, *Gemeineuropäisches Sachenrecht, Band I*, (Munich, CH Beck, 2015).

law has been described as 'national law par excellence'.[4] In conjunction with the work on the DCFR and the nascent European property law discussions, it became obvious that there was an important dividing line between Nordic functionalism and continental substantialism. The differences are considered so profound that a dialogue would almost seem impossible. Gretton finished his book review of an attempt to reach a dialogue between Faber and Martinson with the following words: 'Not all gaps are bridgeable.'[5]

Despite Gretton's demotivating words, this text will try to bridge the gap. It is important to point out already at this stage that, from a continental substantialist perspective, it is about ownership, whereas from a Nordic functionalist perspective, it is not about ownership, or at least it should not be about ownership.

The text that follows below is rather brief and its main focus is Nordic functionalism, since most readers will probably read it through their own substantialist lens, probably without even knowing that they are substantialists. The text starts off with a setting of the scene (Section II), where attempts at a dialogue, the feelings and the difficulties are presented followed by an introductory presentation of three somewhat elusive differences between functionalism and substantialism. Under Section III, focus is on the (ir)relevant question of ownership and Nordic property law images. Section IV is devoted to necessary theoretical issues, ie method and research questions as well as the unorthodox approach of seeking assistance from interdisciplinary fields. Section V contains a concluding application that will bring the discussion full circle and hopefully also show how the gap between functionalism and substantialism can be bridged, while at the same time highlighting their differences.

II. IN PREPARATION: SETTING SOME KIND OF SCENE

A. Attempts at a Dialogue, Feelings and Difficulties

Establishing a good dialogue between functionalists and substantialists has proved difficult. Attempts may result in something that could best be described with the conversational device non sequitur, or turn into more or less hidden disagreements. The first case describes what you might call two parallel monologues, where it is clear that the interlocutors do not understand each other but still keep up appearances. In the second case,

---

[4] Milo, MJ, 'Property and real rights', in Smits, J (ed), *Elgar Encyclopedia of Comparative Law* (Cheltenham, Edward Elgar Publishing Ltd, 2006) pp 587–601 (587); van Erp, S, 'European Property Law' (**) pp 1–2 who argues that property law has been "nationally oriented".

[5] Gretton, G, 'Book review', (**) pp 169–170.

they actually believe that they are having a fruitful conversation, a comparative property law dialogue.

The discussions have to a certain extent been emotional—for some it is possibly a matter of identity and perceived progressiveness[6]—and the tone has at times also been harsh. The substantialist approach has from the Nordic standpoint inter alia been criticised for being 'hocus-pocus law'.[7] The DCFR discussions of the new millennium can be seen as a journey back in time. The Nordic statements on the other hand, can be perceived as superior and missionary.[8] It follows that this might almost be regarded as a religious battle—and thus a topic that a functionally educated PhD candidate would do well to steer away from, provided they do not instead choose a functionalist perspective and unreservedly join the unified crowd of critics. But all PhD candidates are not that sensible.[9]

The functionalist view has mainly been represented by Swedish jurists: Håstad, Martinson, Andreasson and Lilja.[10] They have all in one way or another had some contact with the DCFR project.[11] Jurists outside this limited circle have not chosen to grapple with these issues. A plausible reason for this is that the differences between 'us' and 'them' are so huge that it is hard to participate in the discussions. Another plausible reason is that they

---

[6] See, eg, Samuelsson, J, *Tolkning och utfyllning* (n1) p 390 et seq.

[7] See Faber, W, 'Scepticism about the Functional Approach' (**) p 99 note 10: 'Typical reactions are, for instance, that linking practical consequences to a "transfer of ownership" concept would be "hocus-pocus law", a "step backwards for 100 years" (in case people want to be very polite: for 50 years) or that someone adhering to such an approach is "not discussing real questions"'. See also the important text in Lilja, M, 'Sweden' (**) p 17 note 41 with examples and further references. The text is written in a (self-)critical manner.

[8] Gretton, G, 'Book review' (**) pp 169–170: 'Martinson disavows the role of the missionary, but the disavowal is unconvincing: he seems to be saying that the Swedish approach is best'. The missionary role is familiar in Swedish literature. Besides the missionary Lundstedt in Ross, A, 'Tû-Tû', *ScStL* 1957 pp 138–153 (the original text was in Danish and the English version was also published in HarvLRev 1956–57 pp 812–825), we also meet a missionising attitude in Samuelsson, J, *Tolkning och utfyllning* (**) p 391. Faber (see the previous footnote) finishes his quotation with the following words: 'I wish to clarify, however, that this observation in no way relates to Claes Martinson's contribution to this volume'. And Martinson himself makes clear what his intention with the text was, see Martinson, C, 'The Scandinavian Approach to Property Law, Described through Six Common Legal Concepts', *Juridica International* 2014, p 16 note 4.

[9] See Sandstedt, 'Sakrätten, Norden och europeiseringen' (translation of the full title by Martinson: 'Property Law, the Nordic Legal Culture and the Europeanisation—Nordic Functionalism Meets Continental Substantialism'). See the two different book reviews by Martinson in *SvJT* 2014 pp 662–672 and in English in *EPLJ* 2014 pp 280–284.

[10] Here I only mention literature in English. An original national report for Sweden on DCFR Book VIII was written by Martinson with the help of Andreasson and it was published by Peter Lang Verlag. Martinson, C, 'How Swedish Lawyers Think' (**) pp 69–95; Håstad, T, 'General Aspects of Transfer' (**) pp 37–44; Håstad, T, 'Derivative Acquisition' (**) pp 725–741; Lilja, M, 'Sweden' (**) pp 1–204.

[11] Håstad was a member of The Study Group on a European Civil Code and member of the advisory councils for Books V, VII, VIII and IX; Martinson and Andreasson have been in contact with Salzburg and DCFR Book VIII and Lilja was a researcher in the Salzburg working team and wrote the Swedish national report to DCFR Book VIII.

do not have even a rudimentary understanding of what this alleged battle is about. The battle is not about concrete results, but about something entirely different, something more elusive. The differences are more profound than a discussion about a consensual or a delivery system ie is a contract enough to transfer ownership or creditor protection or is some form of delivery required? Moreover, for many people they are more or less invisible.

The attempted dialogue is difficult for non-participants, but the participants themselves have difficulties with it as well as with the understanding of the opposite approach. The difficulties may be explained as follows:

— the functionalism–substantialism dichotomy and the differences between the two approaches are unknown to most jurists and to a great extent also touch on implicit aspects;

— that these are relevant differences can by many jurists instead be intuitively perceived as an over-dramatization;

— it is important to find a good and accepted methodological tool and fitting criteria for comparison to be able to analyse and deal with the essentially different approaches;

— therefore, the differences must be explained in a clear way and this also includes the need to create a reasonably clear picture of your own functionalism, both in terms of the explicit and implicit features;

— after having achieved this, the counter-intuitive gaze can be directed towards your own approach; and

— the research method requires, finally, that one manages to keep substantialism and functionalism apart.

B. Functionalism and Substantialism

One important dividing line regarding the basic understanding and hence perspective and perception mainly in the area of property law, can as mentioned above be drawn between functionalism and substantialism; a unitary approach is set against a more fragmented approach.[12] This statement is to some degree a simplification, since, numerically-speaking, there is not one functionalism or one substantialism. Perhaps it is more a case of two different models that are set against each other. They hardly exist in reality in their purest form, but the description still shows an important dividing

---

[12] The dichotomy is presented in many different ways: In Lurger and Faber, *Principles of European Law* (n 3) p 409 et seq (Comments no 4), the words used are 'unitary' and 'functional'; Håstad has used the opposites, 'unitary rule' and 'split approach' ('General Aspects of Transfer' (**) p 38)), 'unitary rule' and 'issue-by-issue approach' ('Derivative Acquisition' (**) p 725); van Vliet uses the same words as in *Principles of European Law*, ie 'unitary' and 'functional', but specifies for his part that one rather should call the latter 'fragmented', see *van Vliet, L,* 'Acquisition and Loss of Ownership of Goods—Book VIII of the Draft Common Frame of Reference', *ZEuP* 2011 p 294.

line, that cannot be trivialized. Within the national discourse, there may be gradations and different opinions with alien unreflective tendencies. There are also gradations concerning functionalistic consciousness or orthodoxy. Non-functionalist elements may also be present.

There are several differences which can be presented in various ways. As an introduction, the following three differences are presented.

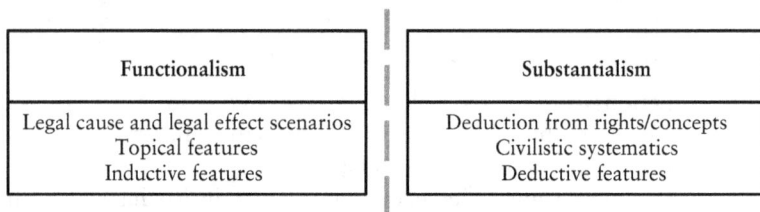

Functionalism	Substantialism
Legal cause and legal effect scenarios Topical features Inductive features	Deduction from rights/concepts Civilistic systematics Deductive features

Legal problems are formulated as functionalist legal cause/legal effect scenarios and also solved in that manner and not through the deduction of substantialism from rights or concepts. Functionalism shows clear topical features compared with the civilistic systematics and inductive features instead of deductive features of substantialism.

The three differences above can also be presented as images. In this text, one set of images will have to suffice. The images are not unfamiliar in legal literature[13] and are normally used to describe differences at a purely theoretical level. The two images show legal cause/legal effect scenarios versus deduction from rights or concepts. They show that the same legal result can be achieved in two different ways. The most important difference is the existence of the intermediate concept 'right' in the substantialist image on the right. It does not exist in the functionalist image. For the present text, this is the important difference, even though other aspects could also be discussed about the images.[14]

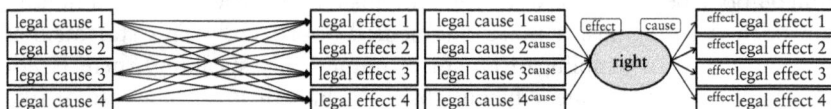

That this is supposed to be a Nordic feature is also stated in the literature. Håstad, to mention a key name, has expressed the following in a Nordic

---

[13] See, eg, Brouwer, B and Hage, J, 'Basic Concepts of European Private Law', *ERPL* 2007 pp 3–26 (16 et seq).

[14] The number of rules needed to achieve the same results differs. Moreover, the images are deceptive at a more down-to-earth level, since they might indicate that the same results also are achieved, which must absolutely not be the case.

context: 'The rules are formulated in a simple manner with legal cause and legal effect and without begriffsjurisprudential circumlocutions.'[15]

The begriffsjurisprudential circumlocution would, in this case, be the intermediate concept 'ownership'.

Håstad has also mentioned our topical features. He has used the words 'issue-by-issue approach' and he has explained that each possible collision should be solved 'on its own merits in each situation etc'.[16] Instead of a statement supporting our inductive features, one statement against deduction shall be presented. This idea stems from Undén: 'To the extent that, for example, remaining natural law ideas relocate ownership and place it above the positive law as an a priori principle, it is important to underline the unscientific nature of such an approach.'[17]

Fundamental differences have been demonstrated. If you do not embrace these differences, the other approach will seem strange.[18]

III. OWNERSHIP AND NORDIC PROPERTY LAW PICTURES

A. The (Ir)Relevant Ownership

Now that it has been pointed out that the intermediate concept is not (or should not be) a part of functionalism, something must of course be said about ownership. Ownership is not central to today's functionalist property law discourse, which instead focuses on the collisions. That is normally not something that is reflected on within the framework of one's own paradigm. This makes it difficult to participate in today's Europeanization discussions, which seem to be about something long since done—and also about something that we do not see.

In addition to the fact that the Nordic countries do not have a civil code with a definition of ownership, as found for example in s 903 BGB or

---

[15] Håstad, T, 'Nordiska önskemål vid en integration av säkerhetsrätten', ['Nordic wishes in case of an integration of the law of security rights'] in Tuominen, S (Red), *Civilrättens integration ur nordisk synvinkel*, [*The Integration of Private Law from a Nordic Perspective*] (Helsingfors, 2001) pp 49–73 (53): 'Reglerna formuleras enkelt med rättsfakta och rättsföljder utan begreppsjuridiska omskrivningar.'

[16] Håstad, 'Derivative Acquisition' (**) 725 and Håstad, 'General Aspects of Transfer' (**) 39. Also see Martinson, 'Bridging the Gap' (**) 282: 'Scandinavian lawyers approach legal issues on an "issue by issue" approach and they strive for keeping the problems apart without connecting the solution of one problem to the solution of another. Therefore, a Scandinavian lawyer would not involve a superstructure, such as the ownership, in the solution of the described problems. The Scandinavian lawyer would in principle deal with the problems independently from each other.'

[17] Undén, Ö, *Svensk sakrätt I. Lös egendom*, 5th edn, (Lund, Gleerup, 1966) p 59: 'I den mån exempelvis kvarlevande naturrättsliga idéer förflytta äganderätten ovanom den positiva rättsordningen såsom en apriorisk princip, är det angeläget att understryka det ovetenskapliga i detta betraktelsesätt.'

[18] Or the differences will be defined away. See below in Sections IV B (i)–(iii). This is how the brain makes information understandable.

Article VIII–1:202 DCFR, the reason stems from a down-to-earth and pragmatic approach. The jurists focused on real problems, without placing individual problems in a system and creating abstractions.[19] In addition, a large part of Nordic property law has evolved through case law and literature. With Hägerström and his followers Lundstedt and Ross, the criticism of the concept of a right became philosophical. Ownership was particularly exposed. It was declared to be non-existent, or, in Ross' own words, Tû-Tû. Over time, the criticism often turned into banter. Subsequently, the knowledge of these 'achievements' became so self-evident, that it was relegated to a footnote on 'the so-called rights debate'.[20] In the preliminary final step in current teaching literature, the development seems to have reached its completion. The rights, Tû-Tû and the rights debate have come to an end and are not even mentioned; they have been relegated to a position of implicit knowledge. We act and react in a certain way and do not care about the reason why.[21] All of a sudden, there are discussions about the Europeanization of property law and the chosen approach with which to deal with the matter does not correspond to our image of normality.

For today's attempted dialogue, we must again look back in time. Lundstedt, who was Hägerström's most litigious disciple in Sweden, demanded that the rights terminology should not even be used. Undén, a property law jurist, stuck to the old terminology, but explained that it was a functional concept now, not a substantial one as it used to be.[22] Undén's books were leading in Sweden for decades and have consequently shaped a large number of jurists. In 1973, Hessler published his book on property law. He embraced Undén's understanding of a right as a functional concept and, therefore, also explained the following:

> 'A "right" in a legal sense is today not perceived, as perhaps was the case earlier, as something substantial, as a more or less mysterious "lump" that is located with a person, but that may be transferred to someone else by that person and is subsequently to be found there. The concept of a right is what is normally called a functional concept.'[23]

In connection with this, he explained that ownership is a 'convenient form of expression' to express that 'with some factual circumstances, legal facts,

---

[19] See, eg, the Nordic work on a common Sale of Goods Act.

[20] Håstad, T, *Sakrätt avseende lös egendom*, (Stockholm, Norstedts, 6th edn, 1996) (with a supplement from March 2000) p 22 note 1. In the first edition of the book from 1982, the same reference is found on p 19 note 1. It has been included in all editions since the start.

[21] This has also been mentioned by both Martinson and Andreasson, see below in Section IV B(i).

[22] Samuelsson, *Tolkning och utfyllning* (**) p 302 et seq.

[23] Hessler, *Allmän sakrätt* (**) p 17: 'En "rättighet" i juridisk mening uppfattas ju numer inte, såsom kanske tidigare, som något substantiellt, som en mer eller mindre mystisk' klump' som befinner sig hos någon person, men som kan av honom flyttas över till någon annan och då alltså istället befinner sig där. Rättighetsbegreppet är vad man brukar kalla ett funktionsbegrepp.'

some legal consequences are connected'.[24] He also clarified the following: 'But what must above all be noted here is that "ownership" is not something independent, that stands as it were between legal fact and legal consequence and which these two are affiliated to in some way.'[25]

Against that background the following contemporary statement by Håstad is more understandable: 'It also seems unnecessary or actually dubious to insert the word *owner* or *ownership* as a resting point between the fact that creates a certain legal result and the result itself.'[26]

B. A Nordic Property Law Image and Property Law Collisions

i. Hessler's Image

While Undén in his books chose to depict the various property rights in a traditional manner, Hessler instead chose to base his book on the various possible collisions. Hessler's collision perspective has had a great influence on Swedish property law of today. His work has even been declared to be a contribution to the completion of functionalist property law.[27] Nordic property law and the various collisions are often presented using images. One of Hessler's central images specifically concerns ownership, namely situations where the A-claim with Hessler's words 'is ownership'.[28]

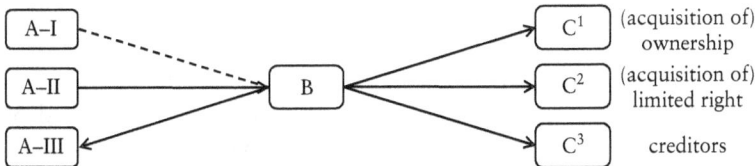

A–I = the general case of ownership for A (but B has stolen or found A's property, or possesses it without a contract on transfer); A–II = A has transferred to B, but has a 'reclaim' (due to an invalid contract, avoidance or *actio pauliana*); A–III = A has acquired the property from B.

[24] Hessler, *Allmän sakrätt* (**) p 17. Here I use the term legal fact as a translation of 'rätts-fakta', but I might as well have used the term legal cause which I would normally use in this context.

[25] Hessler, *Allmän sakrätt* (**) p 18: 'Men vad som här framförallt bör observeras är att "äganderätt" inte är något självständigt, som [så att säga] står emellan rättsfaktum och rätts-följd och till vilket dessa är på något sätt anknutna.'

[26] Håstad, 'Derivative Acquisition' (**) p 726 et seq.

[27] Martinson, 'Ejendomsrettens overgang' (**) p 7: 'At a certain point in time during the seventies, our functional approach thus became generally accepted, the established way of thinking.' ('Någon gång på sjuttiotalet har vår funktionella approach således blivit allmäng-ods, det gängse sättet att tänka.') In Martinson, 'How Swedish Lawyers Think' (**) p 70 with further references in note 4, this view is confirmed and he states that 'the last shakes in the emancipation procedure could be said to have ended as late as the 1970-ies'. In the footnote, the reference inter alia is to Hessler.

[28] Hessler, *Allmän sakrätt* (**) p 68.

The image shows three different A-claims and three C-claims. A denotes the earlier claim. In the middle is B, who is the cause of the collision between A and C. According to Hessler, the image describes an ownership collision; however, it is based on the fact that A claims ownership. The result of the collision is formulated preferably in terms of 'better right' or 'priority'. At the same time, it is important to be aware of the fact that an ownership is unmistakably looming in the background, namely the A–I case. But the original ownership of A–I is not part of the solution—and because of that and the fact that the parties are denoted A, B or C—the ownership disappears into the background.

ii. Basic Property Law Collisions: Creditor Protection and Good Faith Acquisition

Nordic property law deals with two basic questions, namely creditor-protection and good faith acquisition cases; in the latter case, it is normally either the dogmatic main case (A–I against C^1)[29] or double dispositions, ie double sales or with DCFR-words 'Multiple transfers', (A–III against C^1).[30] The main creditor-protection issue concerns creditor protection for things that have been handed over to someone else (A–I or A–II against C^3), or creditor protection for goods that have been acquired from another party (A–III against C^3). A simplified and normally used version merely calls the involved parties A, B and C.

iii. An Important Reminder

An important reminder is that each collision is formulated as a legal cause/ legal effect scenario, that each collision is supposed to be resolved on its own premises, regardless of how other collision cases are resolved and that the solution is not linked to the question of ownership.

IV. METHOD, RESEARCH QUESTIONS AND INTERDISCIPLINARY HELP

A. Finding the Right Method and Research Questions

In comparative law, the functional method occupies a central position, as a mantra for the alleged supporters or a red rag to the critics.[31] Here, the

---

[29] This text will deal with the collision A–II against C^1 below in Section V. This is a collision that, if mentioned at all, is mostly dealt with in few words.

[30] In the DCFR, these are seen as two different questions depending on whether the first contracting party has acquired ownership or not. The 'Multiple transfers' are seen as a special constellation under the rules on 'Transfer of ownership based on the transferor's right or authority' and dealt with in Article VIII–2:301 whereas 'Good faith acquisition of ownership' is dealt with in the third chapter of Book VIII. In Sweden and Norway, on the functionalist other hand, this is not the case.

[31] See the introductory sentences in Michaels, R, 'The Functional Method of Comparative Law', in Reimann, M and Zimmermann, R (eds), *The Oxford Handbook of Comparative*

method serves as a vague inspiration for this text's initial research question. But it is only a vague starting point and the use of an alleged functional method has also been criticised by Kötz himself for focusing too much on the problem and its solution, and forgetting what lies between the two. He has likened it to a black box and pointed out that the content of the black box is often more interesting than a comparison of the alleged solutions of different jurisdictions to a problem that is being investigated.[32]

Here, we are dealing with problems of communication and understanding, not different solutions. The difficulties concern differing basic understanding, perspective and perception. These aspects can be placed inside the black box. Therefore, inspiration has inter alia been sought in the legal formants approach that is also used by the Common Core Project. The project's main focus is on what lies inside the black box.[33]

Finding the right methodological research questions not only requires some methodological insights, but also knowledge about relevant similarities and differences between functionalism and substantialism. The chosen similarity serves as *tertium comparationis*. Creditor protection is central to Nordic property law and also interesting for substantialists. The research question about creditor protection is admittedly broad, especially when you consider the more narrow factual approach used by the functional method in comparative law. But on the other hand, it ensures that you find research material. This is research question 1.

The two following research questions deal with relevant differences. Research question 2 examines other functions that, from a substantialist perspective, can be derived from ownership. It takes the substance of ownership and its function as an intermediate concept into account and can in some ways be seen as a matter of legal dogmatics. Research question 3 is one of terminology and deals with the terms 'owner', 'ownership' and 'transfer of ownership'.

Research questions 2 and 3 are linked to research question 1 to ensure that the same things are being investigated. It is primarily other traces of ownership-functions, which are connected with creditor protection even though that is not supposed to be the case, that are interesting; the same goes for an 'owner' linked to creditor protection. But also an 'owner' without creditor protection can be interesting and be more than a non-discovery, since it would show how flexible functionalists can handle concepts.

Law, (Oxford, OUP, 2006) pp 340–382 (340): 'THE functional method has become both the mantra and the bête noire of comparative law. For its proponents it is the most, perhaps the only, fruitful method; to its opponents it represents everything bad about mainstream comparative law.' The footnote has been omitted.

[32] Kötz, H, 'Abschied von der Rechtskreislehre?', *ZEuP* 1998, pp 493–505 (505).

[33] See the important articles by Sacco, R, 'Legal Formants: A Dynamic Approach To Comparative Law', Installment I, *American Journal of Comparative Law* 1991 pp 1–34 and Installment II pp 343–401. See also Bussani, M and Mattei, U, 'The Common Core Approach to European Private Law', *Columbia Journal of European Law* 1997–98 pp 339–356.

B. How to Approach and Understand Profound Differences: Interdisciplinary Assistance

i. Introduction

The following may seem unorthodox, but it must be remembered that it has been said that the differences between the two traditions are unbridgeable. The differences concern basic understanding, perspective and perception. The unorthodox part starts off gently with legal reflections.

National law can be seen as its own paradigm with its own discourse and discursive conditions. The discourse, like human communication in general, does not only have an explicit, visible side, but it also contains many, more or less hidden aspects, and these are implicit. As long as you remain within the framework of your own paradigm, it is unproblematic; the basic understanding of the paradigm is shared with the partner in dialogue, including the implicit aspects. And the legal discourse has long been conducted at the national level; the property law discourse has even been extremely national. Words like globalization and especially Europeanization have become common even among lawyers, although a career in law is still largely national.

It is often assumed to be more difficult to understand foreign law than domestic law, which also explains why most jurists keep to their domestic law. One relevant reason for the difficulties is that the outsider lacks the insider's gut feeling for the implicit aspects of foreign law. Misunderstandings and misinterpretations may be due to a lack of unseen pieces of the puzzle, or due to the fact that the outsider even ignores visible aspects because they are assumed to be irrelevant in accordance with the outsider's own domestic law. Such experiences can be a reminder that the researcher's domestic legal system can also contain many hidden aspects.

The above is not unknown in legal theory. Tuori talks illustratively of the levels of the law and their different types of knowledge, namely the visible and explicit discursive knowledge of the surface level and the implicit practical knowledge of the lower levels of the law. Practical knowledge is what makes the dialogue function, but at the same time it is largely hidden because it is not pronounced.[34]

Further, many comparatists have also discussed these matters. Sacco calls the hidden aspects 'cryptotypes' and Bussani and Mattei speak of 'hidden data' and 'automatic assumptions'.[35] The comparatist's duties include making such aspects visible and thereby contributing new knowledge.

It must also be pointed out that an awareness of the strong imprint of one's own law is important. It is likely to be perceived as the natural, normal standard, or perhaps even as the only possible standard, but that in itself

---

[34] Tuori, *Critical Legal Positivism* (n 1) p 150 et seq.
[35] Sacco, 'Legal Formants' (n 34) pp 352 et seq.

does not have to be a conscious choice.[36] Inspired by Frankenberg, you can speak of a 'Home Law' paradigm.[37] Two essentially different 'Home Law' paradigms have been presented in a somewhat abstract form using different images.[38] The images show differing basic assumptions, perspective and perception, but making these aspects visible does not mean that the problem is solved. The strong imprint of one's own paradigm is not overcome so easily.

ii. Interdisciplinary Assistance

So far the comments have more or less been legal. Similar comments and more elaborate theories can be found in other sciences where the other, eg foreign cultures, is the object of study and which are, therefore, accustomed to dealing with various meetings between different basic understandings. Mainstream legal science and practice is, on the other hand, more or less a mono-paradigm and provides little help in solving this problem. Legal comparisons are to a large extent concerned with the visible aspects of the surface level.

According to the jurist and legal anthropologist Fikentscher, the 'Home Law' paradigm (in his books: 'Ethnocentrism') appears in the way that 'the researcher uses his or her own categories, experiences, and even bias while problematizing, concluding, reasoning, or systematizing the study of another culture'.[39]

---

[36] Kamba, WJ, 'Comparative Law: A Theoretical Framework', *Int&CompLQ* 1974 pp 485–519 (491): 'When one is confined to the study of one's own law within one's own country and, thus within one's own cultural environment, there is a strong tendency to accept without question the various aspects (norms, concepts, and institutions) of one's own legal system. One is inclined to think that the solutions of one's own legal order are the only possible ones'. See also Husa, J, 'Turning the Curriculum Upside Down', *GermanLJ*, 2009 pp 913–926 (917 after note 17) with a reference to Kamba: 'So, it is not claimed that one necessarily prefers one's own law knowingly, but that one is in an epistemic sense inclined to do that'. Similar statements concerning our property law functionalism have been given by Martinson and Andreasson in Swedish. See Martinson, C, 'Funktionalismen och bättre rätt till fast egendom', *SvJT* 2008 pp 669–687 (669): 'Functionalism has become an obvious starting point requiring neither justification nor does it have to be treated as a specific phenomenon.' ('Funktionalismen har blivit en självklar utgångspunkt som varken behöver motiveras eller ens behandlas som ett särskilt fenomen.') and Andreasson, J, 'Inlösen, äganderättsövergång och "legal transplants"', *SvJT* 2005 pp 522–538 (526 et seq) who mentions Hessler's, Rodhe's and Håstad's great importance for Swedish property law and, thereafter, asserts the following: 'The influence of these descriptions can be alleged to have been so dominant that it is perceived as quite strange to even think about alternatives.' ('Inflytandet av dessa beskrivningar kan nog utan vidare påstås ha varit så dominerande att det upplevs som ganska främmande att ens reflektera över alternativ.') As mentioned both Martinson and Andreasson have been in contact with Salzburg and DCFR Book VIII.

[37] Frankenberg, G, 'Critical Comparisons: Re-thinking Comparative Law', *HarvIntLJ* 1985 pp 411–455 (423) and in 'Stranger than Paradise: Identity & Politics in Comparative Law', *UtahLR* 1997 pp 259–274 (265).

[38] See the images in Section II B.

[39] Fikentscher, W, *Law and Anthropology: Outlines, Issues, and Suggestions*, (Munich, Bayerischen Akademie der Wissenschaften, 2009), Chap 6 p 5, at www.works.bepress.com/wolfgang_fikentscher/. The definition in his earlier book, *Modes of Thought: A Study in the*

In cognitive anthropology, the concept of cultural models is used, and according to Quinn and Holland, cultural models are: 'presupposed, taken for granted models of the world that are widely shared [...] by the members of a society and that play an enormous role in their understanding of that world and their behaviour in it'.[40]

According to D'Andrade, a cultural model is: 'a cognitive schema that is intersubjectively shared by a social group. Because cultural models are inter-subjectively shared, interpretations made about the world on the basis of a cultural model are experienced as obvious facts of the world.'[41]

These three statements give us an idea of the understanding of reality held by a discrete group. This understanding is highly imprinting, but it is only shared by the other members of the group, which causes problems of understanding when it is confronted with something alien.

The quotations can serve as a thought-provoking eye-opener, if you are trying to get to grips with studying something outside your own 'Home Law' paradigm. The quotations demonstrate that there are different paradigms—and a meeting with another paradigm has even been called a discovery by Fikentscher.[42] These statements may give rise to a 'eureka' moment, but do not say much about how to proceed.

Additional help can be provided by other sciences with a cognitive focus, such as cognitive psychology. It can provide a more concrete, but at the same time collectivist, translation of the discursive conditions of a legal paradigm, which consist of the implicit and explicit understanding of the paradigm—and hence also its perspective and perception. The paradigm can metaphorically be treated as an anticipatory schema.

Cognitive psychology is the study of mental processes, inter alia information processes. The legally relevant aspects of the study of information processes can be divided into: (1) perception processes, (2) thought processes, and (3) memory processes. Translated into legal research the issues in turn will be: (1) which material the researcher selects and how it is perceived (perception process), (2) how this material is analysed and which conclusions that are drawn from it (thought process), and (3) how the researcher remembers the foreign material and how memory with time can increasingly be adapted to the researcher's own paradigm (memory processes).

The 'Home Law' paradigm is, as mentioned above, highly imprinting and this relates to perception, thought and memory. Reality and foreign

Anthropology of Law and Religion, (Tübingen, Mohr Siebeck, 1995) was slightly shorter, see p 117: 'the researcher uses his or her own bias while problematizing, concluding, reasoning, or systematizing the study of another culture.'

[40] Quinn, N and Holland, D, 'Culture and cognition', in Holland, D and Quinn, N (eds), *Cultural Models in Language & Thought*, (Cambridge, CUP, 1987) pp 3–40 (4).

[41] D'Andrade, RG, 'Cultural Cognition', in Posner, MI (ed), *Foundations of Cognitive Science*, (Cambridge, Massachusetts, MIT Press, 1989) pp 795–830 (808).

[42] Fikentscher, *Modes of Thought* (n 40) pp 131 and 136 et seq.

legal material can be distorted. Keywords are anticipatory schema, cognitive assimilation, confirmation bias, belief bias, false consensus bias, illusory correlation and different memory errors. The material presented above hopefully provides a slightly more concrete picture of possible errors in research.

iii. Lessons Learned

It is now time to return to the functionalism–substantialism dichotomy. The interdisciplinary outlook used to explain the strong imprint of the 'Home Law' paradigm has hopefully made clear that when the functionalist studies the alien substantialism, this is done through a functionalist lens, ie on the basis of the differences described initially. The same goes for the substantialist's study of functionalism. We are outsiders in relation to the unfamiliar, not insiders. The functionalist converts, or tries to convert, the substantialist material to legal cause/legal effect scenarios and tends to perceive associated issues as being topically separated.

Ownership is important also in this context. It is not a (relevant) part of the functionalist solutions and, consequently, nothing that we would notice, nor understand the great relevance of.[43] For the substantialist, on the other hand, ownership is central. It is probably easier for the substantialist to notice certain differences. From the substantialist's viewpoint, something seems to be missing in the functionalist images. And it has been stated that it is easier to discover that something visible, as well as central, is missing in the functionalist images, than it is for the functionalist to notice something invisible, or to notice additional information deemed irrelevant.[44]

To use images to depict the differences and quotations from other sciences does not mean that the problems of understanding have been solved. It has initially only drawn attention to the fact that there is a problem of understanding—which is something of which a jurist who has tried taking on a cross-border dialogue need not be in doubt about—and it has been pointed out how other sciences can be helpful. Practical comparative experience is of course also important, and in my case also the reason for attempting to understand and solve the above-mentioned problems of understanding.

Furthermore, despite knowing that one's own outsider perspective is erroneous, it takes a great deal of effort to come to terms with it. Understanding that functionalism and substantialism are essentially different is a good starting point, but still just a starting point. To proceed, the researcher needs

---

[43] This is paradoxical and complicated. We often do not notice the relevance of ownership. At the same time, the intermediate concept of ownership is criticized by some conscious functionalists. See also Section III A above.

[44] Nelken, D, 'Legal culture', in Smits, J (ed), *Elgar Encyclopedia of Comparative Law*, 2006 pp 372–381 (377): 'Similarities and differences often come to life for an observer when they are exemplified by "significant absences".'

to understand the explicit and implicit aspects of his/her own paradigm, and ideally you should also try to understand the other paradigm.

In the present case, the functionalist researcher must not only become aware of his/her own 'Home Law' paradigm, but also manage to understand the substantialist images of the legal reality and, to some extent, manage to internalise them, and, at the same time, be able to keep his/her own functionalist images of the legal reality in mind, all for the sake of comparison.[45] The same goes for the substantialist. Finally, interdisciplinary assistance might make it easier to keep the two paradigms apart.

A jurist who seeks assistance from other sciences meets several obstacles. First, the researcher must understand that he needs assistance, and why he needs it and where he can find it. Then the researcher has to understand the assistance that comes from without and manage to transform it into a tool for his/her own legal research. This can be time consuming and the result is also uncertain. A 'cost benefit' analysis will probably be carried out more than once while the work is in progress. In addition, you might have to handle the doubts of a more traditional legal environment. The researcher might have to refer to comparatists who support a broader research approach using other sciences.[46] In view of the relevant audience, it should be borne in mind that the results should look legal and be presented in a way that is understandable for your own discipline and, in this case, jurists.

V. CONCLUDING APPLICATION

A. Introduction

Finding a gap between abstract theory and practical application is not uncommon. What the theorist produces is not applied in practice. The theorist and the practitioner are frequently two different individuals working in two different genres. But theories should preferably also be useful and it is desirable that the researcher who presents the theory also shows how it can be used, and sometimes even why it should be used. Theorists with an interest in practice and practitioners with theoretical interests are called for.

However, at this point an attempt shall be made to let theory and more down-to-earth application unite. The attempt will seek to illustrate how the method and the unorthodox interdisciplinary theory are being used. In addition, it will show that they are needed to bridge the gap between functionalism and substantialism and also to illustrate their differences. The examples

---

[45] The above might be a good description of comparative legal schizophrenia.

[46] See, eg, Palmer, VE, 'From Lerotholi to Lando: Some Examples of Comparative Law Methodology', *AmJCompL* 2005 pp 261–290.

that will be used concern the assumed fundamental questions of causality or abstraction.

B. Comparative Legal Dogmatics: Causality or Abstraction Principle?

Contemporary works on comparative law also contain sections on comparative property law. In different handbooks, both van Vliet and van Erp deal with the question of a causality or an abstraction principle and the same subject matter is also to be found in the DCFR context.[47] This question may, therefore, seem important—but it may equally tell us something about which questions the authors deem to be important comparatively speaking. The question is similarly raised in a comparative context in German literature.[48]

Conversely, this question of causality and abstraction is barely mentioned in Nordic literature, but a researcher who wants to participate in the European discussions should preferably know which matters are being debated and further contribute to matters assumed to be relevant from the Nordic perspective. A spontaneous answer from a functionalist jurist would probably be that Nordic law adheres to the more down-to-earth and natural principle, as much as the researcher would perhaps dislike the term principle. The answer is in my opinion more complicated than that, because such an answer tends to ignore the fundamental and profound differences between functionalism and substantialism.

Some basic explanations: The causality and abstraction principles deal with the issue of the real transfer (according to property law) and its relation to the obligation, mostly the contract. This explanation might already sound archaic and strange, especially to West Nordic jurists. In the Norwegian-Danish national report, it is claimed that the category of property right does not exist, which means that a principle of division (of obligatory and property rights) does not exist, which in turn means that '[a] principle of abstraction or a "causal" system would be even less meaningful'.[49]

---

[47] van *Vliet*, 'Transfer of movable property' (**) p 730 et seq); van Erp, 'Comparative Property Law' (**) p 1060 et seq; Bartels, S, 'An Abstract or a Causal System', in Faber, W and Lurger, B (eds), *Rules for the Transfer of Movables: A Candidate for European Harmonisation or National Reforms?*, Munich 2008 pp 59–67; Lurger and Faber, *Principles of European Law* (n 3) p 454 et seq (Comments no 82 et seq); Drobnig, U, 'Transfer of Property', in Hartkamp, AS, Hesselink, MW, Hondius, EH, Mak, C, du Perron, CE (eds), *Towards a European Civil Code*, Nijmegen 2011, pp 1003–1023 (1015 et seq); van Vliet, L, 'Transfer', in van Erp, S and Akkermans, B (eds), *Cases, Materials and Text on Property Law*, (Oxford, Hart Publishing, 2012) p 823 et seq.

[48] See, eg, Ferrari, F, 'Vom Abstraktionsprinzip und Konsensualprinzip zum Traditionsprinzip—Zu den Möglichkeiten der Rechtsangleichung im Mobiliarsachenrecht', *ZEuP* 1993 pp 52–78.

[49] Færstad, JO, 'Norway and Denmark', in Faber, W and Lurger, B (eds), *National Reports on the Transfer of Movables in Europe*, Vol 5, Munich 2011, pp 205–301 (223).

The abstraction principle (*Abstraktionsprinzip*) is originally a German phenomenon and linked to the principle of division (*Trennungsprinzip*).[50] According to the principle of division, a transfer is divided into two parts: the obligatory contract and the real agreement. This clear division of the law of obligations and the law of property is in accordance with Roman law as understood by the Historical School (*Historische Schule*),[51] but it is also a prerequisite for the abstraction principle; in accordance with the latter, the two areas of law are independent of each other. The (in)validity of one contract or agreement does not influence the (in)validity of the other.[52] The principle also has the effect of maintaining the dividing line between the two areas of law, which was one of the aims of the principle.[53]

The causality principle is less complicated. It is not necessary to keep a clear division between the two areas of law, or even talk about a principle of division, but any such discussion can be had using the old concepts around *titulus* and *modus* or *iusta causa traditionis*. *Titulus* and *modus* imply a division. A transfer requires a valid basis and tradition. The latter need not be physical. *Iusta causa traditionis* explains that the transfer requires a legal basis.[54]

The difference between the abstraction and the causality principles becomes clear in a case where the obligatory contract is invalid (and the delivery has taken place). With a causality principle, the invalidity of the contract also affects the delivery. The transferor can, therefore, recover the good under property rules (and has a right of separation; with functionalist words: he has creditor protection). With an abstraction principle, the delivery is unaffected by the invalidity of the contract. But the delivery has taken place without legal ground and shall be returned in accordance with the rules on unjust enrichment in ss 812 et seq BGB. This claim for restitution is just an obligatory claim (the transferor has no right of separation if the transferee enters bankruptcy; with functionalist words: he does not have creditor protection). Consequently, the question of creditor protection is treated differently under an abstraction principle than under a causality principle—but is not the only question where that is the case.

---

[50] In English, see Füller, 'The German Property Law' (**) p 200 et seq.

[51] Therefore, the Historical School discarded *ius ad rem*, see, eg, Wieling, *Sachenrecht* § 1 II 3 c, p 21. In Swedish literature, see Forssell, H, 'Tredjemansskyddets gränser: en studie av principen "köp bryter lega" och indelningen i sakrätter och obligatoriska rättigheter', Stockholm 1976, Norstedts, pp 16 and 48.

[52] In English, see Füller, 'The German Property Law' (**) p 201 et seq; Baur, JF and Stürner, R, *Sachenrecht*, 18th edn, Munich 2009, § 5 no 40 et seq; Füller, JT, *Eigenständiges Sachenrecht?*, Tübingen 2006, p 112 et seq; Wieling, HJ, *Sachenrecht* (Springer, 2007), § 1 III 1 d, bb, p 33.

[53] See, eg, van Vliet, 'Iusta Causa Traditionis' (**) p 367 note 114, with further references.

[54] van Vliet, 'Iusta Causa Traditionis' (**) p 342 et seq on *iusta causa* and p 361 et seq on *titulus* and *modus* and Savigny); Wieling, *Sachenrecht* (n 53) § 1 III 1 c, p 31 et seq.

The above-mentioned difference also relates to ownership. Either it reverts back or is considered to have never passed; alternatively, it stays unaffected by the invalidity of the obligatory contract. And the question of good faith acquisitions can also be linked back to the question of ownership. For the substantialist, this is the starting point for both the question of creditor protection and that of good faith acquisition. Under the abstraction principle, C acquires the good from the owner B and the rules on good faith acquisition do not apply. Under a causality principle, on the other hand, C acquires from the non-owner B and, therefore, must fulfil the requirements under good faith acquisition rules to be protected against A.

To answer the question whether we have an abstraction or a causality principle and narrow it down to central property law matters, we should at least find an answer to both the question of creditor-protection and that of good faith acquisition. The answer does not have to be without ambiguity—and the research method also presupposes that two separate questions, which are independent from each other, are examined and conflated.

The PEL/Acq states the following: 'The principle of abstraction is employed in German law and, following this model, in Greece and Estonia. The other European countries can be said to employ a causal transfer model, although the question is not identified as a particular issue in all legal systems.'[55]

The possible answer might be that Swedish or Nordic property law more or less resembles one of the two principles, but without actually referring to a principle.

C. A Swedish (and a Nordic) Answer

i. Introduction

In contemporary literature, the question of creditor protection and that of good faith acquisition are treated separately.[56] They are topically separated and the answer to one collision is irrelevant to the answer to the other collision, even though more recently published books do not say so explicitly.[57] The two possible collisions could, in a functionalist way, be presented through the following two legal cause/legal effect scenarios:

— If the contract between A and B is invalid, then A has creditor protection against C (ie a right of separation if B goes bankrupt).

---

[55] Lurger and Faber *Principles of European Law* (n 3) p 454 (Comments no 82).

[56] See Millqvist, G, *Sakrättens grunder*, 7th edn, Stockholm 2014, Norstedts (Chapter 2 on good faith acquisition and Chapters 3 and 4 on creditor protection; see also the basic remark on p 16) and, Zetterström, S, *Sakrättens fyra huvudfall*, 4th edn (Uppsala, Iustus, 2016). According to its title, the book deals with the four main cases in property law.

[57] See above in Section III A, where it is explained that this no longer needs to be mentioned. It is the new normality.

— If the contract between A and B is invalid, then C must make a good faith acquisition to be protected against A.

To examine a possible common answer, a method of induction can be used, even though the answers are supposed to be independent of each other. For the benefit of the substantialist, it is important to note that this is a different approach. The substantialist would instead focus on the question of who the owner is, A or B, placing the solution in a civilistic system and subsequently deducing the answers to both questions from the said ownership.

Case law will be used for the Swedish creditor-protection question and the preparatory works to the Good Faith Acquisition Act[58] for the question of good faith acquisition. Norwegian law will just receive a brief mention.

ii. *Invalidity and Creditor Protection: Does the Transferor have a Right of Separation or Not?*

The current problem typically concerns the situation where A–II and B have entered into a purchase agreement, the good has been handed over to B, B has not paid, the contract can be declared invalid, and B's creditors C[3] claim a better right to the goods than A–II. A fairly uniform literature assumes that A–II has creditor protection, ie a right of separation.[59]

NJA 1985 p 178 is a case from the Swedish Supreme Court which dealt with a collision between the seller A–II and the buyer B's creditors, C[3]. B, in this case, was the company Kalmar varv, a shipyard, and A–II was Järnsida, a company delivering sheet metal. A–II had called off delivery to B after B declared that it called off payments due to financial problems. Later on, a reconstruction of B, which at that time also involved the Swedish government, seemed to be more or less certain and B informed A–II about the solved financial problem. A–II resumed delivery of sheet metal on credit. Surprisingly for both A–II and B, the reconstruction was called off and B went bankrupt.

A–II claimed that the contract was invalid and that they, therefore, had a right of separation. The Supreme Court deemed the contract to be invalid in accordance with the doctrine on presupposed conditions. The Court also found that A–II had a right of separation. The Court arrived at this result without having to deal with the question of ownership. Initially, the Court mentioned the predominant position in the literature, namely that a party as a result of contractual reversion 'has a right to recover individualized property that still exists in principle and is protected against the other party's creditors,

---

[58] Lag (1986:796) om godtrosförvärv av lösöre [Act (1986:796) on good faith acquisition of movable property].

[59] See, eg, Sandstedt, *Sakrätten* (**) p 448 et seq.

ie enjoys a right of separation'.[60] The Court subsequently mentioned some cases that the literature had deemed to be uncertain borderline cases and the weighing of interests between A–II and C[3]. The Court found that no circumstances contradicted a right of separation 'regardless of whether the recovery was claimed before or after the opening of the bankruptcy'.[61] The Supreme Court's solution is functionalistic; it is a legal cause/legal effect scenario and consequently no ownership to which the solution is connected, is mentioned.

Further in NJA 1995 p. 162, also a case decided by the Supreme Court, the invalidity of a contract led to creditor protection for A–II. B had already been sentenced for deceit in a criminal procedure. The Court followed this criminal sentence and explained that s 30 of the Contracts Act[62] on fraudulent deception was covered by the provision in the Criminal Code.[63] The Supreme Court explained the following: 'The right, in connection with invalidity, to recover individualized property that still exists may be asserted against the creditors of the other party also when the recovery was claimed after the enforcement.'[64]

The earlier Supreme Court judgment was confirmed, but not mentioned. The Court of Appeal, on the other hand, stated that A–II should have asserted his claim before the enforcement, which seems contrary to the statements of the Supreme Court in 1985, although these statements concerned bankruptcy, not enforcement. In addition, the creditor, namely the Swedish National Tax Board, and the Enforcement Authority considered that the good could be seized for B's tax debts.

The answer to this question should be similar under Norwegian law.[65]

iii. Invalidity and Good Faith Acquisition: Must the Subsequent Transferee Acquire in Accordance with the Good Faith Acquisition Act or Not?

To answer the question about invalidity and the possible applicability of the Good Faith Acquisition Act, we must examine the preparatory works underpinning the said Act. They state the following:

'The provisions of the Act also apply in cases when the person who disposes of the property has come across it through a legal act which for one reason or another is

---

[60] NJA 1985 p 178 (192). The whole sentence (without references): 'Den övervägande uppfattningen i svensk doktrin är att den part, som vid avtals återgång har rätt att återfå individualiserad egendom som finns i behåll, i princip är skyddad mot medkontrahentens borgenärer, dvs åtnjuter separationsrätt'.

[61] NJA 1985 p 178 (193). The whole sentence: 'Tillräcklig anledning saknas då att inte medge separationsrätt, och det oavsett om krav på av talets återgång framställs före konkursutbrottet eller först därefter.'

[62] Lag (1915:218) om avtal och andra rättshandlingar på förmögenhetsrättens område [Act (1915:218) on contracts and other legal acts in the area of patrimonial law].

[63] Brottsbalk [Criminal Code] (1962:700).

[64] NJA 1995 p 162 (164).

[65] Sandstedt, *Sakrätten* (**) p 450 et seq and the latest Norwegian text on the subject matter, Ørjasæter, Jo, 'Foreldelse, ugyldighet og vindikasjon', *Jussens venner* 2015 p 119–149 (133).

invalid, for instance, if he has acquired the property from a minor or a bankruptcy debtor or if his acquisition is invalid under Chapter 3 of the Contracts Act.'[66]

This picture is confirmed also in the older preparatory works, but in a less clear form, and can be traced back to somewhat vague statements in the preparatory works to the Contracts Act.[67] This picture is also confirmed in the literature. If the contract is invalid, a good faith acquisition is required to protect C. As has been pointed out, this is a legal cause/legal effect scenario. However, the text in s 2 para 1 of the Act presents a different picture:

> 'Where a person has acquired personal property by means of a transfer from any other person who had possession of the property but was neither the owner of the property nor authorized to dispose of it in the manner that has occurred, title to the property shall vest in the acquirer, where such property has come into his possession and he was in good faith.'

If the provision is carefully studied, especially from the functionalist's perspective, it is clear that an owner is present, which the outsider Faber also has observed.[68] In the provision, only the non-owner ('was neither the owner') is mentioned, but logically someone also has to be the original owner according to the Act. With the intermediate concept of an owner, the provision looks substantialist, but this is not identified by the functionalist property jurists, who automatically translate it into a legal cause/legal effect scenario. The same applies to the property jurists with experience of the European discussions.[69]

Two further aspects of the above-mentioned statement in the preparatory works are of interest: firstly, the text presents a legal cause/legal effect scenario ('The provisions of the Act apply' when B has acquired the property 'through a legal act which [...] is invalid') and secondly, the quoted statement is not connected with the prerequisite owner, but instead with the question of how B gained possession of the property. According to the preparatory works and the literature, the question of ownership is not relevant for this matter, but the provision itself shows a different picture.

The answer to this question should be fairly similar under Norwegian law, at least with a focus on a yes/no answer.[70]

iv. A Careful Induction: Proprietary Effects of Invalidity

Two separate questions that are supposed to be resolved with an 'issue-by-issue approach'—our topical features—thus lead to the following

---

[66] Prop. 1985/86:123 (Om godtrosförvärv av lösöre [Good Faith Acquisition Act]) p 19.

[67] SOU 1984:16 (Förvärv i god tro) pp 30, 75 and 195; SOU 1965:14 (Godtrosförvärv av lösöre [Good Faith Acquisition Act]) pp 43 et seq.

[68] Faber, 'Scepticism about the Functional Approach (**) p 115.

[69] Lilja, 'Sweden' (**) p 56 et seq and Martinson, 'How Swedish Lawyers Think' (**) p 75.

[70] Sandstedt, *Sakrätten* (**) p 447 et seq.

conclusion: In the creditor-protection collision between A–II and C³, the first has a right of separation and in the good faith acquisition collision the same A–II can recover the good from C¹, unless the latter has made a good faith acquisition. On the issue of terminology, it can be noted that A–II, in the creditor-protection case, has a right of separation,[71] which is not arrived at through ownership. In the other question, the same A–II, according to s 2 para 1 of the Good Faith Acquisition Act, should be the owner by default; as it is clear that B is not.

Based on the key questions outlined in property law you could induce the solutions and speak of invalidity with proprietary effects (*sakrättsligt verkande ogiltighet*). According to our functionalist legal cause/legal effect scenarios ownership is not included—and the literature does not include ownership either—even though there should be one for the good faith acquisition question. The picture induced, invalidity with proprietary effects, seems to comply with the causality principle, at least when focus is on the two solutions.

D. Ownership and the Question of Whether We Have a Causality Principle

A Nordic researcher would probably often base the answer on just one of the questions, either creditor protection or good faith acquisition, and believe—our perception turns the question into a topical feature—that this is a comprehensive reply. This is at most a half causality principle. By considering both questions we have been able to achieve a whole causality principle, at least within the central areas of property law.

But still, one important difference remains. It is easier to illustrate the difference with two images. The functionalist image is presented on the left and, on the right, the substantialist counterpart.

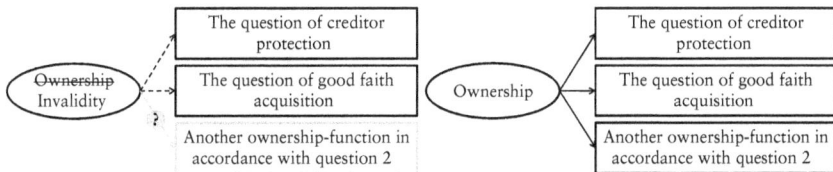

The two topically separated legal cause/legal effect scenarios have been induced to a whole proprietary causality principle picture. But from the material produced, you cannot deduce an answer to another question, which a substantialist would connect with ownership.

---

[71] *Separatist* in some Norwegian literature and sometimes *den separationsberättigade* in Swedish literature.

6

Private International Law Aspects of Substantive Law Harmonisation

CAROLINA SAF*

I. INTRODUCTION

THIS CHAPTER DEALS with the private international law aspects of the Commission's Proposal for a Regulation on a Common European Sales Law (CESL)[1] and, in particular, its introductory Regulation (Reg CESL)—the '*chapeau* rules', to which the CESL is included as Annex I.

The CESL is an optional regime of uniform rules directly applicable to the cross-border sale of goods for the European Union (EU). Its purpose is to simplify the legal environment for businesses entering into cross-border transactions with both consumers and other businesses. This means that the CESL will govern cross-border contracts that fall within the sphere of private international law (PIL). Furthermore, as a directly applicable second regime for the international sale of goods, the scope of the CESL will also coincide with that of the 1980 UN Convention on the International Sale of Goods (CISG)[2] as regards commercial sales contracts.

Consequently, both the interplay between the CESL and the CISG *inter se*, and the interplay with relevant choice-of-law rules in contract will be dealt with.[3] Those rules are found in the Rome I Regulation on

---

* Doctoral Candidate at Stockholm University and Lecturer in Law at Örebro University. Jur.kand. (LL.M.) (Stockholm), and LL.M. in International Business Law (London).
[1] Proposal for a Regulation of the European Parliament and of the Council on a Common European Sales Law, COM(2011) 635 final.
[2] 1980 United Nations Convention on the Contracts for the International Sale of Goods, adopted on 11 April 1980, 1489 UNTS 3, (1980). It entered into force on 1 January 1988.
[3] The CESL governs the following matters: pre-contractual duties to provide information; the conclusion of a contract including formal requirements; the right of withdrawal and its consequences; avoidance of the contract as a result of mistake, fraud, threat or unfair exploitation and the consequences of such avoidance; interpretation; contents and effects, including those of the relevant contract; the assessment and the effects of unfairness of contract terms; the rights and obligations of the parties; remedies for non-performance; restitution after avoidance

the law applicable to contractual obligations (Rome I),[4] the 1955 Hague Convention on the Law Applicable to International Sales of Goods (the 1955 Hague Convention),[5] and the Rome II Regulation on the law applicable to non-contractual obligations (Rome II)[6] as regards pre-contractual duties to provide information (*culpa in contrahendo*).

This chapter was presented as a paper at the Swedish Network for European Legal Studies spring conference on 'Harmonization—the Future of European Private Law?' on 22–23 April 2013 in Stockholm, and following that the European Parliament adopted an amended text of the proposed CESL on 26 February 2014 (EP Amendment)[7]—drawing on the recommendations presented by the Committee on Legal Affairs and the Committee on the Internal Market and Consumer Protection.[8] Furthermore, the new Commission announced on 16 December 2014 that a modified proposal would be submitted as part of the Digital Single Market Strategy, 'in order to fully unleash the potential of e-commerce in the Digital Single Market'.[9] Whether the Commission will reach its aim to conclude inter-institutional negotiations on a modified proposal in 2015 remains to be seen.

Several of the amendments adopted by the European Parliament in 2014 concern the topic of this chapter and are, therefore, included under the relevant headings below, albeit that most of these amendments are clarifications rather than substantial changes to the proposed CESL. One important and

---

or termination or in the case of a non-binding contract; prescription and preclusion of rights; and sanctions available in the event of breach of the obligations and duties arising under its application.

[4] Regulation (EC) No 593/2008 of the European Parliament and of the Council on the law applicable to contractual obligations (Rome I) [2008] OJ L177/6. It applies to international contracts concluded after 17 December 2009.

[5] The 1955 Hague Convention on the Law Applicable to International Sale of Goods (*Convention sur la loi applicable aux ventes à caractère international d'objets mobiliers corporels*), concluded on 15 June 1955, 510 UNTS 149, No 7411 (1964). It entered into force on 1 September 1964. It is available in French only at www.hcch.net/upload/conventions/txt03en.pdf and an unofficial English translation is available at www.jus.uio.no/english/services/library/treaties/11/11-02/law-international-sales.xml.

[6] Regulation (EC) No 864/2007 of the European Parliament and of the Council on the law applicable to non-contractual obligations (Rome II) [2007] OJ L199/40. It applies to non-contractual obligations that arose after 11 January 2009, see Case C-412/10 *Deo Antoine Homawoo v GMF Assurances SA* [2011] ECR I-11622.

[7] European Parliament legislative resolution of 26 February 2014 on the proposal for a regulation of the European Parliament and of the Council on a Common European Sales Law (COM(2011) 0635—C7-0329/2011—2011/0284(COD)) (Ordinary legislative procedure: first reading), Document P7TA(2014)0159 (EP Amendment).

[8] Report on the proposal for a regulation of the European Parliament and of the Council on a Common European Sales Law (COM(2011) 0635—C7-0329/2011—2011/0284(COD)) (Ordinary legislative procedure: first reading), Document A7-0301/2013.

[9] Communication from the Commission to the European Parliament, the Council, the European Economic and Social Committee and the Committee of the Regions, Commission Work Programme 2015, A New Start, COM(2014) 910 final, p 6 including Annex II: List of withdrawals or modifications of pending proposals, 12.

substantial amendment is the proposed reduction of the scope of the CESL to distance contracts and in particular online contracts, as well as digital content and related services provided using a cloud, although it has also been proposed that the review should take into account the possibility to widen its scope to cover on-premises contracts.[10] Notably, the aim of the new Commission is to 'simplify the rules for consumers making online and digital purchases [and] facilitate e-commerce',[11] so the modified proposal might contain fewer general provisions of substantive contract law in comparison with the proposed CESL.[12]

Another important amendment is the explicit classification of the CESL as a directly applicable second regime, ie that it in practice constitutes a uniform law that in effect takes precedence over the choice-of-law rules in the 'intra-Union context' where all parties to the contract are habitually resident in Member States.[13] In the 'external context', where at least one party is habitually resident in a Member State and *at least one* is habitually resident in a non-Member State, the CESL is indirectly applicable as an integral part of the *lex contractus*. This line of argument will be developed in more detail in Section IV.E.ii below.

Recital 9 Reg CESL including EP Amendment 2

(9) This Regulation establishes a Common European Sales Law **for distance contracts and in particular for online contracts**. It **approximates** the contract laws of the Member States not by requiring amendments to the **first** national contract-law regime, but by creating a **second** contract-law regime for contracts within its scope. This *directly applicable* second regime **should be an** *integral part* of the legal order applicable in the territory of the Member States. In so far as *its scope allows* and where parties have *validly agreed* to use it, the Common European Sales Law **should apply instead of the first national contract-law regime within that legal order** [ie the *lex contractus*, see Recital 10]. It should be identical throughout the Union and exist alongside the pre-existing rules of national contract law. The Common European Sales Law should apply on a voluntary basis, upon an express agreement of the parties, to a cross-border contract. (emphasis added)

II. DIFFERENT WAYS OF ACHIEVING HARMONISATION

There are different ways of and aspects to achieving harmonisation—or unification—of the national law of different states, whether it be in an

---

[10] EP Amendments 1–2 and 26 regarding Recitals 8–9 and Art 1(1) Reg CESL.

[11] Communication from the Commission to the European Parliament, the Council (n 9) 6.

[12] Pinkel, T, 'Book review: Javier Plaza Penades and Luz M. Martinez Velencoso (eds.), European Perspectives on the Common European Sales Law, Springer 2015' (2014) 10 *Hanse Law Review* 99.

[13] EP Amendment 2 regarding Recital 9 in conjunction with EP Amendment 6 regarding Recital 12 Reg CESL (changes indicated in bold).

international setting, such as the Hague Conferences on Private International Law or the United Nations and the UNCITRAL, or a regional setting such as the EU. Firstly, harmonisation can be either in the form of an approximation of the national laws aimed at fulfilling certain agreed objectives, such as a model law or an EU directive, or in the form of a set of uniform rules, such as a legislative convention or an EU regulation. The suitability of each form depends on the underlying purposes of the intended legislative act—uniform rules are usually preferable if legal certainty and foreseeability are important for the actors, such as traders pursuing cross-border trade encompassing several countries. Naturally, political concerns will also affect the chosen form and extent of harmonisation. In the context of the EU, the legal basis in the Treaty on the Functioning of the European Union (TFEU)—Article 114 TFEU has been chosen for the CESL—together with the principle of subsidiarity in Article 5 of the Treaty on European Union will play a vital role, too, although such matters fall outside the scope of this chapter.[14]

Secondly, in the international—or perhaps rather the cross-border—setting of private law, the question is whether to harmonise the choice-of-law rules or the substantive rules of the participating states. Replacing the former with harmonised common rules is usually perceived as less intrusive, since it is both a smaller area of law and the national character of private law will be preserved and respected. Accordingly, the harmonisation is achieved through the application of uniform choice-of-law rules, in order to ensure that the same national law is determined as the applicable law to the parties' legal relationship, or the legal situation at hand. The purpose here is thus twofold: (i) to prevent the parties from forum shopping, ie choosing the forum country on the basis of the choice-of-law rules used; and (ii) to reduce the parties' transaction costs in that only one regime of choice-of-law rules will be applied.

However, harmonisation through a uniform choice-of-law regime cannot fully address the transaction costs relating to the need of private actors to inform themselves of the different legal systems so identified, even if the parties are allowed full party autonomy regarding the choice of applicable law (*lex electa*). Accordingly, from the perspective of reducing the private actors' transaction costs, at least in the long run, the best option would be a common regime of uniform substantive rules of private law replacing the national ones and thus making the application of choice-of-law rules as well as foreign law less frequent. Experience shows, however, that it is difficult to agree on the contents of such a replacement regime, often rendering its scope fairly narrow and, consequently, national private law still has to be applied to important legal issues, and there is also the problem of ensuring its uniform application and interpretation in all the participating states.

---

[14] For an analysis of the chosen legal basis, see Low, G, '*Unitas via Diversitas*. Can the Common European Sales Law Harmonize through Diversity?' (2012) 19 *Maastricht Journal* 132.

Thirdly, it is also possible to harmonise through the provision of an optional regime of uniform rules of substantive private law.[15] Even though an additional regime may at first seem counterintuitive—harmonisation through diversity appears illogical—it has the advantage of both offering a common regime and preserving the national regime already in place, which makes it easier for the regime to be accepted by both private actors and participating states.

One important practical aspect is how the optional instrument comes into play, ie whether the private actors must contract into the instrument or contract out of it. For example, Article 8 Reg CESL requires that the parties make an explicit agreement on its use, whereas Article 6 CISG provides that the parties 'may exclude the application' of the CISG thus making it prima facie applicable within its scope.

Another important and closely related aspect is whether it is possible for the private actors to make a direct choice of the optional instrument under the choice-of-law rules. That is to say, whether the optional instrument should constitute its own legal order or form an integral part of the national legal system—a second national regime in all participating states. Other EU optional instruments in the fields of company law and intellectual property law are optional pan-European regimes independent of the national law of the Member States.[16] This solution is sometimes described as the '28th regime-model', since it provides for a (sui generis) legal order that can be chosen alongside the national laws of the 27 Member States under the rules of PIL, whereas the integrated solution is referred to as the '2nd regime-model'.[17]

As far as the CESL is concerned, the Commission has opted for the 2nd regime-model, so as not to disturb the PIL system and, in particular, the

---

[15] Notably, it is of no importance for the characterisation as 'optional' whether such a uniform regime allows for contractual deviations (default rules) or is mandatory in character once chosen.

[16] Council Regulation (EEC) No 2137/85 of 25 July 1985 on the European Economic Interest Grouping (EEIG), [1985] OJ L199/1; Council Regulation (EC) No 1435/2003 of 22 July 2003 on the Statute for a European Co-operative Society (SCE), [2003] OJ L207/1; and Council Regulation (EC) No 40/94 of 20 December 1993 on the Community trade mark, [1994] OJ L11/1. See also Low, '*Unitas via Diversitas*' (n 14) 135.

[17] See eg Fornasier, M, '"28" versus "2. Regime"—Kollisionsrechtliche Aspekte eines optionalen europäischen Vertragsrechts' (2012) 76 *RabelsZ* 401; Fogt, MM, 'Private International Law Issues in Opt-Out and Opt-In Instruments of Harmonization: the CISG and the Proposal for a Common European Sales Law' (2012) 19 *Columbia Journal of European Law* 83, 111 et seq; Low, '*Unitas via Diversitas*' (n 14); Rühl, G, 'The Common European Sales law: 28th Regime, 2nd Regime of 1st Regime?' (2012) 19 *Maastricht Journal* 148.

Note that the term 28th regime really only makes sense from an EU law perspective—27 Member States and the EU. However, from a PIL perspective, it is not without its problems: (i) choice-of-law rules are universal in character and are thus not limited to the law of a Member State (including a pan-European regime); and (ii) there are Member States that have more than one legal system, such as Spain and the United Kingdom. See also Rühl, G above at 150 note 7, including further references.

choice-of-law rules in the Rome I Regulation on consumer contracts.[18] In this context, Gisela Rühl has also submitted the term '1st regime-model' in order to describe 'a uniform law that defines its own scope of application and that will accordingly apply if the parties validly agree on the application of the [uniform law].'[19] That is to say, a uniform law—such as the CISG—that is directly applicable within its scope without recourse to choice-of-law rules and the national *lex contractus*. The advantages of the uniform-law-approach in comparison with the merely indirectly applicable 2nd regime-model, and with the 28th regime-model, will be discussed below. It is noteworthy, however, that the European Parliament has already proposed the following amendment to Recital 9:[20]

> This *directly applicable* second regime should be an integral part of the legal order applicable in the territory of the Member States. Insofar as *its scope allows* and where parties have validly agreed to use it, the Common European Sales Law should apply instead of the first national contract-law regime within that legal order. (emphasis added)

Finally, the success of an optional uniform instrument will in practice depend on how well it is received by the private actors; otherwise the optional instrument will, as a matter of routine, not be used, as often is still the case with the CISG.[21] Thus, its success very much depends on the provision of an appropriate legal infrastructure to support the uniform instrument. The most obvious support is an efficient mechanism to ensure a uniform interpretation and application in practice, which is more easily achieved within the EU as compared to the international arena, given the role of the national courts of the Member States and the Court of Justice of the European Union (CJEU), including the practice of national judgment report systems. Even so, it also requires educating the judges and a court system more accommodating to commercial and private law disputes, perhaps even a specialist CESL court at the European level. Furthermore, the practitioners must be educated and new model contract terms developed for different areas of trade, and academics need to include the instrument in teaching and research.[22]

---

[18] Consideration 10 Reg CESL.

[19] Rühl, 'The Common European Sales' (n 17), 161 including note 44.

[20] EP Amendment 2 regarding Recital 9 Reg CESL.

[21] De Ly, F, 'Opting Out: Some Observations on the Occasion of the CISG's 25th Anniversary' in Franco Ferrari, F (ed), *Quo Vadis CISG?*, (Munich, Sellier, 2005); Ziegel, J, 'The Scope of the Convention: Reaching Out to Article One and Beyond' (2005–06) 25 *Journal of Law and Commerce* 59–73; Saf, C, 'CISG—a Uniform Law within the Sphere of Conflict of Laws' in Kleineman (ed), *CISG Part II Conference, Stockholm 4–5 September 2008* (Stockholm, Iustusförlag, 2009) 94; Smits, JM, 'The Common European Sales Law (CESL) Beyond Party Choice' (2012) 20 *Zeitschriftfür Europäisches Privatrecht* 904–917, 913; Fogt, 'Private International Law Issues' (n 17) 90–91.

[22] Smits, 'The Common European Sales' (n 21).

III. INSTRUMENTS GOVERNING THE INTERNATIONAL SALE OF GOODS

Among the Member States of the EU, there are four instruments already in force applicable to contracts for the sale of goods—three choice-of-law instruments and one uniform law instrument. They are as follows: (i) the 1955 Hague Convention on the law applicable to international sales of goods, specifically non-consumer sales contracts—Contracting Member States are Denmark, Finland, France, Italy, Sweden;[23] (ii) the Rome I on the law applicable to contractual obligations—in force in all Member States but Denmark[24] together with its old incarnation, the 1980 Rome Convention,[25] to which Denmark (and all the other Member States) are Contracting States;[26] (iii) the Rome II on the law applicable to non-contractual obligations as regards *culpa in contrahendo*[27]—in force in all Member States but Denmark;[28] and finally (iv) the 1980 CISG constituting a uniform law for contracts for the sale of goods, specifically non-consumer sales contracts—all Member States but Ireland, Malta, Portugal and the United Kingdom are Contracting States.[29]

Before dealing in more detail with the interplay and interrelation of all the instruments above as well as the CESL in section IV below, a brief account for the choice-of-law rules for sales contracts and consumer sales contracts will be given to provide for a private international law background.[30]

---

[23] The other Contracting States are Norway, Switzerland and Niger. It can also be noted that the Member State, Belgium, has done the sensible thing and denounced the 1955 Hague Convention entirely (on 19 February 1999, effective from 1 September 1999).

[24] Recital 46 Rome I and the Protocol on the position of Denmark annexed to the Treaty of Amsterdam, [1997] OJ C340. See also Protocol on the position of Denmark annexed to the Treaty on the Functioning of the European Union (consolidated version) (TFEU) [2012] OJ C326.

[25] The 1980 Rome Convention on the Law Applicable to Contractual Obligations (consolidated version) [1998] OJ C27/34. It entered into force on 1 April 1999.

[26] See Art 28 of the Rome Convention and inter alia Council Decision 2007/856/EC, [2007] OJ L 347/1. In addition, the Rome Convention still applies within the non-European territories of the Member States, see Art 24 of Rome I including the reference to Art 299 of the EC Treaty—now Art 355 TFEU.

[27] Art 1(2)(i) Rome I explicitly excludes 'obligations arising out of dealings prior to the conclusion of a contract' from the scope of Rome I, and the same applies also to the 1980 Rome Convention; see the Proposal for a Regulation of the European Parliament and the Council on the law applicable to contractual obligations (Rome I), Explanatory Memorandum, COM(2005) 650 final, p 5.

[28] Recital 40, Rome II and the Protocol on the position of Denmark annexed to the Treaty of Amsterdam, [1997] OJ C340.

[29] There are 83 Contracting States altogether as of 23 July 2015; see the UNCITRAL Secretariat status table at www.uncitral.org/uncitral/en/uncitral_texts/sale_goods/1980CISG_status.html.

[30] The PIL concepts of 'public policy' (*ordre public*) (Art 6 of the 1955 Hague Convention, Art 21 Rome I and Art 26 Rome II) and 'overriding mandatory provisions' (Art 9 Rome I and Art 16 Rome II) are beyond the scope of this chapter for two reasons: (i) the CESL, once agreed, cannot offend against either PIL concept before a Member State court, as it is an integral part of the domestic law of all the Member States; (ii) neither concept plays an important role for sales contracts; and for the 'unwitting' consumer, Art 6 Rome I provides even better protection.

A general requirement for PIL instruments to come into play at all is that there is an international, or cross-border, element. The legal situation or relationship must be connected to more than one country, or legal system (legal order) rather—a situation 'involving a conflict of laws'. This requirement is easily fulfilled: whenever there is any doubt as to which law should govern the transaction, the choice-of-law rules are applicable.[31] For instance, the fact that the forum is foreign in relation to the parties and their contract will suffice, since this involves a choice between the law of the forum—the *lex fori*—and the law applicable to the contract—the *lex contractus*. In this context, it is of no regard that the connection to the other country is not substantial, since once the choice-of-law rules come into play, their focus is on finding the strongest connection. Accordingly, a weak connection to another law will fulfil the international element, but it will have no practical bearing on determining the applicable law.

An important characteristic of the traditional choice-of-law rules is that they are universally applicable. That is to say, where states have agreed on a common uniform choice-of-law regime, there is (as a general rule) no requirement as to the reciprocal application of those rules, such as the parties having their places of business or habitual residences in a Contracting or Member State. It is sufficient that the international element is present and that the court deciding on the applicable law is situated in a Contracting or Member State, so that the choice-of-law regime forms part of the *lex fori*. Obviously, the material scope of the instrument must also be fulfilled.[32]

Under EU private international law, 'sales contracts' cover not only business-to-business contracts (sometimes referred to as 'B2B') or 'contracts between traders' in the terminology of the CESL, but also contracts between private parties (sometimes referred to as 'C2C', although slightly misleading as the parties are no consumers but rather non-merchants or non-traders). That is to say, there is no separate merchant law, distinct from non-merchant law. 'Consumer sales contracts' are defined as 'a contract concluded by a natural person for a purpose which can be regarded as being outside his

---

[31] Guiliano, M and Lagarde, P, *Council Report on the Convention on the law applicable to contractual obligations*, [1980] OJ C282/3, 10; Bogdan, M, *Svensk internationell privat- och processrätt*, 8th edn, (Stockholm, Norstedts Juridik, 2014) 244; Philip, A, *Dansk international privat- og procesret*, 2nd edn (Copenhagen, Juristforbundetsförlag, 1972) 325; Saf, C, *A Study of the Interplay between the Conventions Governing International Contracts of Sale—Analysis of the 1955 Hague Convention on the Law Applicable to Contracts of International Sales of Movable Goods; the 1980 Rome Convention on the Law Applicable to Contractual Obligations; and the 1980 United Nations Convention on Contracts for the International Sale of Goods*, (1999) on www.cisg.law.pace.edu/cisg/biblio/saf.html, section 4.2.1. See also further in section III.A below.

[32] Article 1 of the 1955 Hague Convention; Arts 1 Rome I and Rome II, respectively. The wording in the 1980 Rome Convention is even clearer referring to '*any* situation' (emphasis added). See Art 2 Rome I and Art 3 Rome II; and Guiliano and Lagarde, *Council Report on the Convention* (n 31) 13.

trade or profession (the consumer) with another person acting in the exercise of his trade or profession (the professional)' (sometimes referred to as 'B2C'), see section III.B below.

A. Determining the *Lex Contractus* for Sales Contracts

Clearly, choice-of-law issues regarding contracts of international sales of movable goods fall within the scope *materiae* of both the 1955 Hague Convention and the Rome I, which means that there is a conflict of norms. Under Article 25(1) Rome I, earlier conventions on the same subject matter are given precedence.[33] This would also follow from the principle of *lex specialis derogat lex generalis* under public international law. As regards matters falling outside the scope *materiae* of the 1955 Hague Convention, eg formal validity, Rome I is applied as *lex generalis*.[34]

Accordingly, in Member States that are also Contracting States to the 1955 Hague Convention, those choice-of-law rules will be applied instead of Rome I, which at least, in some cases, means that the outcome will differ. From the perspective of uniformity alone—not to mention the advantage of a more elaborate regime—those Member States would be well advised to follow the example of Belgium and denounce the Convention.

i. The Parties' Choice of Law

The first and most important rule is the principle of party autonomy, an old and well-established choice-of-law rule in contract law. Accordingly, both the 1955 Hague Convention and Rome I[35] provide for the parties to

---

[33] The same provision is found in Art 21 of the Rome Convention.
See also Art 351 [ex 307] TFEU, which encompasses the general international law principles of *pacta sunt servanda* and *res inter alios acta*. Due to the universal character of the conflicts instruments, it is impossible to identify any reciprocal treaty obligations that could be modified under the law of treaties as between the Member States only. Thus, eg the Rome I cannot be given precedence as a modification to an existing convention between both Member States and Third States in accordance with Art 41 (per analogy) of the 1969 Vienna Convention on the law of treaties. See further Saf, [The Community Regime on Free Movement of Judgments and Cross-border Service—Denmark included], (2007) *Europarättslig Tidskrift* 632, 635 et seq. including footnotes. Furthermore, the exception in Art 25(2) Rome I, requiring the Member States to apply Rome I instead of an existing Convention exclusively between Member States, does not apply since several of the Contracting States to the 1955 Hague Convention are Third States. Under international law, Art 25(2) Rome I cannot affect the application of such a Convention, so the provision would be characterised as a joint declaration by all Contracting States to allow departures from the Convention without breaching its treaty obligations. See the 1980 Declaration regarding the non-application of the 1955 Hague Convention to consumer contracts, section III.B below.
[34] See inter alia Saf, *CISG* (n 21) 101–102.
[35] The remarks on Rome I applies mutatis mutandis also to the Rome Convention. For a more detailed account of the latter, see eg Saf, *Interplay* (n 31).

conclude an agreement on the applicable *lex contractus*—the *lex electa*. In principle, the parties' choice is free, so there is no need to show any real or substantial connection to the chosen *lex contractus*. However, it must be observed that the parties can only choose the law of a country (*'la loi interne du pays'*), ie it is not possible to make a direct choice of an a national or non-State or supranational body of law, such as the CISG or the CESL. Such regimes can only be indirectly chosen as an integral part of the *lex contractus*. A different matter is that the parties may incorporate by reference such a body of law or an international convention.[36] Another different matter is that the European legislator could either change Rome I or make the CESL admissible and subject to Rome I.[37]

Article 2 of the 1955 Hague Convention

La vente est régie par la loi interne du pays désigné par les parties contractantes.

Cette désignation doit faire l'objet d'une clause expresse, ou résulter indubitablement des dispositions du contrat.

Les conditions, relatives au consentement des parties quant à la loi déclarée applicable, sont déterminées par cette loi.[38]

In comparison with Article 2 of the Hague Convention, the provisions in Article 3 Rome I is more elaborate: on the one hand, allowing for *depeçage* (different laws governing different parts of the contract) and altering the *lex contractus* during the contractual timeframe—both logical extensions of the principle of party autonomy, and, on the other hand, stricter in limiting the parties' choice of a non-Member-State law in the intra-Union situation as regards mandatory EU law.

Article 3 Rome I—Freedom of choice

1. A contract shall be governed by the law chosen by the parties. The choice shall be made expressly or clearly demonstrated by the terms of the contract or the circumstances of the case. By their choice the parties can select the law applicable to the whole or to part only of the contract.

---

[36] Article 2 para 1 (*e contrario*) of the 1955 Hague Convention and Recitals 13–14 and Art 3(3) (*e contrario*) Rome I.

[37] See Recital 14 Rome I. See also Rühl (n 17) 153; Fogt (n 17).

[38] Article 2 of the 1955 Hague Convention:

'A sale shall be governed by the domestic law of the country designated by the Contracting Parties.

Such a designation must be contained in an express clause, or unambiguously result from the provisions of the contract.

Conditions affecting the consent of the parties to the law declared applicable shall be determined by such law.'

2. The parties may at any time agree to subject the contract to a law other than that which previously governed it, whether as a result of an earlier choice made under this Article or of other provisions of this Regulation. Any change in the law to be applied that is made after the conclusion of the contract shall not prejudice its formal validity under Article 11 or adversely affect the rights of third parties.

3. Where all other elements relevant to the situation at the time of the choice are located in a country other than the country whose law has been chosen, the choice of the parties shall not prejudice the application of provisions of the law of that other country which cannot be derogated from by agreement.

4. Where all other elements relevant to the situation at the time of the choice are located in one or more Member States, the parties' choice of applicable law other than that of a Member State shall not prejudice the application of provisions of Community law, where appropriate as implemented in the Member State of the forum, which cannot be derogated from by agreement.

5. The existence and validity of the consent of the parties as to the choice of the applicable law shall be determined in accordance with the provisions of Articles 10, 11 and 13.

The main difference between the 1955 Hague Convention and Rome I regarding the PIL requirements for the parties' choice of law is that under Rome I it is sufficient that it was 'clearly demonstrated by the terms of the contract or the circumstances of the case', whereas the former requires that the choice must at least 'unambiguously result from the provisions of the contract'. That is to say, in order to ascertain whether there is an implied choice by the parties only the contract itself can be examined under the 1955 Hague Convention, which means that an express choice of law in a related transaction between the same parties cannot be inferred as an implied choice.[39] Furthermore, where the implied choice is 'clearly demonstrated' but 'not unambiguous', it will be upheld under Rome I, whereas under the 1955 Hague Convention, the default rules will determine the *lex contractus*—albeit it still remains to be seen whether this difference will actually emerge in practice.[40]

An implied choice of law can be inferred from, inter alia, a jurisdiction clause,[41] ie that the parties intended the *lex fori* to also be the *lex contractus*, the usage of a particular standard agreement or legal concepts or terms that belong to a specific legal order. Arguably, an otherwise valid choice of the CESL (but for a Member State *lex contractus*) would also qualify as an implied choice of 'Member State' law in the external context, at least if one particular Member State can be identified, which would be the case where

---

[39] Plender, R and Wilderspin, M, *The European Private International Law of Obligations*, 3rd edn (London, Sweet & Maxwell, 2009), para 1–052.

[40] Saf, *Interplay* (n 31) section 5.2.3; Philip, A, *EU-IP: europæisk international privat-ogprocesret*, 2nd edn (Copenhagen, Jurist- ogøkonomforbundetsforlag, 1994), 137.

[41] Recital 12 Rome I.

eg the buyer is habitually resident in a Member State.[42] Furthermore, on the basis of the identicalness of the CESL in all Member States, it is submitted for the purposes of applying the CESL, that where several of the parties to the 'external contract' are habitually resident in different Member States, it is not necessary in practice to determine which Member State law, including the CESL, has been impliedly chosen, since the identical uniform contents of the CESL in effect precludes a conflict of laws between those Member State laws.[43]

Rome I also extends the scope of the international choice-of-law to encompass the parties' choice of a foreign law in a domestic setting, albeit that the party autonomy is limited in that the parties can only contract out of the domestic default rules. Hence, their domestic contract will be governed by both the domestic and the foreign mandatory provisions—cumulative application. The same limitation applies mutatis mutandis to intra-Union contracts with regard to mandatory EU law. Under the Hague Convention, this is not possible, but the parties' choice will be regarded as an incorporation by reference of the foreign law as contractual provisions and as such there will be no mandatory character left of that law (apart from binding contractual terms if valid under the parties' domestic law).

Apart from fulfilling the PIL requirements stated in Article 2 of the Hague Convention and Article 3 Rome I, respectively, the parties' choice-of-law agreement must also be validly entered into as a matter of national substantive contract law, ie substantive or material validity. Under both instruments, the national law governing the substantive validity of the parties choice-of-law agreement—as well as the rest of their agreement—is the chosen *lex contractus*.[44] In addition, Rome I contains a specific safeguard rule regarding the existence of consent in Article 10(2), which applies to both the choice-of-law agreement as well as the actual contract:

Article 10 Rome I—Consent and material validity

1. The existence and validity of a contract, or of any term of a contract, shall be determined by the law which would govern it under this Regulation if the contract or term were valid.
2. Nevertheless, a party, in order to establish that he did not consent, may rely upon the law of the country in which he has his habitual residence if it appears

---

[42] See Recital 25 Reg CESL. See Cuniberti, G, *Common European Sales Law and the Third State Sellers* on conflictoflaws.net/2012/common-european-sales-law-and-third-state-sellers/; Rühl (n 17) 158. See also Fogt (n 17) 115 (similarly).

[43] See (a fortiori) EP Amendment 3 regarding Recital 10 Reg CESL on the (in practice non-) application of the cumulative rule in Art 6(2) Rome I on mandatory consumer protection rules, dealt with in Section III.B.

[44] Article 2 para 3 of the Hague Convention and Arts 3(5) and 10 Rome I, respectively. See also eg Saf, C, 'Sweden—The Validity of a Collective Labour Agreement Resulting from a Swedish Blacking—*The Rickmers Tianjin* 2007 AD Nr 2' (2007) IX *Yearbook of Private International Law* 481.

from the circumstances that it would not be reasonable to determine the effect of his conduct in accordance with the law specified in paragraph 1.

The purpose of Article 10(2) Rome I is to protect an inexperienced actor (whether professional or not) from the situation where her unwitting conduct, of which an eloquent silence may form part, is construed as a valid acceptance under the *lex contractus*. Under this unreasonableness test rule, all circumstances should be taken into account and particularly the parties' previous practices *inter se* and their previous business relationships, in order to prevent any abuse of the safeguard rule.[45]

ii. The Absence of Choice

Where the parties have not made a choice-of-law agreement, the *lex contractus* must be determined using the objective connecting factors stated in the default rules. The underlying principle here is that the contract—just like any legal relationship or legal situation—should be governed by the law of the country with which it is most closely connected. For a sales contract that would be the law of the seller, and Article 3(1) of the 1955 Hague Convention contains a strict rule to that effect:

Article 3 of the 1955 Hague Convention

A défaut de loi déclarée applicable par les parties, dans les conditions prévues à l'article précédent, la vente est régie par la loi interne du pays où le vendeur a sa résidence habituelle au moment où il reçoit la commande. Si la commande estreçue par un établissement du vendeur, la vente est régie par la loi interne du pays où est situé cet établissement.

Toutefois, la vente est régie par la loi interne du pays où l'acheteur a sa résidence habituelle, ou dans lequel il possède l'établissement qui a passé la commande, si c' est dans ce pays que la commande a été reçue, soit par le vendeur, soit par son représentant, agent ou commis-voyageur.

S'il s'agit d'un marché de bourse ou d'une vente aux enchères, la vente est régie par la loi interne du pays où se trouve la bourse ou dans lequel sont effectuées les enchères.[46]

---

[45] Guiliano and Lagarde (n 31) 28.

[46] Article 3 of the 1955 Hague Convention:

'In default of a law declared applicable by the parties under the conditions provided in the preceding Article, a sale shall be governed by the domestic law of the country in which the vendor has his habitual residence at the time when he receives the order. If the order is received by an establishment of the vendor, the sale shall be governed by the domestic law of the country in which the establishment is situated.

Nevertheless, a sale shall be governed by the domestic law of the country in which the purchaser has his habitual residence, or in which he has the establishment that has given the order, if the order has been received in such country, whether by the vendor or by his representative, agent or commercial traveller.

However, there is one exception to this rule: the *lex contractus* will be the buyer's law where the seller or her representative receives the buyer's order in the country of the latter. An authorisation simply to receive the buyer's order is sufficient for the exception rule to apply. In this way, a buyer who is unaware of the seller's location abroad will not suffer from any surprise application of foreign law due to the (unknown) international character of the sales contract.[47] The combined effect of these two rules, however, has been criticised for at times producing random and inappropriate results, depending on where the order was received.[48]

Unlike the 1955 Hague Convention, the choice-of-law rules in Rome I are presumptions, albeit very strong ones—'*manifestly* more closely connected' with another country—and it is not settled what is required to rebut them. One suggestion is the situation envisaged in Article 3 para 2 of the 1955 Hague Convention.[49] This means that most sales contracts are governed by the law of the seller's country under Rome I.

Article 4(1)–(3) Rome I—Applicable law in the absence of choice

1. To the extent that the law applicable to the contract has not been chosen in accordance with Article 3 and without prejudice to Articles 5 to 8, the law governing the contract shall be determined as follows:
    (a) a contract for the sale of goods shall be governed by the law of the country where the seller has his habitual residence;

    [...]

    (g) a contract for the sale of goods by auction shall be governed by the law of the country where the auction takes place, if such a place can be determined;

    [...]

2. Where the contract is not covered by paragraph 1 or where the elements of the contract would be covered by more than one of points (a) to (h) of paragraph 1, the contract shall be governed by the law of the country where the party required to effect the characteristic performance of the contract has his habitual residence.
3. Where it is clear from all the circumstances of the case that the contract is manifestly more closely connected with a country other than that indicated in paragraphs 1 or 2, the law of that other country shall apply.

It is submitted that an otherwise valid choice of the CESL (but for a Member State *lex contractus*) could also constitute such a manifest connection in the

---

In case of a sale at an exchange or at a public auction, the sale shall be governed by the domestic law of the country in which the exchange is situated or the auction takes place.'

[47] Prop 1964:149, 23; Bogdan (n 31) 247; Philip, *DIPP* (n 31) 335; Saf, *CISG* (n 21) 103.
[48] See eg Bogdan (n 31) 247 note 66; Saf, *Interplay* (n 31) section 5.3.1.
[49] Saf, *CISG*, (n 21) 104.

external context where the presumptions in paragraphs (1) and (2) point to the law of a non-Member State. However, this suggestion does not successfully tackle the problem of applying the CESL where the default rules of the Hague Convention identify the law of a non-Member State as the *lex contractus*, since they are strict rules. Accordingly, it is better to regard the otherwise valid choice of the CESL as an implied choice of a Member State law, since this secures a uniform application in all the Member States regardless of which choice-of-law regime is applied.

'Habitual residence' is generally defined in Article 19 Rome I as the place of central administration for legal persons and the principal place of business for natural persons doing business. If the seller has more than one place of business, the establishment concluding or performing the contract will be treated as the place of habitual residence (Article 19(2) Rome I). Notably, there is no general definition for the habitual residence of private persons (non-traders). Arguably, this is a question of fact and, thus, needs no legal definition. Suffice it to say that in this context, there can only be one such place. The relevant point in time is at the conclusion of the contract.

Both instruments have a specific provision for auction sales: the law of the country where the auction takes place. At a traditional auction ('in real life'), this would truly be the *lex loci contractus*, whereas the cross-border element becomes even more present at online auctions where bidders from the entire world may participate.

B. Determining the Law Applicable to Consumer Sales Contracts

Only Rome I applies to all consumer contracts, since the 1955 Hague Convention is no longer applied to consumer sales at all—in this regard the instrument was considered obsolete and two sets of rules unreasonably complicated for consumers. Thus, there is no norm conflict as regards such contracts.[50]

Under EU law, the 'consumer sales contract' is an autonomous concept with an independent meaning, which refers to a contract between a professional seller or trader and a consumer whatever the (non-business) purpose of the contract. This non-business purpose must also have been known to the professional trader at the time of entering into the contract. At least,

---

[50] *La Déclaration et la Recommandation suivantes relatives au domaine de la Convention sur la loi applicable aux ventes à caractère international d'objets mobiliers corporels conclue le 15 juin 1955, Conférence de La Haye, Quatorzième Session 1980, Actes et Documents* II-186, permitting the Contracting States to adopt specific choice-of-law rules for consumer sales without violating their Convention obligations.

See also Section 1 para 2 p 4 of the Swedish Act (1964:528) on the law applicable to international sales of tangible goods; Prop 1997/98:14, pp 23–24; and Saf, *Interplay* (n 31) section 4.3.1.

for PIL purposes, it is enough that the supposed consumer eg orders items usable in her business, uses business stationary, or mentions value added tax deductions, in order to be regarded as having renounced the PIL consumer protection.[51]

A related question is how to characterise dual-purpose contracts, ie contracts concluded for both professional/trade and private/non-trade purposes. The European Parliament has amended the definition in the CESL, so as to align it with that in the Consumer Rights Directive:[52]

Recital 11 a (new)

(11a) The definition of consumer should cover natural persons who are acting outside their trade, business, craft or profession. However, in the case of dual-purpose contracts, where the contract is concluded for purposes partly within and partly outside a person's trade and the trade purpose is so limited as not to be predominant in the overall context of the contract, that person should also be considered as a consumer. In order to determine whether a natural person is acting fully or partly for purposes which come within that person's trade, business, craft or profession, the way in which the person in question behaves towards the contracting party should be taken into account.

Article 2

(f) 'consumer' means any natural person who is acting for purposes which are outside that person's trade, business, craft, or profession; **where the contract is concluded for purposes partly within and partly outside that person's trade and the trade purpose is so limited as not to be predominant in the overall context of the contract, that person shall also be considered to be a consumer;** (See the wording of recital 17 of Directive 2011/83/EU).

In comparison, the CJEU has held regarding the jurisdiction rules—which holds equally true for identical wording in the Rome I, see Recital 7 Rome I—that where the contract has such a dual purpose, the professional purposes must be of 'negligible importance' for the contract as a whole to be characterised as a consumer contract. If this requirement is not fulfilled, the contract will not fall within the scope of the special consumer PIL regime, but will instead be governed by the regular PIL rules.[53]

---

[51] Case C-464/01 *Gruber v Bay Wa* [2005] ECR I-439, paras 50–53; and Case C-269/95 *Benincasa v Dentalkit* [1997] ECR I-3767 (no consumer when contract relates to future professional activities).

[52] EP Amendments 5 and 32 regarding Recital 11 a (new) and Art 2(f) of the Reg CESL; Recital 17 of the Directive 2011/83/EU of the European Parliament and of the Council of 25 October 2011 on consumer rights, amending Council Directive 93/13/EEC and Directive 1999/44/EC of the European Parliament and of the Council and repealing Council Directive 85/577/EEC and Directive 97/7/EC of the European Parliament and of the Council [2011] OJ L304/64.

[53] See Case C-464/01 *Gruber v Bay Wa* [2005] ECR I-439, paras 40–45.

Accordingly, where a dual-purpose contract has a predominant private purpose but the professional purpose is still of non-negligible importance, the regular rules in Articles 3 and/or 4 Rome I will apply to determine the *lex contractus* as explained in the previous section. This does not mean, however, that the consumer is deprived of all—if any—substantive consumer protection. The contract still falls within the substantive consumer contract definition and thus the consumer will enjoy the consumer protection provided by the *lex contractus*, ie either the law of the professional seller under Article 4(1)(a) or the *lex electa* under Article 3 Rome I. Where the parties have made a valid agreement to apply the CESL, its consumer provisions will apply accordingly.

Furthermore, it is not enough for jurisdiction and choice-of-law purposes that the contract can be characterised as a consumer contract in its narrow PIL sense. In order for the special consumer PIL regime to apply, the professional (trader) must also have actively approached the consumer in the consumer's country, either through the professional's local establishment in, or by her directed commercial activities towards that country, and the contract at issue falls within the scope of such activities.

Article 6 (1)–(3) Rome I—Consumer contracts

1. Without prejudice to Articles 5 and 7, a contract concluded by a natural person for a purpose which can be regarded as being outside his trade or profession (the consumer) with another person acting in the exercise of his trade or profession (the professional) shall be governed by the law of the country where the consumer has his habitual residence, provided that the professional:
   (a) pursues his commercial or professional activities in the country where the consumer has his habitual residence, or
   (b) by any means, directs such activities to that country or to several countries including that country, and the contract falls within the scope of such activities.
2. Notwithstanding paragraph 1, the parties may choose the law applicable to a contract which fulfils the requirements of paragraph 1, in accordance with Article 3. Such a choice may not, however, have the result of depriving the consumer of the protection afforded to him by provisions that cannot be derogated from by agreement by virtue of the law which, in the absence of choice, would have been applicable on the basis of paragraph 1.
3. If the requirements in points (a) or (b) of paragraph 1 are not fulfilled, the law applicable to a contract between a consumer and a professional shall be determined pursuant to Articles 3 and 4.

The provision requires neither a distance contract nor a causal link between the trader's directed commercial activities, eg an internet site, and the conclusion of the consumer contract. However, it must be shown that such activities are directed to the consumer's state and in that regard such a link is a good indication.[54] Accordingly, 'both the establishment of contact at a distance, … the reservation of goods or services at a distance, or a fortiori the conclusion of a consumer contract at a distance, are indications that the contract is connected with such an activity'.[55]

Furthermore, it is not enough that the trader's or its intermediary's website can be accessed in the consumer's state, nor that the website contains contact details such as an email address, or the use of a language or a currency generally used in the trader's state. Instead, it must be apparent from the actual contents of the website and the trader's overall activity that the trader intends to conclude contracts with consumers in that state. The CJEU has stated the following non-exhaustive list of website activities that indicate 'directed commercial activity':[56]

> [T]he international nature of the activity, mention of itineraries from other Member States for going to the place where the trader is established, use of a language or a currency other than the language or currency generally used in the Member State in which the trader is established with the possibility of making and confirming the reservation in that other language, mention of telephone numbers with an international code, outlay of expenditure on an internet referencing service in order to facilitate access to the trader's site or that of its intermediary by consumers domiciled in other Member States, use of a top-level domain name other than that of the Member State in which the trader is established, and mention of an international clientele composed of customers domiciled in various Member States.

Notably, the rule of the consumer's law in Article 6 does not prevent the parties from making a valid choice of another law than the objective 'consumer *lex contractus*'. However, its effect will be limited, because it is not allowed to contract out of the mandatory rules of the consumer *lex contractus*. Thus, there will be a cumulative application of the mandatory rules under the consumer *lex contractus* and those of the *lex electa*. In relation to the CESL, Article 6(2) Rome I will have no practical relevance in the intra-Union context.[57] For example, where the consumer is habitually resident in one Member State, the *lex electa* is the law of another Member State and there is a valid agreement to apply the CESL, its mandatory consumer provisions would apply undisturbed, since the regime—'the protection afforded'—is identical under both laws.[58] If the consumer is instead habitually resident in

---

[54] Case C-218/12 *Emrek* [2013] ECR 666.

[55] Case C-190/11 *Mühlleitner* [2012] ECR 542, para 44.

[56] Joined Cases C-585/08 and C-144/09 *Pammer and Hotel Alpenhof* [2010] ECR I–12527, in particular para 93.

[57] Recital 12 Reg CESL, including the clarifications made by EP Amendment 6.

[58] The identicalness of the CESL in consumer contracts is guaranteed by Art 8(3) Reg CESL, where it is stated that 'in relations between a trader and a consumer the Common European Sales Law may not be chosen partially, but only in its entirety'.

a non-Member State and the *lex electa* is the law of a Member State includ-ing a valid choice of the CESL, paragraph 2 will operate as usual.

Finally, where it is the consumer who has actively approached the (inactive) professional in another country, which is greatly facilitated in this digital age, the regular rules in Articles 3 and/or 4 Rome I will apply, see paragraph 3. As has already been explained, this means that it will be the consumer protection provided by the regular *lex contractus*, ie either the law of the professional seller or the *lex electa*.

C. Determining the Law Applicable to *Culpa in Contrahendo*

Pre-contractual liability means per se that there is no contract in place between the parties at that point in time. Accordingly, *culpa in contrahendo* is characterised as a non-contractual matter and as such governed by the choice-of-law rules in Rome II. Hence, neither the 1955 Hague Convention nor Rome I are applicable. However, its close relationship to the contrac-tual legal sphere is clear from the chosen connecting factor—the negotiated (hypothetical) contract:

Article 12 Rome II—*Culpa in Contrahendo*

1. The law applicable to a non-contractual obligation arising out of dealings prior to the conclusion of a contract, regardless of whether the contract was actually concluded or not, shall be the law that applies to the contract or that would have been applicable to it had it been entered into.
2. Where the law applicable cannot be determined on the basis of paragraph 1, it shall be:
   (a) the law of the country in which the damage occurs, irrespective of the country in which the event giving rise to the damage occurred and irre-spective of the country or countries in which the indirect consequences of that event occurred; or
   (b) where the parties have their habitual residence in the same country at the time when the event giving rise to the damage occurs, the law of that country; or
   (c) where it is clear from all the circumstances of the case that the non-contractual obligation arising out of dealings prior to the conclusion of a contract is manifestly more closely connected with a country other than that indicated in points (a) and (b), the law of that other country.

The reference to the hypothetical *lex contractus* in paragraph (1) means that in practice the relevant rules in Rome I will be applied to the choice-of-law question. In the rarer cases where the hypothetical *lex contractus* cannot be ascertained, the *lex loci damni*—the law of the country in which the direct effect took place—will apply to cross-border negotiations, see paragraph (2)(a). It falls beyond the scope of this chapter to deal with the rather complicated question of where exactly this place of direct effect is.

Finally, it is also possible for the parties to agree on the applicable law under Article 14 Rome II, although the freedom of choice for non-contractual obligations is more limited than its counterpart in Rome I. Only parties pursuing a commercial activity may enter into a freely negotiated choice-of-law agreement ex ante, eg in a letter of intent, whereas other parties must wait until after the event giving rise to the damage occurred. On the other hand, the counter-party is often not known before this point in time anyway.

IV. THE SCOPE AND INTERPLAY OF THE INSTRUMENTS

In order to establish the interplay *inter se* of the instruments governing international sales of tangible goods (including related matters such as *culpa in contrahendo*), their respective scope must be determined, including any provisions explicitly addressing those issues. Since the CESL is the focus of this chapter, its terminology has been chosen to describe the various aspects of defining the scope of the respective instruments, even though this terminology does not entirely correspond with the one used within the field of private international law.

Accordingly, Article 3 Reg CESL states four aspects of scope: 'cross-border contract' and 'the territorial, material and personal scope' that must all be fulfilled before the parties can opt into the CESL in accordance with Article 8 Reg CESL. The general requirement that the *lex contractus* must be the law of a Member State follows from the character of the CESL as a contract-law regime (see Recital 9). The first aspect—'cross-border contract'—corresponds with the PIL concept of 'international element' or 'situation involving the conflict of laws', although it is more limited as it requires that the parties are habitually resident or otherwise settled in different states.

The second aspect—the 'territorial scope'—refers to the requirement of a geographical link of the parties to a Member State, ie habitual residence in a Member State. In PIL terminology, however, this is usually referred to as the 'personal scope', since it relates to the parties' personal connection to a particular country.[59] In the PIL context, 'territorial scope' is instead used to describe the geographical area in which the legal instrument will be applied by the participating states and their courts, ie in the traditional sense of the law of the treaties.[60]

The third aspect—'the material scope'—refers to the material law contents of the CESL, which is the usual meaning of the term. However, it is

[59] See Case C–412/98 *Group Josi Reinsurance Company SA v Universal General Insurance Company (UGIC)* [2000] ECR I-5925.
[60] See Art 24 Rome I.

more narrowly construed in the CESL in comparison with at least the PIL terminology. In the CESL, it is used only to describe sales contracts, contracts for the supply of digital content and related service contracts, whereas the distinction between 'merchant' and consumer contracts, respectively, is construed as the fourth aspect—'personal scope'—relating to the legal character of the parties—rather than the character of the contractual relationship. Thus, from a PIL perspective, the terms 'material' and 'personal scope' in the Reg CESL are both referring to the material scope.

A. The Interrelation of the Instruments

Before the interplay of the instruments can be explored, the interrelation of the instruments has to be established and to what extent there really is a norm conflict at a more general level.

i. *General Characteristics of the Instruments*

The 1955 Hague Convention, Rome I, and Rome II are all multilateral instruments on uniform choice-of-law rules relating to various aspects of an international contract for the sale of tangible goods, including related matters such as *culpa in contrahendo*. Through the application of these uniform choice-of-law rules, the same national law will be identified as the *lex contractus*, regardless of in which Contracting or Member State the forum is situated. The instruments as such are mandatory in the sense that the parties cannot choose other choice-of-law rules; the instruments must be applied by the courts of a Contracting or Member State. However, the principle of party autonomy is still recognised in that the choice-of-law rules allow the parties to agree on the applicable law.[61]

The CESL and the CISG, on the other hand, are multilateral instruments on uniform substantive (material) rules relating to various aspects of an international contract for the sale of tangible goods, widely defined. They are uniform sales law regimes incorporated into the national substantive laws of their Contracting/Member States; as such, they form an integral part of those laws yet remain an autonomous body of law.[62] Accordingly, the CESL and the CISG will correspond with what is usually meant by the *lex contractus*. Neither of the instruments is mandatory, since the parties can agree on the use of the respective instrument: under Article 6 CISG, the parties can opt out of the CISG in its entirety. A different matter is that some of the provisions are mandatory, once the regime has been

---

[61] Art 2 Hague, Art 3 Rome I, and Art 14 Rome II, respectively.
[62] See eg Fogt (n 17) 96.

chosen.[63] In this regard, Article 6 CISG allows the parties to derogate from all provisions.

ii. The Primacy of the Instruments inter se

In determining the interrelation of the instruments *inter se*, it must first be established that matters of PIL (choice-of-law) and those of substantive law do not concern the same subject matter. This means, for instance, that Article 90 CISG (cited in full below) does not give precedence to eg the 1955 Hague Convention, as the latter does not concern the same subject matter. Accordingly, since there is no overlapping scope, there can be no norm conflict as such between choice-of-law regimes on the one hand, and uniform substantive law regimes on the other.[64] The interplay between choice-of-law rules and rules providing for the direct application of a uniform substantive law regime will be discussed in section V.E below.

Secondly, EU-law instruments do not constitute international law despite their supranational character under the EU Treaties, but are regarded as national (domestic) law under the law of treaties. This is also the major reason why the 1955 Hague Convention takes precedence over Rome I as regards sales contracts, although the outcome would remain the same if Rome I were an international instrument, as was explained above in Section III.A.

The CISG contains two provisions dealing with the interplay with other uniform private law regimes: Articles 90 and 94 CISG. The former provision states:

Article 90 CISG

This Convention does not prevail over any international agreement which has already been or may be entered into and which contains provisions concerning the matters governed by this Convention, provided that the parties have their places of business in States parties to such agreement.

Since Article 90 CISG only gives precedence to 'international agreements', it cannot give precedence to the CESL. However, the non-application of

---

[63] See Art 6 CISG, and Arts 3 and 8 Reg CESL, respectively.

[64] Re the CISG: Prop. 1986/87:128, p 159; Honnold, JO, *Uniform Law for International Sales under the 1980 United Nations Convention*, 3rd edn, (Hague, Kluwer Law International, 1999), §§ 464–464.3; Bonell, MJ and Liguori, F, 'The U.N. Convention on the International Sale of Goods: A Critical Analysis of Current International Case Law—1997 (Part 1)' (1997) *Revue de droit uniforme/Uniform Law Review* 385, para 3.1(a) including note 46; Fogt (n 17) 96 and 101 including notes 31 and 44, respectively. Re the CESL: Recital 10 Reg CESL including Amendment 3.

Against, Schlechtriem, P, Schwenzer, I and Hachem, P, in Schwenzer, I (ed), *Schlechtriem & Schwenzer: Commentary on the UN Convention on the International Sale of Goods (CISG)*, 3rd edn (Oxford, Oxford University Press, 2010), Article 90 para 8.

Article 90 CISG does not mean that the CESL cannot apply instead of the CISG. Instead, the technical legislative solution in the CESL is to draw on the provision on party autonomy in Article 6 CISG:

Article 6 CISG

The parties may exclude the application of this Convention or, subject to article 12, derogate from or vary the effect of any of its provisions.

Under Article 6 CISG, it is possible for the parties to contract out of the CISG in its entirety, which in effect equals the parties' choice with a proper choice-of-law clause.[65] The 'non-choice' can be either explicit—stating either that the CISG does not apply, or that a specific domestic sales law regime applies; or implicit through the use of contractual terms referring to the domestic regime or a domestic standard agreement.[66] Accordingly, it is stated—or re-stated rather—in Recital 25 Reg CESL:

(25) Where the United Nations Convention on Contracts for the International Sale of Goods would otherwise apply to the contract in question, the choice of the Common European Sales Law should imply an agreement of the contractual parties to exclude that Convention.

According to Recital 25, the parties' choice to opt into the CESL will also mean opting out of the CISG.[67] Because such an opt-out means that the CISG is no longer applicable, the validity, and the other contractual aspects, of the 'CESL/non-CISG' agreement will be governed by the *lex fori* including its choice-of-law rules as well as the rules on the application of the CESL. That is to say, the agreement to opt into the CESL must fulfil the requirements of Articles 3 (scope) and 8 (agreement) Reg CESL including references, as well as the general requirement that the *lex contractus* is the law of a Member State under the choice-of-law rules of the *lex fori*.

In relation to the CISG, the proposed CESL will have a regional application, which means that it would fall within the scope of Article 94 CISG. This provision allows Contracting States to make a unilateral declaration in favour of the regional regulation:

Article 94 (1)–(2) CISG

(1) Two or more Contracting States which have the same or closely related legal rules on matters governed by this Convention may at any time declare that the Convention is not to apply to contracts of sale or to their formation

---

[65] Bonell, MJ in Bianca-Bonell, *Commentary on the International Sales Law* (Milano, Giuffrè, 1987) 53–54; Saf, *CISG* (n 22) 107.

[66] Bonell (n 65) 54.

[67] The agreement to use the CESL also means opting out of the 'first national contract-law regime', ie the domestic contract law of the *lex contractus*. See Art 11 and Recitals 9–10 Reg CESL including EP Amendments 73–74 and 3–4.

where the parties have their places of business in those States. Such declarations may be made jointly or by reciprocal unilateral declarations.

(2)   A Contracting State which has the same or closely related legal rules on matters governed by this Convention as one or more non-Contracting States may at any time declare that the Convention is not to apply to contracts of sale or to their formation where the parties have their places of business in those States.

Article 94 CISG complements Article 90 CISG in that harmonisation which is not based on a treaty may also be respected and given precedence. There is, however, no need to make such a declaration by virtue of the solution in Recital 25 Reg CESL. It is also questionable whether this would be at all advisable, since it will work as a reservation against the application of the CISG. That is to say, its effect would be to at least prima facie exclude the application of the CISG where the parties have their places of business in different Member States. Consequently, the parties' choice would be limited to the domestic law regime and the CESL regime, and the only way for them to opt into the CISG would be to choose as the *lex contractus* the law of a CISG State that is a non-Member State, since it is not possible to choose the CISG directly under Article 2 1955 Hague Convention and Article 3 Rome I, respectively.[68]

In conclusion, the CISG takes precedence over the CESL, but since the parties can contract out of the CISG by virtue of Article 6 CISG, they can choose the CESL (within its scope and provided the *lex contractus* is a Member State law)—or any other domestic regime—before the CISG.[69] This is also the most appropriate legislative choice, since the choice-of-law instruments do not allow for a direct choice of the CISG.

B. Cross-Border Contracts—'International Scope'

The requirement of an international, or cross-border, element is easily fulfilled in the area of private international law. In fact, it is safe to say that whenever there is any doubt as to which law should govern the transaction,

---

[68] Evans, M in Bianca-Bonell, *Commentary on the International Sales Law* (Milan, Giuffrè, 1987) 652–653; Schlechtriem, Schwenzer, Hachem, *Commentary on the UN Convention* (n 64), Art 94 paras 6–7. Where the law of a Reserving State is identified as the *lex contractus*, Art 94(2) will in this respect have the same effect as a reservation under Art 95 against the application of Art 1(1)(b), but to a geographically limited area and with the difference that it should be upheld by any court in any country.

Against: Fogt (n 17) 102 et seq—arguing that an Art 94 reservation together with transforming the CESL into an opt-out regime is a better solution for regional unification. It is submitted, however, that this suggestion fails to take the overall aim of the CESL of providing an *optional* regime into account.

[69] Art 90 CISG in conjunction with Recital 25 Reg CESL.

the choice-of-law rules are applicable.[70] A different matter is that an insubstantial connection to the law of a particular country will have no bearing on determining the *lex contractus*.

The situation is different under both the CISG and the CESL. According to Article 1 CISG and Articles 3 and 4(1) Reg CESL, respectively, the instruments will only apply when the parties have their places of business—or habitual residences—in different states. In addition, in the amended CESL, a distance contract is required, ie that the parties were present in different states when concluding the contract.[71] In other words, only a concrete international, or 'cross-border', criteria of a constant nature will suffice. Under the CISG, the relevant point in time to determine whether it is a cross-border contract is at the conclusion of the contract, whereas under the CESL, it is the time of the agreement on the use of the CESL, since it is an opt-in instrument. This could of course be at an earlier time than the conclusion of the contract.

Where the cross-border dimension is unknown at the relevant point in time, neither of the instruments will apply.[72]

C. Territorial Scope (ie Personal Scope)

As was explained at the beginning of this section, the term 'territorial scope' in Article 3 Reg CESL is misleading from a PIL perspective, since it refers to what is known as 'personal scope' in the latter field of law. Be that as it may, traditional choice-of-law rules are of universal—'non-territorial'—character: they will apply 'in situations involving a conflict of laws', which means that the only geographical ('territorial') connection needed for the application of the 1955 Hague Convention, Rome I and Rome II, respectively, is that the court seized with the dispute is situated in a Contracting or Member State. That is to say, there is no reciprocity requirement, such as the parties having their places of business or habitual residences in a Contracting or Member State.[73]

Both the CISG (prima facie) and the CESL, however, require that the parties have a geographical/'territorial' connection to a CISG State and a Member State, respectively.

---

[70] Giuliano and Lagarde (n 31) 10. Bogdan (n 31) 244; Philip (n 31) 325; Saf, *Interplay* (n 31) section 4.2.1. See further section III.A above.

[71] EP Amendment 60 regarding Art 4(1) Reg CESL.

[72] Article 1 CISG; and Arts 3, 4(6) and 8 Reg CESL in conjunction.

[73] Article 1 of the 1955 Hague Convention, Arts 1 Rome I and Rome II, respectively. The wording in the 1980 Rome Convention is even clearer referring to '*any* situation' (emphasis added). See Art 2 Rome I and Art 3 Rome II; Guiliano and Lagarde (n 31) 13.

Article 1 of the CISG

(1) This Convention applies to contracts of sale of goods between parties whose places of business [or habitual business][74] are in different States:
  (a)   when the States are Contracting States; or
  (b)   when the rules of private international law lead to the application of the law of a Contracting State.

According to Article 1(1)(a) CISG, the uniform sales law regime will be 'directly applicable'—ie without recourse to any choice-of-law rules—where all parties have their places of business in different CISG States. If a party has more than one place of business, Article 10 CISG provides that the relevant place is the one 'which has the closest relationship to the contract and its performance, having regard to the circumstances known to or contemplated by the parties at any time before or at the conclusion of the contract'.

In addition, the CISG can also be 'indirectly applicable' in situations where the geographical connection is not present and the CISG forms part of the *lex contractus* as identified by choice-of-law rules (see Article 1(1)(b) CISG). This means that it is possible for parties with no connection to a CISG State to choose the CISG as their applicable sales regime, albeit indirectly. The concepts of direct and indirect applicability, respectively, will be discussed more in depth in Section V.E below.

The 'territorial scope' of the CESL, ie the parties' geographical connection to the EU and its Member States, is stated in Article 4 Reg CESL:

Article 4(1)–(4) Reg CESL incl EP Amendment 60—Cross-border contracts

1.   The Common European Sales Law may be used for distance contracts which are cross-border contracts.
2.   For the purposes of this Regulation, a contract between traders is a cross-border contract if the parties have their habitual residence in different countries of which at least one is a Member State.
3.   For the purposes of this Regulation, a contract between a trader and a consumer is a cross-border contract if:
  (a)   either the address indicated by the consumer, the delivery address for goods or the billing address are located in a country other than the country of the trader's habitual residence; and
  (b)   at least one of these countries is a Member State.
4.   For the purposes of this Regulation, the habitual residence of companies and other bodies, corporate or unincorporated, shall be the place of central administration. The habitual residence of a trader who is a natural person shall be that person's principal place of business.

In comparison with the CISG, the territorial requirement is stricter, since an opt-in requires that at least one party must have a territorial (geographical) connection to a Member State. If this connection is lacking, it is not

---

[74] See Art 10 CISG.

possible to opt into the CESL at all. Furthermore, the contract must be a distance contract, including online contracts, ie it cannot be an on-premises contract.[75] These requirements apply to commercial sales and consumer sales contracts alike, but the connections used are different.

For traders the 'habitual residence' is the relevant connection, ie the place of central administration or the principal place of business. If a trader has more than one place of business, Article 4(5) Reg CESL provides that the relevant place is the 'branch, agency or any other establishment' where the contract is concluded in the course of the operations of that establishment. This is the same connection as is used in Article 19 of Rome I and Article 23 of Rome II as well as in Article 7(5) of the Brussels Ia Regulation,[76] so it should have the same autonomous meaning—primarily referring to the typical foreign branch of a company.[77] However, unlike Rome I and Rome II—referring to both the conclusion of the contract and the responsibility of performance—the provision only refers to the place of business where the contract is concluded, which corresponds with the rule in Article 4(6) Reg CESL on the relevant point in time (above).

The relevant connection for a consumer is an address: either the address indicated by the consumer—presumably for contact, the delivery address for the goods or the billing address. Since there is no reference to any more objectively substantial connection than address details, it would seem that the consumer could create the necessary cross-border character unilaterally by indicating a fake address in another state in her dealings with the trader. As long as the delivery address and the billing address are genuine, the practical performance of the transaction will still function properly.

D. Material and 'Personal' Scope

As was explained at the beginning of Section IV, the terms 'material scope' and 'personal scope' in Article 3 Reg CESL are slightly misleading, since in effect they refer to different aspects of what is commonly referred to as 'material scope'. The distinction made in the CESL is that only the type of

---

[75] EP Amendment 29 regarding Art 2(p) Reg CESL: '"distance contract" means any contract between the trader and the consumer **or another trader** under an organised distance sales scheme concluded without the simultaneous physical presence of the trader or, where the trader is a legal person, a natural person representing the trader and the consumer or **the other trader**, with the exclusive use of one or more means of distance communication up to and including the time at which the contract is concluded'.

[76] Regulation (EU) No 1215/2012 of the European Parliament and of the Council of 12 December 2012 on jurisdiction and the recognition and enforcement of judgments in civil and commercial matters (recast) [2012] OJ L351/1 (Brussels Ia).

[77] See eg Case 33/78 *Somafer* [1978] ECR 2183, Case 139/80 *Blanckaert & Willems* [1981] ECR 819 and Case 14/76 *De Bloos* [1976] ECR 1497.

contract is described as 'material scope', whereas the 'personal scope' relates to the legal character of the parties—traders and consumers, respectively—rather than the character of the contractual relationship—commercial, private and consumer contracts, respectively.

The 1955 Hague Convention applies to international sales of goods: both commercial ones and private ones as well as auctions, but not to consumer sales contracts. Matters included are eg formation and substantive validity. Rome I applies to international contracts—both sales contracts and consumer contracts as well as auctions. Matters included are eg formation and formal and substantive validity. Furthermore, the *lex contractus* itself governs eg interpretation, performance, breach of obligations, prescription and limitation of actions, nullity of the contract. Finally, Rome II applies to eg *culpa in contrahendo* and the scope of the law applicable encompasses eg basis and extent of liability, existence, the nature and the assessment of damage or remedy claimed and the prescription and limitation of actions.[78]

Under Article 1(1) and (3) CISG, the uniform sales law applies to international contracts of sale of goods regardless of the nationality or the civil or commercial character of the parties, ie both commercial and private contracts fall within its scope. The legal issues governed by the CISG are the formation of contract and the sale of goods. Matters explicitly excluded from its scope are consumer sales contracts, and sales by auction, as well as the validity of the contract (formal and substantive) and proprietary matters, see Articles 2 (a)–(b) and 4 CISG, respectively.

According to Articles 5 and 7 Reg CESL, the CESL may be used for sales contracts, contracts for the supply of digital content and related service contracts, but only if the seller/supplier is the trader (and it is a distance contract). Even where such contracts are linked to another contract or form part of a mixed-purpose contract, the CESL may be used—provided those elements are divisible and if so they are deemed to be a linked contract. The linked contract will be governed by its *lex contractus*, so the situation is really one of *depeçage*.[79]

Trader contracts and consumer contracts fall within the scope of the CESL, but not contracts between non-traders (private parties), see Article 7 Reg CESL. This exclusion is questionable, since non-traders involved in—probably more sporadic—cross-border trade could really benefit from a regime that comes in 24 languages and is easily accessible online. Notably, the European Parliament has also proposed to remove the requirement that at least one party must be a small or medium-sized enterprise in an all-trader

---

[78] Re 1955 Hague Convention, see Arts 1–3 and 5; re Rome I, see Arts 1 and 10–12; and re Rome II, see Arts 1, 12 and 15.

[79] EP Amendments 64–68 regarding Art 6 Reg CESL.

contract.[80] Another proposed amendment introduces a new provision stating the material scope of the CESL, which for obvious reasons corresponds with that of the *lex contractus* as determined under the choice-of-law rules.

Article 11a (new) Reg CESL, EP Amendment 74—Matters covered by the Common European Sales Law

1. The Common European Sales Law addresses in its rules the following matters:
    (a) pre-contractual duties to provide information;
    (b) the conclusion of a contract including formal requirements;
    (c) the right of withdrawal and its consequences;
    (d) avoidance of the contract as a result of mistake, fraud, threat or unfair exploitation and the consequences of such avoidance;
    (e) interpretation;
    (f) contents and effects, including those of the relevant contract;
    (g) the assessment and the effects of unfairness of contract terms;
    (h) the rights and obligations of the parties;
    (i) remedies for non-performance;
    (j) restitution after avoidance or termination or in the case of a non-binding contract;
    (k) prescription and preclusion of rights;
    (l) sanctions available in the event of breach of the obligations and duties arising under its application.

Furthermore, Article 11 Reg CESL has been amended so as to make the CESL applicable to matters of *culpa in contrahendo* also in situations where no contract was actually concluded, provided the negotiations were entered into with reference to the CESL. However, where the trader has also made reference to other legal regimes, the applicable law will be determined under the choice-of-law rules, ie Article 12 of the Rome II.[81]

E. The Applicability of the CESL in Comparison with the CISG

There are essentially three different ways to make the CESL applicable to those private actors interested in contracting into the uniform regime. They have been presented in Section II as the '28th regime-model', the '2nd regime-model', and the '1st regime-model'. The terms refer to whether the optional instrument should constitute its own legal order—the independently applicable '28th regime-model', or form an integral part of the national legal system in all participating states—the indirectly applicable '2nd regime-model'

---

[80] The requirement, that at least one party must be a small or medium-sized enterprise where all parties are traders for the CESL to apply, has been abolished in EP Amendment 70 regarding Art 7 Reg CESL.

[81] EP Amendments 73–74 regarding Art 11 Reg CESL—Consequences of the use of the Common European Sales Law.

and the directly applicable '1st regime-model' (uniform-law model). It will be argued that the CESL is a '2nd regime-model', which is directly applicable in the uniform-law sense in the intra-Union context, ie where all relevant connections are to Member States, whereas it is indirectly applicable in the external context when the *lex contractus* is the law of a Member State.

i. 'Independently Applicable' as Lex Contractus *through* the Choice-of-Law Rules

The European legislator has already discarded the '28th regime-model' and instead opted for the '2nd regime-model', but the former will still be dealt with briefly to explain why it is not an appropriate solution. One major problem with the '28th regime-model' is that the choice-of-law instruments do not allow for a direct choice of a non-State body of law, and a pan-European regime would be just that. Even if the CESL itself were to contain provisions allowing the parties a direct choice of the CESL regime in line with Recital 14 Rome I, five Member States would still have to apply the 1955 Hague Convention instead of Rome I to determine the *lex contractus*.[82]

Furthermore, the contents of the two choice-of-law regimes are not identical, so even in the intra-Union context the parties would have to take both of them into account to ensure the applicability of the CESL.[83] The problem of non-uniform choice-of-law rules is an even stronger argument in the external situation, ie where only at least one party is habitually resident in a Member State, since other PIL instruments will come into play before non-Member State courts as part of the foreign *lex fori*.

Finally, there are important restrictions to party autonomy under, particularly, Rome I, notably Article 6(2) on consumer sales contracts and Article 3(3) on domestic contracts.[84] Either provision only allows for partial contracting out of the objective *lex contractus*, leading to a cumulative application of mandatory rules of the former law and the CESL as an autonomous *lex electa*.

ii. 'Indirectly Applicable' as Part of Lex Contractus *via the* Choice-of-Law Rules as Compared to 'Directly Applicable' as the Uniform Law Regime

As has been indicated, the European legislator has opted for the '2nd regime-model', so as not to disturb the PIL system and in particular the

---

[82] See section III.A.i above; Rühl (n 17) 151 et seq. See Fogt (n 17) 109 et seq: same conclusions regarding the status of law, but suggesting that it is the proper solution to treat the CESL as 'binding 'Community Rules of Law".

[83] See section III.A (introductory part) above; Rühl (n 17) 154.

[84] See sections III.B and III.A.i respectively above; Rühl (n 17) 158 et seq; Fogt (n 17) 114–115.

choice-of-law rules on consumer contracts in Rome I. That is to say, the CESL can only be indirectly applied as part of the *lex contractus*. A different matter is that, in relation to the domestic contract law regime of each Member State, the parties' valid opt-in clause makes the CESL directly applicable under Article 11 Reg CESL:

Article 11 Reg CESL including EP Amendment 74—Consequences of the use of the CESL

1. Where the parties have validly agreed to use the Common European Sales Law for a contract, only the Common European Sales Law shall govern the matters addressed in its rules, **instead of** the contract-**law regime that would, in the absence of such an agreement,** govern the **contract within the legal order determined as the applicable law.**

In its amended version, it is clear that Article 11 Reg CESL is what is usually called an 'internal choice-of-law rule', ie a rule that distributes legal issues between different bodies (regimes) of law within a legal system.[85] Other examples are Article 1(1)(b) CISG and its corresponding provision in Section 5 of the Swedish Sale of Goods Act (1990:931). The consequences of the '2nd regime-model' are further explained in Recitals 9–10 Reg CESL (Recital 9 is cited in Section I):

Recital 10 Reg CESL including EP Amendment 3

(10) The agreement to use the Common European Sales Law should be a choice exercised within the respective national **legal order** which is **determined as the applicable law** pursuant to Regulation (EC) No 593/2008 or, in relation to pre-contractual information duties, pursuant to Regulation (EC) No 864/2007 of the European Parliament and of the Council of 11 July 2007 on the law applicable to non-contractual obligations (Regulation (EC) No 864/2007), or any other relevant conflict of law rule. The agreement to use the Common European Sales Law **results from a choice between two different regimes within the same national legal order. That** choice, therefore, **does** not amount to, and **should** not be confused with, a choice between **two national legal orders** within the meaning of the conflict-of-law rules and should be without prejudice to them. This Regulation will therefore not affect any of the existing conflict of law rules **such as those contained in Regulation (EC) No 593/2008.**

It follows from Recital 10 Reg CESL that the CESL will be indirectly applicable—ie via the choice-of-law rules—as an integral part of the *lex contractus*, and it can only form part of the *lex contractus* if that law is the law of a Member State—a 'CESL State'. Accordingly, in order to make a valid choice of the uniform regime CESL, the parties must first make sure that the *lex contractus* is the law of a Member State (a 'double choice' or

---

[85] The opinions were divided regarding the initial Proposal for the CESL. See eg Rühl (n 17) 159.

'two-step procedure' due to the opt-in nature of the CESL). This is the same situation mutatis mutandis as is envisaged in sub-paragraph (b) of Article 1(1) CISG:

Article 1(1) of the CISG

(1) This Convention applies to contracts of sale of goods between parties whose places of business [or habitual business][86] are in different States:
   (a) when the States are Contracting States; or
   (b) when the rules of private international law lead to the application of the law of a Contracting State.

Under Article 1(1)(b) CISG, the CISG will be indirectly applicable when the *lex contractus* is the law of a Contracting State—a 'CISG State', provided that the parties' places of business are in *any* different States.

However, the CISG also contains an additional rule in sub-paragraph (a), under which the contract law regime in the CISG will be 'directly applicable' where the parties have their places of business in different Contracting States—'CISG States'.[87] That is to say, the CISG constitutes a combined '1st and 2nd regime' model, since the regime can be either directly applicable under Article 1(1)(a) CISG or indirectly applicable under Article 1(1)(b) CISG.

The provision in Article 1(1)(a) CISG is also one of the major differences between the CESL and the CISG: that there is no explicit distinction in Article 4(2) Reg CESL between, on the one hand, the intra-Union situation where all parties are habitually resident in different Member States— see Article 1(1)(a) CISG—and on the other, the external situation where at least one party is habitually resident in a Member State and at least one party is habitually resident in a non-Member State—see Article 1(1)(b) CISG.

Arguably, this is due to the fact that the CISG is an opt-out instrument, and as such it needs an explicit provision (an independent starting point) for its application. However, such a binding obligation to apply the CISG prima facie to cross-border sales can only be laid upon Contracting States to the CISG. Hence, the reciprocal requirement in Article 1(1)(a) CISG that all parties must have their (relevant) places of business in different Contracting

---

[86] See Art 10 CISG.

[87] Arguably, Art 1(1)(a) CISG constitutes a 'unilateral choice-of-law rule', but the question of its proper characterisation falls outside the scope of this chapter. Suffice it to say that unilateral choice-of-law rules are a common feature in international conventions on uniform law, where they perform the task of determining when the uniform law is applicable. As provisions of *lex specialis*, unilateral choice-of-law rules take precedence over the regular universal choice-of-law rules and the latter must no longer be applied. A different view is that the presence of a common uniform regime rules out a conflict of laws, thereby making the choice-of-law rules inapplicable. Either way, the end result is the same: the uniform regime takes precedence over both the universal choice-of-law rules and the domestic substantive law regime.

States (CISG-States) for the CISG to apply directly and without recourse to the choice-of-law rules.[88]

Regarding the CESL, however, there is no need for an independent starting point, since its application depends on the parties opting into the CESL in accordance with Articles 8 and 3 Reg CESL and the general requirement of a Member State *lex contractus*. Instead there are other ways in the intra-Union situation to achieve the same goal as Article 1(1)(a) CISG, ie the de facto direct application of the uniform regime without recourse to the choice-of-law rules, since the only legal order that can be determined as the *lex contractus* in the intra-Union situation is the law of a Member State and as such it contains the identical uniform contract law regime: the CESL. This is indicated in Recital 12:

Recital 12 Reg CESL including Amendment 6

(12) **Once there is a valid agreement to use the Common European Sales Law, only the Common European Sales Law should govern the matters falling within its scope.** Since the Common European Sales Law contains a **comprehensive** set of **uniform** harmonised mandatory consumer protection rules, there will be no disparities between the laws of the Member States in this area, where the parties have chosen to use the Common European Sales Law. Consequently, Article 6(2) of Regulation (EC) No 593/2008, which is predicated on the existence of differing levels of consumer protection in the Member States, has no practical **relevance to** the issues covered by the Common European Sales Law, **as it would amount to a comparison between the mandatory provisions of two identical second contract-law regimes.**

Recital 12 simply points out that where all parties to a consumer contract are habitually resident in Member States, opting into the identical uniform contents of the CESL de facto prevents Article 6(2) Rome I from coming into play even if the *lex electa* is eg the trader's law, as a 'conflict of laws' never arises. The identicalness of the CESL in consumer contracts is guaranteed by Article 8(3) Reg CESL, where it is stated that 'in relations between a trader and a consumer the Common European Sales Law may not be chosen partially, but only in its entirety.'

Furthermore, a CESL opt-in clause in the intra-Union context, where all parties to a trader contract are habitually resident in Member States and there is either no *lex electa*, or the *lex electa* is the law of a Member State—ie all relevant connecting factors point to Member States—the CESL is in practice directly applicable in virtually the same manner as the CISG is under Article 1(1)(a) CISG. That is to say, the uniformity of the CESL prevents in effect 'a conflict of laws', and thus it will not be necessary to identify which

---

[88] Notably also, the court must be situated in a Contracting State, as Art 1(1)(a) CISG must form part of the *lex fori* in order to create an obligation on the part of the national court to apply it.

Member State law is the actual *lex contractus* under the choice-of-law rules in order to establish that the CESL is applicable.

Accordingly, the reference in the Amended Recital 9 Reg CESL to the CESL and its application as being both 'directly applicable' and an 'integral part' of the *lex contractus* is not as inconsistent as it prima facie may seem in comparison with Article 1(1)(a)–(b) CISG. A different matter is whether a new proposal ought to be drafted with a specific provision for the direct application of the CESL in intra-Union situations and another provision for the indirect application in external situations.[89] Arguably, the private actors are better served with a good practice handbook and a clear model agreement.

F. The 'Entirely Domestic Setting' in Article 13 Reg CESL

Article 13 Reg CESL provides the individual Member States with the opportunity to extend the application of the CESL to intra-State trade within that Member State:[90]

Article 13 Reg CESL—Member States' options

A Member State may decide to make the Common European Sales Law available for:

(a)   contracts where the habitual residence of the traders or, in the case of a contract between a trader and a consumer, the habitual residence of the trader, the address indicated by the consumer, the delivery address for goods and the billing address, are located in that Member State;

In other words, an extension under Article 13 Reg CESL removes the cross-border requirement stated in Article 4(1) Reg CESL (see Section IV.B above), so that the CESL can be used for distance contracts in what is referred to as an 'entirely domestic setting'.[91] Notably, the territorial link to the extending Member State means that it is not possible for parties habitually resident in another non-extending Member State to make the extended CESL applicable as part of the *lex electa*.

However, all situations covered by Article 13 do not constitute an 'entirely domestic setting', since the concept of cross-border is much more limited under the CESL in comparison with the PIL rules. Thus, the Article 13 extension also brings the CESL fully in line with the international scope

---

[89] Rühl (n 17) 161–162.

[90] Since Amendment 70 regarding Art 7 Reg CESL has abolished the requirement that at least one party to a trader contract must be a small or medium-sized enterprise ('SME'), there is no longer any need to allow for an extended application of the CESL to non-SME trader contracts by the individual Member States under Art 13(b) Reg CESL.

[91] Explanatory Memorandum to the CESL (n 1) 12.

of the choice-of-law rules. Without the extension, the CESL could, for instance, not be opted into in the situation where the foreign trader has a branch in the same Member State in which the trader or consumer is habitually resident, since that branch is the only relevant connection to establish the cross-border scope under Article 4, see Article 4(5) Reg CESL. The same applies where eg the contracting parties are established in the same Member State and the contractual performance is taking place in a foreign country, or that the prima facie domestic contract belongs to an international contractual setting. That is to say, those cross-border elements are only given any relevance under the PIL rules.

This leads to the awkward situation that where there are both an international element and a 'local connection' present, the parties can agree both on jurisdiction under Article 25 BIa and the *lex electa* under Article 2 1955 Hague Convention or Article 3 Rome I, but the possibility to opt into the CESL is ruled out without the extension in Article 13 Reg CESL.[92]

Consequently, where a trader is seeking to do cross-border business with either other traders or consumers and wishes to rely—or even keeps relying—on the CESL, that trader is well advised not to set up a branch in the other party's Member State, unless that Member State has opted for the Article 13 extension. This is both counter-productive and counter-intuitive from the perspective of private actors involved in cross-border trade, so hopefully all Member States will make use of this option to extend the scope of the CESL. An even better solution from a uniformity perspective would be to make the extension permanent, at least for trader contracts. It could also be an advantage for the online consumer—the CESL could apply to all online purchases.

V. CONCLUSIONS

In general, the CESL fits well within the 'sphere of private international law' in those situations where the contracting parties have their (relevant) habitual residences in different (Member) States, ie within the narrow scope of 'cross-border contract' in the CESL.

However, one major problem is the situation involving both an international element and a 'local connection'—ie the parties' relevant habitual residences are in the same (Member) State. Unless the scope of the CESL is extended to match that of PIL, there is a risk that the purpose to enable traders, in particular SMEs, to rely on a common set of rules and use the

---

[92] A different matter is that under the PIL rules, the 'local connection' will be given effect under the default rules, constituting a ground for jurisdiction under Art 7(5) Brussels Ia as well as the relevant connecting factor regarding the *lex contractus* under Art 3 of the 1955 Hague Convention, and Arts 4(1)(a)–(b) and 6(1)(a)–(b) in conjunction with Art 19(2) Rome I.

same contract terms for *all* their cross-border transactions will not be fulfilled. In addition, there is a risk of locked-in business expansion, since the establishment of a branch in the Member State where the trader's cross-border customers are, will prevent the use of the CESL (subject to Article 13 Reg CESL).

Trader contracts still suffer from the non-uniformity of the two choice-of-law regimes in different Member States, but the '2nd regime' model chosen for the CESL does not make things worse, as a '28th regime' model would. Furthermore, the interplay of the CESL and the CISG is straightforward. The chosen legislative solution to use the opting-out mechanism in the CISG and leave the practical choice between the two regimes to the contracting parties is both elegant and legally sound. It preserves the status quo of the CISG as the primary uniform law regime for international sales of goods and does not jeopardise the private actors' possibilities to use the CISG by default, as a declaration under Article 94 CISG would have done. Compared to the CISG, the CESL is a more complete regime, covering a number of issues not regulated by the former. Whether this would make the proposed CESL more attractive only time will tell. Under Article 8(3) Reg CESL including EP Amendment 72, parties to trader contracts have at least the possibility of combining the CESL with either the CISG or a domestic regime (*depeçage*).

Furthermore, it has been shown that in practice there is really no major difference between the '2nd regime' model chosen for the CESL and the combined '1st and 2nd regime' model of the CISG. In the intra-Union context, the valid opting into the CESL in effect means that it is unnecessary to determine which Member State law constitutes the *lex contractus* (including *lex electa*), since the identicalness of the uniform CESL rules out any conflict of laws. Thus, the same result is achieved as under Article 1(1)(a) CISG. In the external context, the parties must make sure that the *lex contractus*—either as *lex electa* or under the default rules—is the law of a Member State in order to validly opt into the CESL. This situation corresponds with the rule in Article 1(1)(b) CISG, apart from the additional requirement that at least one party must be habitually resident in a Member State.

Accordingly, there is really no need to alter the proposed CESL into an explicit '1st and 2nd regime' model. It is submitted, however, that the most important pre-condition that the *lex contractus* must be the law of a Member State in order to be able to opt into the CESL should also be explicitly stated in Article 3 Reg CESL, and not just follow from the Recitals.

Regarding consumer contracts, the use of CESL as such is unproblematic. The fact that the CESL in certain cases would not be as protective to the consumer as the domestic regime of the Member State *lex contractus* under Article 6 Rome I, is of no concern from a PIL perspective. The agreement to opt into the CESL is a question of substantive law—an internal choice-of-law-regime issue; and it is well within the prerogative of the legislator to provide for different protective regimes within the same legal order.

Finally, another major problem, in my opinion, is that the CESL is not open to non-trader contracts. Those contracts can also be of high value, such as in the case of the sale of pedigree cat. One of the major advantages with the CESL is namely that it is available in 24 languages and those are easily accessible online in one place. Accordingly, the transaction costs for a non-trader doing cross-border business on a more sporadic, or even a one-off, basis would be greatly reduced if the CESL were made available.

7

Global Business: National Law, EU Law and International Customs and Contracts

LARS GORTON[*]

I. BUSINESS AND EU LAW

A. Starting Point[**]

PRODUCTS HAVE BEEN traded and exchanged for as long as there have been people and societies.[1] Originally, trade took place between individuals but later it increasingly developed to involve business entities and states. Gradually, different services also came to be part of the exchange including the trade in intellectual property rights. Hence, business has evolved over the centuries, and the legal framework has developed in various ways in order to meet the particular needs that have arisen at different times and with respect to different trades and traditions. Some legal techniques and instruments have a very long history, whereas other circumstances have led, in more recent times, to new and/or changed methods.[2]

As a basis for my observations below, I would like to refer to some of the works of the late Clive M Schmitthoff who debated the question of a new

---

[*] Professor Emeritus associated with the Stockholm Centre for Commercial Law, Stockholm University, Sweden.

[**] The footnotes below may be regarded as being rather haphazard, and reference is mostly made to Swedish and English legal sources.

[1] In recent years there has also been a huge growth in the exchange of services and questions related to intellectual property (licences with respect to patents, trademarks, knowhow). Eric Runesson in his book *Licens till patent och företagshemligheter i avtals- och kontraktsrätten* (Stockholm, Norstedts, 2014) analyses and discusses contractual aspects related to certain intellectual property rights.

[2] Patrick Glenn in his *Legal Traditions of the World*, 4th edn (Oxford, OUP, 2010) makes several references to the question of tradition in a legal context. He speaks about 'legal traditions' rather than 'legal systems'. Here, I do not specifically delve into the various theories that have been developed in this context, and without going into the particularities of this debate, the problems below that are related to commercial transactions will also be discussed to a certain extent against the background of various legal traditions and developments.

lex mercatoria in various writings dating back to the 1980s, inter alia (but not only) in some Gresham lectures.[3] He there on p 18 et seq refers to the distinction between 'the law applying to home transactions and that applying to international business.' On p 19 he explains that international trade law has developed in three stages, the first being the period of the medieval law merchant, the old *lex mercatoria,* and the second being the period when the old *lex mercatoria* was incorporated into the national systems of law during the 17th through to the 19th centuries. On p 20 he subsequently adds: 'In the third, contemporary, period we find a conscious and deliberate return to the international spirit of our subject.' These are words expressed in the 1980s. There have since been several new trends. Of course, Schmitthoff in this article mainly discusses different trends related to private law matters, but in his book on export trade he also deals with other legal aspects besides private law.[4]

Today, the perspective could be widened to also cover 'trade matters' (a broader perspective which could be called the macro perspective) and various other administrative law matters, and thus the topic now appears in a somewhat different light. The overall view varies over time also due to changes in economic political ideas. Even if this particular aspect is not discussed here at any length, the indirect influence of the economic political sphere related to the conduct of trade by and among states since the beginning of time and, from a European perspective, since the 15th century cannot be ignored.[5]

Trade patterns based on the ideas of mercantilism and liberalism have also been relevant from my more narrow perspective. At the end of the 1990s and the beginning of the 2000s, there have been a number of problems in relation to the World Trade Organization (WTO) system, which have

[3] See, eg, Schmitthoff, *Commercial Law in a Changing Economic Climate,* 2nd edn (London, Sweet & Maxwell, 1981). Schmitthoff belonged to an important group of legal scholars who fled Germany during the 1930s and 1940s and who came to provide the development of legal scholarship, particularly in the UK and the US, with a deep knowledge of continental law combined with their later acquired equally deep knowledge of English and US law respectively. Schmitthoff discussed related problems in several other works, one of which will be mentioned below.

[4] The first edition of *Schmitthoff: The Law and Practice of International Trade* was published in 1948, and the latest 12th edn by Carol Murray, David Holloway and Daren Timson-Hunt was published by Sweet & Maxwell in 2012. Apart from extensive sections on various private law matters related to sales, carriage, insurance and payments, the book also covers matters related to the WTO (World Trade Organization) and customs law. In the book, there is also a section on 'private international law', a legal area whose importance may have been reduced somewhat by the use of harmonized material rules. As a general observation, it may be said that the later editions of the book are more influenced by the common law perspective than the first editions. As from the latter part of the 1950s, the Treaty of Rome of 1957 as subsequently amended and new Treaties came to have a particular impact on European conditions.

[5] See, eg, Bernstein, *An Exchange. How Trade Shaped the World* (London, Grove Press, 2008).

prevented a new and broader agreement.[6] Instead a growing number of bilateral and multilateral agreements outside the WTO system have gained in importance.[7] In early December 2013, a limited trade agreement was reached within the WTO, which could pave the way for further agreements. Failing the conclusion of a more general global trade agreement, regional and bilateral agreements have for now come into force. Various bilateral trade agreements have been concluded, and there are presently negotiations between the EU and the US for a Transatlantic Partnership for Trade and Tnvestments (TTIP).[8]

Since the creation of the International Centre for Settlement of Investment Disputes (ICSID) Convention in 1966, a growing number of International Investment Agreements have also been concluded. They regularly contain a specific investor-state dispute resolution clause referring such dispute to the ICSID.[9]

One particular business sector, reflecting this twofold evolution, concerns the financial markets, where, not least over the last 20 to 30 years, there has been a growing global development followed by some contraction since the financial crisis in 2007/08. Financial regulation has expanded nationally, regionally and internationally. A particular trend which is not related to *lex mercatoria* in the traditional sense thus concerns the regulatory aspects which developed in the US particularly during the financial crisis in the 1930s.[10] Add to this a further legal area of practical importance with respect to business, namely taxation, where the OECD has played a significant role with respect to the United Nations Model Double Tax Convention

---

[6] The WTO system has its origin in the General Agreement on Tariffs and Trade (GATT) dating back to 1948 and its various so-called rounds. The object of WTO is to simplify free trade and economic development and it has been criticized for promoting trade in favour of the rich countries to the detriment of poorer countries and the environment. There are presently 155 members of the WTO. WTO has its own dispute resolution mechanism. See inter alia Hudgins, 'Regional and Multilateral Trade Agreements: Complementary means to open markets', *Cato Journal* 1995/96 p 231 et seq.

[7] See, eg, Special report on the world economy: *The Gated Globe* (The Economist, 12 October 2013).

[8] One of the most controversial parts of the TTIP agreements concerns the dispute resolution mechanism which is being criticized for allowing disputes to be referred to as 'private' settlements where state interests are involved, and it has been discussed at length in connection with EU/US negotiations. Thus, the Transatlantic Trade and Investment Partnership (TTIP) is still being negotiated and there are intense ongoing discussions on the part of the agreement which deals with the Investor State Dispute Settlement (ISDS). Other similar bilateral trade agreements contain such dispute resolution mechanisms.

[9] The ICSID Convention from 1966 now has 150 contracting states. Several investment disputes have since been settled through the ICSID mechanism. Beside the ICSID Convention, the World Bank harbours a number of organizations established to promote its goals, such as IBRD (International Bank of Reconstruction and Development, IDA (International Development Agency) etc. See inter alia Schreuer, Malintoppi, Reinisch and Sinclair, *The ICSID Convention. A Commentary*, 2nd edn (Cambridge, CUP, 2009).

[10] See, for instance, the Glass Stegal Act 1932 (related to banks) and its repeal in 2009. In the UK, self-regulation has been largely favoured but following EU rules, soft law regulation has been gradually replaced by hard law.

2011 between developed and developing countries. In this connection, there should also be mention of the ongoing discussions with respect to a permanent arbitration panel for international tax disputes. Furthermore, The EU has played a significant role in regulating VAT questions across EU member countries.

The observations below focus on the divisions that still exist between the global, regional and national perspectives, where developments seem to take various routes at the same time. Undoubtedly, national law still plays a fundamental role, and national legal traditions may thus be seen to follow different trends, although there appears to be a greater degree of harmonization aimed at certain legal areas. While there is an increase in the conclusion of new regional and even bilateral agreements between states, there is also, a global trend as exemplified by the ongoing discussions on a Transatlantic Partnership Agreement as well as by the Transpacific Partnership Agreement already concluded. That being said, it is important to recognize that the extent to which there is a global development of law is debatable. The political and economic globalization which has undoubtedly been taking place for a long time is further discussed. Globalization has by no means only brought greatness and happiness; however, a breakdown of international efforts would on balance, in my view, have a generally negative effect on the development of societies worldwide. It has to be recognized that since the 1950s, following decolonization and then, later in the 1990s, with the fall of the Soviet Union, the development can be characterized as a line with several fractures. The present evolution signifies different and partly colliding roads with several rifts in the ongoing and presently probably slowing or changing process of globalization.[11]

In my view, this means that several legal trends may be discerned. From a private law perspective, the role of the Unidroit Principles of Commercial Contracts (PICC) may be recognized as a particular parameter in the extended discussion related to global commercial law matters.[12] Apart from

---

[11] Undoubtedly, there are several trends and it is very hard to determine which parameters have played the more decisive role in this evolution. Of course, the underlying need for peace after World War II was never really fully fulfilled, and the various wishes arising at different times had to face changing political and economic conditions. An important feature of developments is also characterized by the number of new bodies, public and private, specialized and general, regional and international. A large number of bilateral, regional and international treaties of different types covering different areas have been established which have gradually grown in importance. The increasing numbers of non-governmental organizations (NGOs), each with their particular agenda, have also played a greater role.

[12] See Vogenauer and Kleinheisterkamp (eds), *Commentary on the UNIDROIT Principles of International Commercial Contracts (PICC)* (Oxford, OUP, 2009). Where the PICC may be characterized as an international tool, the Principles of European Contract Law (PECL), although in many respects not fundamentally different from the PICC represents a more European perspective just like for that matter the Draft Common Frames of Reference (DCFR) with its more precise goal to lead to a harmonized European law of obligations, which is unlikely to come into being in a near future.

the development of material law rules, it is important to underline that international private law has also expanded in various ways adding to the complexity of the situation.[13]

B. Global Business—Local Law ('Glocal' Law)

The concept of globalization has over the last 30-year period come to be used to describe a particular development and has also been assigned a specific role in international business and trade. As a concept, 'globalization' seems to be fairly well established in the field of business and economics but it is also evolving as a concept in political science. However, even if its use in legal discourse is becoming more frequent, it seems to be less adaptable, in part because law is often connected to a state/nation.[14] My general observations above are based on the perception that private law has developed over a considerably longer period than administrative law and also consists of fairly well-established principles which may in many cases not have changed fundamentally over time, although they are far from identical in different legal orders.[15] Having said that, it goes without saying that the development of private law is also affected by technological, organizational and political development, not least circumstances such as colonization and decolonization. Hence, the different trends have in turn contributed to the development of new legal methods, instruments and techniques with respect to private law matters and not only to those of administrative law character.

From a European perspective, the legal framework, which has developed after the establishment of the EU,[16] has meant that certain new legal methods have come into use, involving in particular certain parts of law but also causing problems in relation to adopted traditional legal doctrines and traditions gradually established and applied in different legal systems. There is not much doubt that the quality in the drafting of legislation emanating from Brussels is to, some extent, adversely affected as a consequence of the collision between different drafting techniques in the different Member

---

[13] In Lindskoug, Maunsbach, Millqvist, Samuelsson, and Voget (eds), *Essays in Honour of Michael Bogdan* (Lund, 2013) several authors have addressed particular questions related to EU law, questions related to choice of law, jurisdiction and the enforcement of judgments.

[14] Just as witnessed at the end of the 19th century, there now seems to be a European security order which is being pulled apart by nationalism, imperialism and globalisation: see Lieven, *Towards the Flame: Empire, War and the End of Tsarist Russia* (Allen Lane, 2015).

[15] Cotterrell, 'What is transnational law', (2012) *Law & Social Inquiry*, 37. See also Senn, Winiger, Fritschi, Avramov, *Recht und Globalisierung/Droit et mondialisation* (Stuttgart, Franz Steiner Verlag, 2010).

[16] See further Bernitz and Kjellgren, *Europarättens grunder*, 5th edn (Stockholm, Norstedts juridik, 2014).

States, language differences and the need to handle various compromises.[17] This is in part due to the need to find compromises and the result of language difficulties but also because the legal methods used and law-making procedures applied may vary between different EU jurisdictions. Furthermore, what is being referred to as the democratic deficiency of the EU has also bred a growing antipathy among several EU nationals vis-à-vis EU institutions including the European Court of Justice.

Commercial law has thus developed in various ways and at different levels and through different methods. Hence, different parameters have contributed to the evolution. Such a development may not have been the same for all business segments. Obviously commercial law is not based only on legislation and case law, but also soft law (customs, practices and standard conditions etc) plays an important role, not least where international business is concerned.[18]

My main objective in this article is to discuss certain elements related to commercial relationships and contracts, and thus I shall not primarily deal with these questions from the EU perspective but rather try to see developments from the angle of the general development of global (international) commercial law. That, however, also means that some EU rules and principles may be mirrored in a global (international) law perspective. It should be underlined that EEC law initially, in the first phase after the Rome Treaty came into force, to a large extent involved matters related to competition law, as far as commercial and trade law were concerned. Competition law would in traditional terminology hardly be regarded as part of *lex mercatoria* in spite of its impact on the development of international business and indirectly on commercial law probably as an effect of US influence on the European development after World War II.[19] Looking at the development of international business entities the efficiency of these rules must, however, be questioned. There are from this perspective undoubtedly differences between different areas of law, where items related to contract law may have to be approached differently to questions related to property law, and also administrative law matters will have to be treated using different methods, as they actually evolved on the basis of specific legal parameters.[20]

---

[17] Undoubtedly, the distinction made in EU law between regulations and directives is important in this context, and it can be noted that the concept of regulation as used in English law is not necessarily the same as the concept of 'regulation' as used in EU law. This has, however, nothing per se to do with poor drafting.

[18] If using common law as a basis, one could possibly say that contracts and standard contracts can be regarded as a kind of hard law from the contracting parties' point of view.

[19] Competition law seems nowadays to have an increasing impact on trade and business.

[20] The efforts needed to create a European Civil Code must, therefore, be seen in relation to the international (global) efforts and, from a European perspective, it is also necessary to recognize the impact of EU law with respect to the development of legal methodology, see in Swedish law, Hettne and Otken Eriksson (eds), *EU-rättslig metod. Teori och genomslag i svensk rättstillämpning*, 2nd edn (Stockholm, Norstedts juridik, 2011).

A particular aspect also concerns the development of infrastructure projects in different markets involving various parts of the relevant legal system.

C. Old Trade Patterns. Is There a Need for Cross-Border (International) Commercial Law? If So, In What Form(s)?

When dealing with trade and business from a historical perspective, it is obvious that several parameters have to be taken into consideration. European continental law broadly evolved from Roman law and eventually came to clash with Germanic customs. Roman Law as saved by the glossators evolved into the *Corpus Iuris Civilis* and remained an important basis for the general development of law in continental Europe, but with respect to commercial matters, certain specific principles developed mainly within that legal area which could be assigned to *lex mercatoria*. In this connection, Roy Goode sets out that:

'[F]or my purposes I shall treat the *lex mercatoria* as consisting of customary commercial law, customary rules of evidence and procedure and general principles of commercial law, including international public policy.'[21]

Lex mercatoria seems to have evolved linked to specific markets, in the old Mesopotamia and the Middle East, and developed later in the Northern Italian city states and in market places in the north western parts of Europe.[22] It seems to have developed around dispute settlement mechanisms often linked to specific markets and also around certain payment instruments (the bill of exchange and the documentary letter of credit) and around certain transport documents (bills of lading) etc. One could say that *lex mercatoria* was function-oriented since it developed out of a need for practical legal solutions.

Hence, *lex mercatoria* may be regarded as some kind of legal tool, which in its old form was not based on a legislative procedure but rather on custom

---

[21] Goode, 'A New International Lex Mercatoria', in *Juridisk Tidskrift* 1999/2000 p 253 et seq. His findings here differ somewhat from those expressed by Schmitthoff in n 3 above. He, for good reason, also finds that 'no two writers are agreed on its meaning.' He also discusses the use of the concept and on p 257 warns against 'too lax an approach by some arbitration tribunals to evidence international trade usage.' In Nordic law, Ole Lando was in my view one of the first to refer to *lex mercatoria* in connection with international commercial contracts, see Lando, 'The Lex Mercatoria in International Commercial Arbitration' (1985) 34 *International and Comparative Law Quarterly* 747. See also Dalhuisen, *Dalhuisen on Transnational Comparative, Commercial, Financial and Trade Law. Vol 1. Introduction— The New Lex Mercatoria and Its Sources*, 5th edn (Oxford, Hart Publishing, 2013), where the author discusses the transnationalization of commercial and financial law.

[22] See the discussion in Sachs, 'From St Ives to Cyberspace. The Modern Distortion of the Medieval "Law Merchant"' (2006) *American University International Law Review* 685. There he concludes that it is hard to transform the old 'law merchant' into a modern framework of 'lex mercatoria'.

and usage and dispute resolution and developing for practical purposes. It is not easy to determine precisely what rules or principles may be regarded as embodied in *lex mercatoria* nor always their precise legal effects, but they may be used as a reference point in a contract law context, and they may possibly be applied by a court or an arbitration tribunal.[23] The specific legal areas where reference to *lex mercatoria* may be particularly relevant date back to the law of sales, the law related to carriage (in particular bills of lading) and the law related to trade and payment (payments, letters of credit, on demand guarantees and bills of exchange—nowadays often jointly referred to as trade finance).[24] In the last few decades, making certain large commercial contracts, including investment contracts, subject to *lex mercatoria* or similar principles is a practice that seems to have become more common.[25]

A different term, anational law, is sometimes used and referred to in this regard.[26] The idea behind this concept is to identify certain principles relevant in a commercial law context, but which are not particularly linked to a national legal system. In one sense, it should be possible to establish (at least to some extent) the existence of such principles but in the case of a dispute under a specific contract, a judge or arbitrator may prefer to resort to principles which they know and which often stem from national rules. Hence, a contract, which is subject to *lex mercatoria* and where a dispute is to be settled by a particular court or by arbitrators in a particular country, may encounter certain problems in the settlement of the dispute.[27] This may also lead to the concept 'anational', which may, from the contract writer's point of view, seem relevant when the contract is negotiated but maybe fading out in the settlement phase if a court is involved in the resolution. In connection with dispute settlement, particularly where courts are involved, a more precise legal framework may be necessary. This being said, it may very well be that, in the case of dispute settlement through arbitration, arbitrators from

[23] See, eg, Preamble to the UNIDROIT Principles of International Commercial Contracts (below referred to as the PICC). The fact that several standard contracts have been developed by the International Chamber of Commerce (ICC) where reference is made to a particular trade usage (rather than *lex mercatoria*) or the PICC also merits a mention, see further below under sections 2 and 3.
[24] Lindskog, *Betalning: om kongruent infriande av penningskulder och andra betalningsrättsliga frågor* (Stockholm, Norstedts juridik, 2014); Adestam, J, *Den dokumentvillkorade garantin.* (Lund, Lund University Publications, 2014).
[25] See below in II.B.
[26] Lando uses the expression in *Den ikke-nationale handelsvoldgift*, Festskrift til Alf Ross, (Copenhagen 1969) 295. See also Meidel, *An Anational Approach to International Contracts* (Oslo, 2007) 14 et seq and Gorton, in *Rättsliga ramar för internationella affärer*, 2nd edn (Stockholm, 2005) who has used this particular perspective. See further *Developing neutral legal standards for international contracts. A-national rules as the applicable law in international commercial contracts* presented to the ICC by the taskforce chaired by Fabio Bortolotti and Franco Silvano Tono di Cigoli.
[27] See further below in II.B.

different countries who are not fully familiar with a particular law, may resort to an a-national perspective of some kind in their reasoning.

D. Certain Terminology

The above indicates that the terminology used to cover the area of law which is discussed here may vary; ranging from international commercial law to transnational business law, and global economic law etc.[28] It is not set in stone that the various terms in use always mean exactly the same thing. Apart from the above-mentioned concepts, there are also terms such as business law, mercantile law, commercial law and trade law. They do not seem to be used fully interchangeably, but in the legal literature the different concepts cover similar features to a large extent. 'Commercial law' and 'mercantile law' seem to cover legal issues which are connected to business activities, while 'trade law' seems to be more geared towards a macro perspective, where also, for example, WTO issues are involved. 'Business' law is perhaps more often used for matters related to business entities (company law, environmental law, labour relations etc), but the terminology is rather ambiguous. It may also be the case that a preferred term is related to a particular jurisdiction and to a particular author.

'International commercial law' may in some instances be used rather than international business law but also the concept of international economic law is sometimes applied, albeit with a slightly different approach.[29] Furthermore, 'global law' seems to be an emerging concept whereas less than 30 years ago the discussion seems rather to have focused on the role of multinational corporations. Transnational commercial law is another concept in use which seems to have a counterpart in transnational corporations.

---

[28] It is also important to mention that in certain legal systems a number of rules have been referred to that part of the code book which has been called commercial law (Handelsrecht, Code de Commerce). In Nordic law, Mäntysaari in a number of articles and studies has suggested a particular legal theory with respect to commercial law, see for instance Mäntysaari, 'Handelsrättens teori: En teoretisk referensram för handelsrättslig forskning', (2011) *Tidsskrift for Rettsvitenskap* 197 et seq, where he has also included a list of references.

It is also important to recognize that 'international law' may have a specific meaning depending on the context of its use.

[29] All these terms are found in different contexts. My impression is that 'trade law' is used when trade matters are discussed related mainly to WTO and other macroeconomic issues, but there are textbooks involving international trade law which also deal with private law transactions between sellers and buyers. My impression is also that economic law was a term used in socialist countries to describe and contain a certain area of law. See, eg, *Schmitthoff: The Law and Practice of International Trade* (n 4); Schaffer, Agusti, Dhooge, and Earle, *International Business Law and Its Environment*, 8th edn (Cengage Learning, 2012) as well as Goode, Kronke, McKendrick and Wool, *Transnational Commercial Law*, (Oxford, OUP, 2007) and Dalhuisen (n 21). In this connection, see also Ramberg, *International Commercial Transactions*, 3rd edn (Stockholm 2004), which covers a more narrow legal area related mainly to sales law and the law of carriage.

If you only take the EU perspective, it is also important to emphasize that commercial law/business law seem to be developing rather broadly at the international level instead of being restricted to a more narrow geographical perspective. With this as the point of departure, it would seem that EU law is geographically and perhaps also functionally too narrow, from the global perspective where the geographical framework should not be restricted by the EU or Europe.[30]

II. SOME FACTORS OF IMPORTANCE

A. The Development of Co-operation Patterns, Documents and Certain Concepts

'EU law' is of course relevant also in the context of commercial law or business law and also in a more international context, but EU law as a particular legal framework covers a much broader legal area than commercial law or business law. One may thus question the extent to which EU law is connected to international commercial law. 'Global commercial law' is a legal framework distinctly different from EU law; broader in geographical coverage but narrower when it comes to the legal areas involved. EU law does cover some of those elements which are attributed to global commercial law, but the geographical perspective is, of course, narrower. 'Global commercial law' may also be approached from an angle where legal parameters of different legal kinds are used. A different perspective appears when concepts such as hard law and soft law respectively are used. Hard law on the one hand consists of national legislation and case law. National legislation is sometimes based on international conventions, which have been transformed into national legislation.[31] However, different kinds of soft law principles have evolved in various forms.[32]

Whether usage and customs should be referred to as soft law or as a particular form of hard law is a matter for discussion, but undoubtedly usage and customs are referred to as something which forms a part of hard law since, in some legislation, explicit reference is made to usage or customs but

---

[30] As mentioned above in n 12, the PICC has been established as a set of international principles. Apart from the PICC, the Principles of European Contract law (PECL) and the Draft Frame of Reference (DCFR) have been designed for European conditions.

[31] Draft conventions, as with draft legislation, are not considered legal sources, although they may have a certain impact on the development of law as an inspiration in the legal development applied by courts or contract draftsmen.

[32] The role of NGOs (non-governmental organizations) may also be important from this perspective.

it may also be the case that soft law is a more recent concept.[33] Other legal items in this context involve the extensive practical use of various international standard contracts. Such standard terms have particular practical importance not because they have the same legal effect as legislation, but because they are actually used as a basis for several types of transactions usually related to specific segments of international business. It should also be mentioned that standard contracts may amount to usage and customs under particular circumstances.[34]

It is debatable whether a distinction should be made between the concepts of usage, customs and practices, and how they relate to hard law and soft law respectively.[35] Soft law as a legal concept has undoubtedly been in use for a rather short period of time, but using international business law as a point of departure, the different concepts referred to above may have to be seen in a particular light. In Swedish law, the question of usage and customs has been discussed in different contexts, and there is reference to both in some Swedish legislation.[36] In this sense, they are undoubtedly a source of law. They also have a great impact on international commercial law.[37]

National legislation based on an international convention is of a principally different character (hard law) than an international standard contract which is basically only important for a court if it has been made explicitly part of the individual contract by the parties (unless of course regarded as

[33] With respect to soft law see, eg, Bernitz, U, *Commercial Norms and Soft Law* (Stockholm, Scandinavian Studies in Law, 2013). There are other articles on this issue where soft law is discussed. See also 'Rättsbildning i en ny miljö—hur har domstolarnas roll och betydelse förändrats? Rapport från Rättssymposium 27–28 november 2003 på Häringe slott', av H Eklund (2003) *Svensk Juristtidning* 205 et seq and also Jessika van der Sluijs, 'Soft-reglering av försäkringsrätten', (2010–2011) *Juridisk Tidskrift* 296 et seq. In Swedish law, Karlgren, *Kutym och rättsregel. En civilrättslig undersökning* (Stockholm, 1960) discusses the particular features and Grönfors, K, *Almén om handelsbruk*, Rättsvetenskapliga studier till minnet av Tore Almén (Stockholm, 1999) p 123 et seq.

[34] See, eg, Cranston, 'The Rise and Rise of Standard Form Contracts: International Commodity Sales 1800–1970', in Cranston, Ramberg, and Ziegel (eds), *Commercial Law Challenges in the 21st Century* (Stockholm, Iustus Forlag, 2007) 11 et seq.

[35] There is a difference in legal quality between local customs and international trade usage. There is, for example, a difference between the Incoterm principles and the local varying port customs which may exist.

[36] In this sense there may be a difference between the Swedish perception of usage and that which is found in the CISG, for example, or the view on usage expressed in the PICC and the PECL. See, eg, Bernitz, *Standardavtalsrätt*, 8th edn (Stockholm, 2013) 41 and 59. Reference has been made to Karlgren, *Kutym och rättsregel* (n 33) and Grönfors, *Almén om handelsbruk* (n 33). In Swedish law, there are many cases where courts (not least the Supreme Court) have taken customs and usages into consideration when deciding a particular case. In order to establish such trade practice, opinions are often requested from different trade organizations.

[37] See further Kozolchyk, *Commercial Letters of Credit in the Americas: A Comparative Study of Contemporary Commercial Transactions*, (Albany, NY, 1966) 75 et seq; Schmitthoff, *Commercial Law* (n 3) 18 et seq. Draft conventions would not be immediate sources of law, but they may prove to have some relevance as food for legal thought in a particular case.

custom between the parties or commercial usage).[38] In some jurisdictions, courts have considered certain standard contracts to be usage or custom under some circumstances and particularly if they are acknowledged as agreed documents. Hence, usage or custom may be referred to and used by a court as a source of law in particular circumstances and also as regards individual contractual relations.[39]

These various parameters may thus give rise to a variety of considerations when determining the framework of 'global commercial law'. Naturally, case law is also in turn relevant to a certain extent in this context. A court in one country may take into account the development of case law in another jurisdiction, even if it is not directly applicable.[40] Naturally, it must then be recognized that arbitration awards have less legal weight than court decisions (particularly those from higher courts).[41]

B. Dispute Settlement

One parameter of particular relevance in this context concerns dispute settlement. Disputes arising under a commercial contract need a mechanism for settlement, and as mentioned above, this was important already in the old *lex mercatoria*. Naturally, today, when there is a question of settlement, whether in connection with the negotiation of a contract or a dispute arising under a contract, both the choice of law and the method of settlement have to be considered.[42] With respect to commercial contracts, there are matters

---

[38] It may, of course, also be made part of the contract implicitly. See for instance the discussion in Bernitz, *Standardavtalsrätt* (n 36) and Ramberg, and Ramberg, *Allmän avtalsrätt*, 10th edn (Stockholm, Wolters Kluwer, 2016) p 27 et seq.

[39] The PECL Art 1:105 and the CISG Art 3 seem to apply similar understanding of usage and custom which may differ somewhat from the Swedish understanding as expressed in the Swedish Contract Act (Avtalslagen) § 1.2.

[40] See, eg, CISG Art 7: 'In the interpretation of this Convention, regard is to be had to its international character and to the need to promote uniformity in its application and the observance of good faith in international trade.' Apart from such provisions in international conventions, courts may also be influenced to some degree by case law in other countries or by principles developed outside their own jurisdiction, so in Swedish law, eg, NJA 2009 p 672 and NJA 2010 p 600. See further Munukka, *Transnational Contract Law Principles in Swedish Case Law—PICC, PECL and DCFR*, Stockholm Centre for Commercial Law. Årsbok IV (Stockholm, 2012) 123 et seq.

[41] Arbitration awards are seldom published (one of the particularities of arbitration proceedings and often regarded to be an advantage) which may affect their legal weight compared to court decisions as far as legal developments are concerned. Notwithstanding this, arbitration in the context of B2B contracts often seems to be the preferred settlement method (but also other dispute resolution methods such as conciliation and mediation are growing in use). It should be underlined that arbitration awards are accounted for in a number of contexts, eg, International Commercial Arbitration Research with various references.

[42] It should be mentioned that the 1958 UN Convention on the Recognition and Enforcement of Foreign Arbitral Awards (New York) besides the CISG is a Convention which has gained most recognition.

which involve not only contractual questions but also questions related to property and insolvency, and in the latter case, the scope of contractual freedom is much more restricted, and also arbitration may not always work as a possible or at least as an efficient method of settlement.

In commercial contracts, a court procedure does not seem to be the preferred method of dispute settlement. In fact, the use of a court procedure to settle a dispute in a commercial contract seems to be universally on the decrease. In a large number of standard contracts, there are provisions specifically setting out that a contract is subject to the laws of a particular country and that a dispute shall be referred to an arbitration tribunal at a certain place and/or to a particular court. This is a solution which has gained in popularity as regards commercial contracts and seems to be based on the assumption that the contractual text is more or less complete and that it can be interpreted in accordance with any law that the parties agree on.

Disputes in connection with commercial contracts are frequently referred to arbitration tribunals, sometimes on an ad hoc basis, often by reference to an ICC arbitration clause or to a specific clause setting out the Stockholm Chamber of Commerce arbitration rules (or any other equivalent dispute resolution entity).[43] Hence, there is, for various reasons, in Sweden as well as in several other countries, a trend towards the use of arbitration as a method for dispute settlement in commercial contracts.[44] There also seems to be a growing number of trade specific private settlement mechanisms.[45] Moreover, it is increasingly common for a commercial contract to explicitly stipulate that before the parties resort to arbitration or court proceedings, they shall first endeavour to settle their differences by agreement.[46] Furthermore, the particular type of settlement mechanism known as ADR (Alternative Dispute Resolution) should be mentioned in this connection.[47] A standard contract may also include provisions on what may be referred to as self-executing contract arrangements. A particular mechanism which

---

[43] The ICC has its own arbitration procedure. Arbitration is also an area where UNCITRAL has been involved with respect to new rules, Model Law as amended in 2010, and also with respect to rules on conciliation. These arbitration rules have been used as models for new national arbitration legislation. In most trading centres, there are thus particular arbitration tribunals eg London, Shanghai, Singapore, Stockholm, Zürich etc. Furthermore, reference may be made to n 8 and n 9 above.

[44] Often costs and time are mentioned as reasons for choosing arbitration instead of ordinary court proceedings. Other factors which are often mentioned are confidentiality and also the possibility to choose arbitrators with particular knowledge.

[45] This seems to be the case with respect to, eg, GAFTA contracts.

[46] One type of clause that may be found in commercial contracts is the following headed settlement of disputes with one section on consultation and one on arbitration. Section 1 reads: 'If any dispute arises out of or relates to the validity, implementation or termination of this Agreement or any of their Appendices, the Partners shall attempt in the first instance to resolve such dispute through friendly consultations....' Such or similar words may be used to express at least a moral obligation on the parties.

[47] In this context, it is important to mention the growing use of conciliation and mediation, particularly in the US and England.

is found in certain commercial contracts may involve a specific method for benchmarking when establishing certain material obligations under the contract.[48]

Another area where specific methods of dispute settlements have evolved, concerns construction and similar contracts.[49] These types of contracts frequently include dispute resolution mechanisms for settling disputes on technical matters aimed at simplifying a dispute settlement and shortening the dispute settlement period (time and costs always being important elements). Apart from these particular dispute settlement procedures, the FIDIC contracts also provide for arbitration as a method of settlement.

Article 41 in the BIMCO Newbuildcon contract (related to shipbuilding) sets out with respect to the governing law: 'This Contract shall be subject to English law unless another law is stated in Box 23 (a) in which case the law stated in Box 23 (a) shall apply.'[50] Article 42 on dispute resolution sets out a choice of solutions but with respect to arbitration, London is specifically nominated. Hence, Box 23 allows the parties to fill in another law to apply and another place for dispute settlement.[51] Article 42 of the Newbuildcon also includes extensive provisions covering various types of disputes to which different terms apply.[52]

In some contracts, there may also be explicit provisions setting out that a dispute shall first be referred to the management board (or similar) of both parties in order to find a common acceptable solution without having to resort to arbitration.[53]

---

[48] See, eg, Gorton, 'Benchmark Clauses—Functions and Drafting: Some Remarks' in *Essays in honour of Michael Bogdan* (Lund 2013) 59 et seq.

[49] It should be recognized, however, that to an increasing extent at least certain disputes in connection with Swedish construction contracts are referred to a general court procedure.

[50] This is a contract which is based on the box layout, nowadays generally adopted in BIMCO documents.

[51] This is a type of solution which is now frequently found in several international standard contracts, which are drafted in English and based on English law and where the choice of law clause sets out that a dispute shall be resolved in accordance with English law. The standard contract, however, also sets out alternatives for the parties to choose and mark. This means that the contract is based on English law, but that it has been drafted in such a way that it could almost equally well, without particular adjustment of the contractual provisions, be made subject to New York law and referred to arbitration in New York or any other law of the choice of the parties. This seems to be an increasingly frequent way of drafting standard choice of law clauses in many charter parties, in the Loan Market Association (LMA) Agreement etc. Particular questions may subsequently arise with respect to the interpretation of the contract. Should English law still have some impact even if the individual contract has been made subject to another law?

[52] Thus, there are particular rules with respect to technical matters (expert determination), and otherwise contractual provisions set out rules on arbitration and mediation.

[53] Evidently, in most cases, both parties would normally have tried to reach an amicable solution before turning to external bodies to solve the problem on their behalf. But, and probably following requirements from East Asian parties, it is gradually becoming more common that the parties set out an explicit method for an amicable settlement.

In several of the various ICC standard contracts, efforts have been made to create alternative methods for the choice of law and dispute resolution provisions. Just to take an example, the ICC franchise contract spells out the following as alternative clauses in Article 31:[54]

'31.A Unless otherwise agreed any questions related to this Contract which are not expressly or implicitly settled by the provisions contained in this contract shall be governed, in the following order:

(a) by the principles of law generally recognized in international trade as applicable to international franchises contracts,
(b) by the relevant trade usages, and
(c) by the Unidroit Principles of International Commercial Contracts.'

Article 31.2 adds:

'In any event consideration shall be given to mandatory provisions of the law of the country where the Franchisee is established which would be applicable even if the contract is governed by a foreign law. Any such provisions will be taken into consideration to the extent they embody principles which are universally recognized and provided their application appears reasonable in the context of international trade.'

It is not easy to establish precisely 'the principles of law generally recognized in international trade as applicable to international franchises contracts', but this may give arbitrators a rather wide discretion to find out and establish those principles applicable in any particular case.

With regard to a very specific area of trade finance, the use of Docdex could be mentioned as a settlement method. This relates to a simplified and hopefully cheaper dispute settlement method in connection with letters of credit.[55] Otherwise, disputes in relation to letters of credit have traditionally been referred to a court procedure, and there is a well of court decisions in this area not least in England but also in the US. In some court decisions, particular reference has also been made to Docdex. There is no particular mention in the UCP or the URDG of the Docdex rules and they are seldom referred to in the individual letter of credit or guarantee documentation, but it would seem that they serve as an option for the parties to use once a dispute has arisen.

As mentioned above in Section I. A, there are dispute resolution mechanisms in different international legal instruments.

[54] Work is presently ongoing in the ICC Commission on Commercial Law and Practice to establish similar standards for the different ICC standard contracts taking into consideration the particularities of the various contract types.
[55] The ICC Rules for Documentary Instruments Dispute Resolution Expertise (DOCDEX) have been in force since 15 March 2002 and provide parties with a specific resolution procedure that leads to an independent, impartial and prompt expert decision settling disputes involving the UCP, URDG, URR and URC (see more on these abbreviations below in 4.9).

III. DEVELOPMENTS IN BUSINESS/LAW

A. Certain Parameters under Development

Following the general observations above, I shall now try to identify some more specific features in the developments discussed in this article. It is obvious that the *lex mercatoria* of the early ancient times is something rather different to what may today be described as a 'modern' *lex mercatoria*. The concept is in use in different contexts, and its modern application and contents seem to be wider than in the past. As mentioned above, Schmitthoff in the 1960s and Goode 30 years later discussed 'a new *lex mercatoria*' as a certain trend with respect to international commercial law. Lando, endorsing the idea of a *lex mercatoria*, also used the concept of 'anational law' as a legal feature which, even if hard to identify specifically, may have some bearing on certain features of the legal developments in this particular context.

In the present context, it is also worth mentioning that reference is made to *lex mercatoria* in both the PICC and the PECL suggesting a certain relationship between them.[56] Below, I shall further illustrate some of these different trends, which may bear some interest in this connection and also try to mirror the variety of items which may be discerned from different angles. As will become apparent below, the ICC, in certain aspects, also plays a particular role in this development.[57] A number of different parameters have contributed to the changes and the evolution.

B. Technological and Organizational Changes

Some of the changes, which have influenced the development of international business, are the consequence of new technology and new business organizations. New technological aspects involve the development of materials, products, methods of distribution and transportation, and during the last 30 years, computerization in a broad sense has also had a particular impact on the changes and has contributed to changes in the organization and management of business. Hence, and without delving further into the various changes, it is perhaps sufficient to underline that they have had a

---

[56] See the preamble of the PICC, 'purpose of the principles', which explicitly sets out that: 'These Principles set forth general rules for international commercial contracts … They may be applied when the parties have agreed that their contract be governed by general principles of law, the *lex mercatoria* or the like.' There is in Art 1:101 PECL 'Application of the Principles' in (3) a similar reference to *lex mercatoria*.

[57] See, eg, Gorton, *Forfaiting, trade finance and the International Chamber of Commerce (ICC)*, Festskrift til Nis Jul Clausen (ed N Dietz Legind, B Mortensen, H Viggo Godsk Pedersen & K Engsig Sorensen), Köbenhavn 2013 p 155 et seq.

fundamental impact also on legal developments and have all contributed to fundamental changes in several respects.

New products which have been brought to light as a consequence of research and development, new transaction forms, new ways of combining public and private co-operation (PPP), but also new forms of co-operation patterns have thus led to fundamental changes in the development of international commerce and also of its legal framework. Competition questions have gained in importance, but also in some businesses there is fierce competition between different entities combined with a need for co-operation.[58]

New transaction forms include the design of more complex individual contracts but also the design of new standard contracts. Another feature is that there are gradually more contractual relations where combinations of contracts are more common also including linked contracts.[59]

It is also obvious from the many forms of contracts designed by the ICC and other international organizations (some acting on a more general basis, others with more specialized functions) in different sectors of trade and business that growing specialization may have contributed to and called for an increasing number of specialized contract forms.

Another feature concerns new forms of co-operation, where it is, however, also necessary to be aware of various competition rules which may aim at increasing competitive behaviour between businesses thus hampering certain types of co-operation. Different forms of joint ventures may, therefore, form an important part of the trend but there are also limits to their use for competitive reasons. This is one example where there is a collision between the doctrines of the freedom of contract and freedom of competition.

Other features concern sourcing and outsourcing respectively. In the latter case, a growing number of specific contracts involve the outsourcing of certain business activities to other entities, often with other owners involved, sometimes established in other jurisdictions with lower employment costs, taxes etc. Such outsourcing may be a consequence of governments or local governments for various reasons selling out publicly owned entities but also where a private company sells a part of a business which is no longer regarded as a core business (often in the form of an MBO, management buyout). Moreover, environmental rules now play an increasingly important role, both in the sense of efforts made to avoid increased costs and as a method of marketing awareness of environmental questions. Furthermore and not least, the development of intellectual property, patents, trademarks, knowhow etc have played a fundamental role.

---

[58] See for instance the rivalry between Samsung and Apple with respect to smartphones at the same time as Apple is an important buyer of Samsung's semiconductors etc.

[59] See, eg, Hellner, Hager, Persson, *Speciell avtalsrätt II. Kontraktsrätt. 2 häftet. Allmänna ämnen*, 5th edn (Stockholm, 2011) pp 23, 137 et seq.

It is thus a manifold trend, and anyone who is interested in dealing with it will have to consider a complex material, where different parts may be chosen for particular scrutiny, but where also a rough overview may be of some value.

C. Some Organizations Playing a Specific Role in the Development of International Commercial Custom and International Standard Contracts

Several trading organizations are contributing in various ways to the development of the legal frameworks of international business. These organizations are involved in different ways and in different businesses, and apart from drafting various standard contracts they may be contributing to the development of different business practices and may also be participating in the promotion of different rules and principles. Some are connected to different products or businesses, such as the Gafta with the different Gafta agreements,[60] but they may also be in organizations where the standard contracts may be related to cover various businesses, such as the ICC and Orgalime (Brussels).[61] In the ICC as well as Orgalime a large number of standard contracts have been drafted, intended for different purposes and for different trades, such as sales contracts, distribution agreements, agency agreements, M&A agreements, license agreements etc. Another international organization with a major impact within its particular area is BIMCO which plays a specific role with regard to the maritime business. BIMCO has thus designed and drafted a large number of transport documents, standard charter parties, ship management agreements, agreements for the sale of vessels and shipbuilding contracts. A further example of such an international organization is FIDIC which plays a specific role with respect to the development of international construction contracts.[62]

It is also important to bear in mind that standard terms may be designed for use in domestic (national) markets or in international markets. Domestic conditions may be quite similar to those that are used internationally, but they may also have been adapted with regard to the particular legal context of the individual country. Nowadays, it seems quite common for international standard conditions to be adapted for national purposes or translated for use in a particular market. This is, for example, the case with the NSAB conditions (Nordiska Speditionsförbundets bestämmelser—Standard

---

[60] Grain, animal feeding stuffs, pulses and rice are often traded internationally under the terms and conditions of the Gafta standard forms of contract, see inter alia Schmitthoff, *The Law and Practice* (n 4) 891.

[61] Schmitthoff, *The Law and Practice* (n 4) 595 et seq and 895 et seq.

[62] See further below in IV.G.

conditions for freight forwarders in the Nordic market). An international organization, the FIATA, has designed specific international conditions for this particular sector, but the FIATA rules have developed separately from the NSAB, although there may have been some discussions between the different groups participating in the drafting of the separate terms. Since the latest version, NSAB 2000, was adopted, there has been ongoing amendment work to achieve an NSAB 2015.[63] The work on such amendments does not always follow the development of the corresponding international terms but rather seems to take its own course in a Nordic context. Sometimes, the international standard contracts are transferred into national terms or rather adopted for use in a particular market, but, in other instances, the national or regional terms have developed into international standard contracts either generally or in any individual case.[64]

D. An Increasing Number of Internal Group Transactions

A particular feature of transnational business is related to globally active business entities which are sometimes very large, and where the commercial activities increasingly take place between the different entities in the group, often through subsidiaries in different countries. The more transactions that are carried out across subsidiaries, the less overall risk the group is exposed to. This also means that there may be less need for an external risk assessment, external trade financing etc. This is a development which does not call for specific legal rules except with respect to taxation considerations as a consequence of transfer prices being set up between the group companies for reasons other than commercial ones, leading, for example, to higher profits for a group company which is based in a country where taxation is lower.[65] Outsourcing may be connected to this development.

Globalized business transactions between group companies are more likely to give rise to practical questions and solutions relating to the different entities within the group, where in most cases no particular legal rules are required.

---

[63] Ramberg, *The Law of Transport Operators in International Trade* (Stockholm, Norstedts juridik, 2005).

[64] The international basis for the NSAB is the FIATA terms (International Federation of Freight Forwarder Associations). The FIATA Combined Transport Bill of Lading dates back to 1975 but was updated in 1993. The FIATA issues a variety of documents related to the freight forwarding business.

[65] See, eg, Arvidsson, *Dolda vinstöverföringar. En skatterättslig studie av internprissättningen i multi nationella koncerner* (Stockholm, Jure, 1990).

E. Some Examples of International Conventions

The growing use of international conventions in the commercial law area
has also to be seen against the background of the growth in national legislation. This development covers questions related to material law as well as
to procedural matters. In international commerce, there was a need for the
harmonization of different rules related to commercial transactions. This
development took off during the nineteenth century initially in the area of
transportation and payments. This process intensified at the beginning of
the twentieth century when international conventions were gradually being
introduced relating to an ocean carrier's liability and the use of bills of lading as well as a number of other topics.[66] At the time, there were far fewer
independent states than there are today.

The Great Depression in the 1930s and the subsequent Second World War
led to a slowdown and even a halt in international commerce and it was
only after 1945 that trade picked up again. The breakdown of the different
colonial systems after the Second World War eventually led to a substantial
growth in the number of independent states, naturally requiring amendments to previous international conventions or the introduction of new
ones. The new geopolitical situation thus also had an effect on the development of international legislative efforts. Similarly, the fall of the Soviet
Union and its satellites had substantial political and legal consequences and
created ground for new legal rules to be adopted.

The work within the United Nations (UNCITRAL, UNIDROIT and
UNCTAD)[67] gradually added a number of new international conventions,
draft conventions and other legal instruments.[68] As mentioned, the GATT
and later the WTO[69] came to lay new ground for multinational business and
international trade, and with the growing number of members this worked
well for some decades albeit with the emergence of several setbacks and difficulties. It is also clear that today, for a variety of reasons, there is a great
deal of tension between several member states and that the growth of global
business has decreased or at least the growth is no longer marked.

---

[66] In Schmitthoff, *The Law and Practice* (n 4) various conventions and model laws are
referred to on p 887 et seq, and in Ramberg, *The Law of Transport Operators* (n 63), there is
a particular focus on conventions and other methods related to the law of carriage.

[67] The United Nations Committee on International Trade Law, the International Institute
for the Unification of Private Law, the United Nations Conference on Trade and Development
respectively.

[68] It is also important to mention the work carried out within and by OECD (the Organization for Economic Cooperation and Development) and the ECE (the European Commission
for Europe) and similar organizations in other parts of the world. Naturally, a draft convention
could hardly be described as a legal instrument but it may nevertheless have some legal effect.

[69] The General Agreement on Tariffs and Trade and World Trade Organization respectively.

Different regional organizations have been established in different parts of the world where the EU has to a certain extent been used as a model for a similar development elsewhere. There is also some co-operation between these regional organizations. The different bilateral or multilateral organizations have been established to work with various trading schemes and operations. The EU and more recently, the advent of several new trading blocs with varying agendas now seem to play a growing role in world trade, raising a number of legal questions.

As far as EU law is concerned, particular mention should also be made of the Rome I Regulation,[70] the Rome II Regulation[71] and the Brussels I Regulation[72] involving questions related to applicable law and jurisdiction. They also cover subjects other than those related to commercial law. Moreover, the New York Convention on the Recognition and Enforcement of Foreign Arbitral Awards (New York, 1958) entered into force in 1959 and has a large number of signatories. It thus also plays an important role particularly with respect to commercial matters. Similarly, the work on the Hague Principles on Choice of Law in International Contracts should also be mentioned in this context.

A large number of international conventions have gradually come into being, in fields such as maritime law, transportation law, sales law, the law on bills of exchange etc, but there have also been efforts to conclude certain conventions, which have, however, so far largely failed. Model laws have also been designed by, for instance, UNCITRAL, the best known is probably the UNCITRAL Model Law on International Arbitration from 1995, amended in 2010.[73] As mentioned above, much of the preparatory work on international conventions in the field of private commercial has been carried out during the last few decades within organizations such as UNCITRAL and UNIDROIT.

Probably the most successful convention in the private law area is the CISG, which has been ratified by more than 80 states although not by the United Kingdom nor by certain commonwealth countries. The CISG has thus a very broad coverage both from a geographical and a political point of view. The Nordic countries initially requested certain exemptions from certain parts of the CISG, but have now largely withdrawn the exemptions.[74]

---

[70] Regulation (EC) no 593/2008 of the European Parliament and of the Council of 17 June 2008 on the law applicable to contractual obligations (Rome I), OJ 2008 L 177/6 related to contractual obligations.

[71] Related to non-contractual obligations.

[72] Regulation (EU) no 1215/2012 of the European Parliament and the Council of 12 December 2012 on jurisdiction and the recognition and enforcement of judgments in civil and commercial matters (recast), OJ 2012 L 351/1.

[73] This Model Law has been used as a model for legislation in several countries like Sweden.

[74] See the discussion in inter alia. *The CISG Part II Conference, Stockholm, 4–5 September 2008*, Kleineman (ed) (Stockholm, Stockholm Centre of Commercial Law, 2009).

Another area where a large number of international conventions have been introduced is maritime law. The first convention related to the liability of the ocean carrier for cargo damage was the Brussels Convention (the Hague Rules) from 1924.[75] This convention was later repealed and, in many countries, substituted by the Hague-Visby Protocol.[76] A similar development has taken place with respect to air law, road and railroad transportation.

The CISG on the one hand, and the various conventions related to the liability of ocean carriers (as well as those related to other carriers) on the other, use different methods of approach. The CISG is based on *non-mandatory* rules representing reasonably balanced risks between seller and buyer interests, whereas the various conventions concerning carrier liability are based on mandatory liability with certain minimum liability (including the limitation of liability) put on the carriers.[77] This is certainly a reason why the transport conventions have been regarded as politically more controversial. The reason for this approach with respect to the mandatory liability of the ocean carrier has been to protect the interests of the cargo owner. That being said, it is also important to bear in mind that the bill of lading conventions (the conventions related to the liability of the ocean carrier) have been introduced also to protect the bill of lading as a negotiable document of title. It is, however, only the Rotterdam Rules which deal in detail with matters such as the effect of documents in relation to the goods covered by and/or represented in the document and also the disposal of cargo when no document has been issued.[78] It is, however, far from certain whether the Rotterdam Rules will reach the stage of a binding convention.

In the financial area there are also certain international conventions related to commercial matters, such as the UNCITRAL 1988 Convention on International Bills of Exchange, which is in force between some countries and the 1988 UNIDROIT Conventions on International Financial Leasing and International Factoring respectively. Some countries have ratified these latter conventions but for various reasons they are not widespread.

Apart from the organizations mentioned here which are public institutions there are also several organizations of a private character which have

---

[75] It followed as an international response to the US Harter Act introduced as mandatory US legislation in 1896.

[76] An amendment was made through the Hague Visby Rules 1968 amended through a protocol, a new convention, the Hamburg Rules 1978 never received many signatories and even fewer ratifying states. More recent efforts have been made to achieve an updated convention in this field, the Rotterdam Rules, which so far have been signed by a few countries only. The future of the Rotterdam Rules seems to be far from certain.

[77] Particularly the original convention from 1924 is sometimes referred to as the bill of lading convention, since one of the aims with the mandatory character of the convention was to protect the bill of lading as a negotiable document of title. The Hague–Visby Rules from 1968 did not have the same focus and the latest efforts, the Rotterdam Rules have a broader scope. See Schmitthoff, *The Law and Practice* (n 4) p 308 et seq.

[78] Chapter 11 of the Rotterdam Rules contains rules on the transfer of rights.

played an important role in the development of legal tools such as standard contracts which naturally have a different legal impact compared to legislation regardless of whether they are based on international conventions or not.

F. Various Commercial Customs, Soft Law Principles and their Use

Of course, private bodies do not have the power to issue statutes but such power is only given to public entities such as national parliaments, the EU or similar entities. The ICC as a private body but also public entities may be involved in the design of soft law principles of various types. One general observation concerns the gradual development of different legislative provisions, of a different character and at different levels, including international conventions, draft international conventions, model laws, and influence from rules and principles etc. In the last decade, a number of principles and rules have been developed which are not legislation, such as the PICC, the PECL and the DCFR.[79] This means that, apart from formal convention work, the legal development has also taken place with other means and also at different levels.

These various steps in the developments play different roles and may have different implications for the contract draftsmen and for the courts (or arbitrators as the case may be). There may be influences from soft law principles on hard law, but legislators may also refrain from taking any legislative steps, since there is deemed to be no particular need for legislation considering the already existing soft law principles, standard contracts, custom and practices etc. The legal development may, therefore, take different routes and its practical significance may also vary depending on the particular legal area concerned.

In this context, it may be appropriate to discuss certain soft law principles, which have evolved gradually. As mentioned above, soft law has evolved in various ways and has been of significant importance in the field of international commercial law whether in the context of *lex mercatoria* or otherwise. Several of the principles emanating from *lex mercatoria* may not necessarily be regarded as part of established trade custom, and a distinction may have to be made between those legal items which are regarded as local trade custom, as broader usage or items which follow from more general principles.[80]

---

[79] Apparently, the US Uniform Commercial Code has been an important source of inspiration for the CISG but also for other ongoing law harmonization work.

[80] See above in II.A.

Some words should also be said about certain rules and principles which have evolved out of custom and usage. The Incoterm rules is one of the best-known and broadly used set of rules which has developed over several decades, the latest version being Incoterms 2010. Incoterms are risk and cost distribution principles related to sales contracts. The Incoterm rules are thus one of the most widespread set of commercial law principles, developed and gradually updated by the ICC. They are being constantly revised and an amended version may be published within the next few years. Whether they should be seen as soft law (commercial usage) or as standard terms with particular coverage may be a case for discussion, but nowadays the Incoterms have certainly worldwide recognition and are applied in a large number of international sales transactions although there are still discussions regarding their interpretation. Another set of widely used principles is the UCP (Uniform Customs and Practice for Documentary Credits—the present version known as UCP 600). They also enjoy worldwide recognition. It is clear, in all circumstances, that the ICC plays a particular role with respect to the development of international trade principles and standard contracts of varying character.

These various items may thus be broken down into *lex mercatoria* principles, international customs and usages, such as Incoterms, the UCP, model laws, standard terms and conditions, and also particular clauses. I shall not delve further into the question whether all these should be regarded as part of soft law or if they should instead be seen as principles of another kind.

Another legal concept which is neither found in the traditional *lex mercatoria* nor is it covered by hard law, concerns the evolution of Corporate Social Responsibility (CSR), which has gradually gained ground in international business.

G. The Use of International Standard Contracts

Even if they are sometimes seen as part of international usage or custom, it is perhaps important to specifically mention standard terms and conditions in order to mirror the diversity of the legal norms of various types, developed alongside international conventions and customs and usages.[81] Standard

---

[81] In Scandinavian legislation, reference is made to customs and usage in eg the Contracts Acts. The Swedish Contracts Act is a joint Scandinavian law project and the Swedish version is 100 years old (it was first enacted in Sweden and later in Denmark, Norway and Finland). On several occasions, the question has arisen as to whether there is a need for reform. In the last few years, this topic has been discussed by, inter alia, Flodgren, *Den svenska avtalslagen snart 100 år—ett välfungerande instrument för dagens ekonomiska liv?* (2012/13) Juridisk Tidskrift, 14 et seq. Two volumes by Scadinavian legal scholars related to Scandinavian contract law were published in 2015, one volume in English and one in the Scandinavian languages, the former *The Nordic contracts act. Essays in celebration of its one hundredth anniversary*

contracts undoubtedly play a specific role in this legal development. It is not always easy to track down the exact difference between international trade custom and international standard contracts. Be that as it may, standard contracts play a fundamental role in a large number of international commercial transactions. While it is often difficult to come to an agreement with regard to international conventions related to a particular area of law (or for that matter national legislation or law-making at the EU level), the creation of new standard form contracts and amendments to them are often easier to agree on. They are generally geared at specific and often rather precise areas. Standard conditions do not, of course, have the same legal weight as legislation but they may have a particular impact on different types of international business transactions, and they are of prime and practical relevance to the specific contracting parties, as long as the principles of freedom of contract and the binding nature of contract are recognized.[82]

A practical advantage with the use of international standard forms is that they are more flexible and easier to amend when the need occurs, and they may thus be more easily adapted to new requirements. They are also often designed to suit the needs of particular businesses. There are, however, certain limitations. Countries may impose legal requirements which set limits on the legal impact of the contractual terms and of the international standard form agreements used in individual cases. A contract, whether individually negotiated or in standard form, will not take over or set aside national obligatory rules of a mandatory character, or rules related to bankruptcy. This means that contract draftsmen will always have to take various legal uncertainties into account when drafting contracts.[83] New technology has also played a role with respect to standard form contracts, and electronic standard forms may thus be used and easily amended in individual cases.

There is an abundance of international standard form contracts used for different businesses, trades and geographical areas.[84] Such standard forms are found in almost all trades covering sales, intermediaries, financing, construction, licensing in connection with intellectual property, chartering matters etc. The various parameters discussed above may apply differently in different situations. In Section IV below I shall describe some of the different types of contracts in use.

(editor Torgny Håstad) and the latter *Aftaleloven 100 år. Baggrund. Status. Utfordringer. Fremtid.* (editors Mads Bryde Andersen, Johan Bärlund, Boel Flodgren and Johan Giertsen).

[82] The use of standard contracts and arbitration is also discussed in Cordero-Moss, *International Arbitration and Commercial Contract Interpretation: Contract Wording, Common Law, Civil Law and Transnational Law.* Essays in honour of Michael Bogdan (Lund 2013) 33 et seq.

[83] In financial matters legal risks have been the object of a study in MacCormack, *Legal Risks in the Financial Markets*, 2nd edn (Oxford, OUP, 2011).

[84] Apart from these, there are also several terms and conditions in use drafted by and for various corporations as house standards, sometimes used on a take-it-or-leave-it basis.

H. Various Intermediaries

Agency questions may involve various parameters, and the concept of agency in common law covers both questions of representation and authority in a broad sense and specific questions related to particular types of intermediaries, such as sales agents.[85] The Geneva Convention on Agency in the International Sale of Goods of 1983 has been signed by some states and has been ratified by even fewer, and the Convention has had little impact except maybe as a source of inspiration. Intermediaries are of different kinds and may have different tasks. Some of them have authority to negotiate for and bind the principal, others not.

The use of intermediaries is by no means a new feature in international business, indeed intermediaries have a long history in the promotion of international business transactions. Intermediaries appear in different trades and have different functions. They appear under different titles, such as agents of various types, commission agents, brokers, factors, freight forwarders, etc.[86] Their role varies from limited negotiations to contracting. In some instances, they appear as independent contractors. Different rules apply to them. The legal requirements differ in different trades and businesses, and an intermediary may thus be entrusted with various degrees and forms of authority. Some intermediaries may negotiate for the principal party but have no authority to negotiate for and bind its principal (such as ordinarily brokers) whereas others may enjoy a rather wide authority. An intermediary will have different practical and legal functions depending on the character of their tasks. Hence, there may be different contractual arrangements and liability rules related to their services. Will they be advisers (for instance financial advisers)? Will they represent and bind the principal in the negotiation and sale of goods? Will they be brokering various deals between different parties but without any authority to sign for and bind the principal? Will they appear in their own name on someone else's behalf? Will they appear as agents for and bind a principal? Will they appear 'as agent only'—implying what? Does the mandate set out a limitation of liability provision?

These different parameters have to be kept in mind when determining the particular functions and the legal framework which apply to different intermediaries in an individual case.

---

[85] See in English law in particular Markesinis and Munday, *An Outline of the Law of Agency*, 4th edn (Oxford, 2005). See also, eg, Grönfors (ed), *Intermediaries in Shipping*, (Gothenburg, 1990).

[86] See Schmitthoff, *The Law and Practice* (n 4) p 743 et seq. In this connection the 'trust' may also be kept in mind, since its functions are well established in English law even in commercial roles whereas it has no immediate correspondence in Scandinavian law.

I. B2C and B2B Relations

The distinction between B2B and B2C contracts is a distinction made and upheld in Europe as a consequence of the consumer protection legislation, which has been introduced gradually since the 1970s.[87] However, the question arises as to whether it will be possible to keep these relationships distinctly separate in the long run, or whether the influence of consumer protection regulation will be such that B2B contractual relations will be affected. In some legal systems (eg, in Germany) the general view in the legal community is that private law should be treated as a unity (see the present German BGB legislation), whereas in other legal systems there are rather strong dividing lines between what is often referred to as consumer law and commercial law. EU Rules are generally geared to B2C relations, but there are in some areas also rules covering B2B relations. Financial law matters often concern B2B matters but then mostly through administrative law rules. Some examples of rules outside the consumer oriented legislation concern competition law and also the EU Directive on Commercial agents specifically cover B2B relations.[88] In a broader perspective DCFR cover B2C as well as B2B relations.

IV. CERTAIN TYPES OF CONTRACTS—DIFFERENT CHARACTERISTICS AND SOLUTIONS

A. Some General Points

In this section, the perspective will be somewhat different, and I shall here discuss specific types of contracts and contractual relations. The list is by no means complete, and there are several more standard documents intended for general use but perhaps more normally intended for specific contractual relations, trades and geographical areas.[89] There are a large number of standard contracts drafted by different organizations or company groups intended for their particular use.

Even if there are a large number of standard contracts which are intended for use in specific trades, the parties will regularly adapt the contractual

---

[87] This development started in the 1970s in Europe and has gradually expanded as a separate legislative area, not least through EU rules. There has thus been a gradual change from a 'caveat emptor' to a 'caveat vendor' perspective with respect to the growing consumer legislation. This is a distinction which is not recognized in the United States.

[88] The latter is of private law character.

[89] In Schmitthoff, *Law and Practice* (n 4) 889 et seq, there is mention of a number of ICC standard contracts but also of standard conditions issued by various trade associations as well as different model contracts drawn up by the United Nations Economic Commission for Europe (ECE). Similarly, in Sweden there is a list of standard contracts published by Teknikföretagen covering various contracts and contract types.

provisions to the individual transaction through various deletions and amendments. Often the contractual relation is based on a document containing the individual particularities of the contract to which is added a reference to the particular standard terms. Hence, a distinction should be made with respect to standard forms of 'take-it-or-leave-it-character', which are normally used together with the individual conditions with respect to the particular transaction, and those standard forms which are rather model forms used as a basis for negotiations and intended for changes and amendments by the parties.[90]

B. Sale and Purchase

Sale and purchase is undoubtedly one of the areas where the number of standard contracts is the largest due to the number of tradesmen, the number of trades and trading areas and the number of products. Several of the standard contracts in use are geared towards particular products whereas others are for more general use and cover different segments of sales. Many of them are intended for international use, but they have also been used as models for regional or national contracts. Some are intended for certain geographical areas only.

One of the sales contracts which has a wide use is one that was designed and drafted by the ICC. It is widely used as a contract but probably more often as a model. The Orgalime S 2012 is also worth mentioning. It is intended for use with respect to the supply of mechanical, electrical and electronic products. This Orgalime form seems to be used more commonly than the ECE conditions which were developed in the early 1950s and came to be used as a basis for several regional standard conditions.[91] The GAFTA conditions have been designed for international sales of food products. They are mainly intended for the trading of different grain and other food products.[92]

Particular agreements have been designed by inter alia the ICC regarding mergers and acquisitions (M&A) and the acquisition (or sale) of a foreign company. A particular form involving the sale of second-hand ships is the Norwegian Sales Form (latest version is from 2012) designed for

---

[90] See, eg, Bernitz, *Standardavtalsrätt* (n 36) 13 et seq, Adlercreutz and Gorton, *Avtalsrätt II*, 6th edn (Lund, Studentlitteratur, 2010) 67 and 75 et seq and Ramberg and Ramberg (n 36) p 150 et seq.

[91] See Ramberg (n 29) p 483 et seq and Schmitthoff, *Law and Practice* (n 4) p 889 et seq. See also Ramberg and Herre, *Allmän köprätt*, 6th edn (Stockholm, Norstedts juridik, 2012) 53 et seq, 64 et seq and 237 et seq.

[92] There are several different GAFTA forms intended for use with respect to different products, see, eg, Schmitthoff (n 4) p 891.

worldwide use and for individual amendments. The Norwegian Sales Form is nowadays also recognized as a BIMCO form. The contracts mentioned here are only a fraction of those which have been drafted for various products and trades.

C. Commercial Intermediaries

Commercial intermediaries play a particular role in international commercial transactions. This is an area where various particular contractual solutions are found. Brokers are mainly intermediaries without particular authority and they may carry out several functions in international trade and transportation, and they often appear 'as agents only'.[93] Commercial agents may be appointed on the basis of nationally designed contracts, but there are also standard contracts which have evolved internationally. Hence, eg, the ICC and Orgalime have both designed their standard forms with respect to commercial agents. Generally, the functions of the principal and the agent are set out as well as their particular duties and liability as well as the contract period and termination provisions.[94]

D. Distribution Agreements

Distributors, as distinguished from commercial agents, act in their own name and on their own behalf, and make their profits (if any) on the difference between the purchase price of the product and the price at which it is sold. Again the ICC and other organizations have designed their particular distribution agreements, which are often used as a kind of model form. Whereas the EU has chosen to protect the commercial agent through certain mandatory protective rules, there is no specific directive on distribution agreements, but in a number of countries, including some Member States, there are national rules allowing the distributors a certain minimum protection.[95] Otherwise, several contractual provisions in agency agreements and distribution agreements are rather similar.

---

[93] See, eg, in *Intermediaries in Shipping* (n 85) where the different roles of the agent are discussed on p 11 et seq.

[94] EU states have introduced agency legislation based on the EU Directive (86/653/EEC) of 18 December 1986 on the co-ordination of the laws of the Member States on self-employed agents aiming at harmonizing the rules applicable to the commercial agent and to protect the rights of the agent through to some extent mandatory rules. The Directive has been amended. See eg Schmitthoff (n 4) p 743 et seq.

[95] There are also competition rules which aim at protecting the market against restrictive trade practices. It must be underlined that the EU rules as well as other competition rules are perhaps particularly important with respect to several of the contract types mentioned here.

E. Licensing Agreements

Licensing agreements are largely tied to intellectual property, eg, patents, trademarks etc. Also knowhow agreements may be the object of a licensing agreement.[96] This again is a legal area where standard form contracts have been designed and drafted by certain trading organizations. Some of these license agreements have been designed by organizations like Orgalime.

It should be emphasized that licensing agreements often require individual solutions. This means that even if the parties have agreed on the use of a particular standard contract, the particular transaction requires individual solutions. It merits to be underlined that intellectual property represents an economic area which is probably one of the fastest growing and, similarly, the legal framework related to this particular field has been expanding significantly during the last couple of decades.

F. Joint Ventures—Co-operation Arrangements

Joint ventures often involve different areas of law. Even if the establishment of a joint venture may be connected to one jurisdiction, the parties to a joint venture agreement are often established in different jurisdictions. Joint ventures have a basis in contract law and in corporate law (company law may be involved as well as rules on partnership). That being said the contractual provisions appearing in the contract may still prevail if they are not contrary to mandatory corporate law provisions.[97]

In many business contexts, joint ventures are found and used as a kind of practical term involving the co-operation between two or several partners from the same but often different jurisdictions. A distinction is often made between 'contractual' and 'equity' joint ventures (JV), depending on whether the JV involves a legal person or not. In a JV agreement, it is common to find a contractual provision of the following or similar type: 'It is specifically agreed between the parties that the particular legislation on partnership in law shall not apply to this agreement', a contractual solution which may prove to have a limited value, at least in some jurisdictions.

---

[96] This is also an area where particular international or for that matter European conventions are found which cover the particular items involved. The study by Runesson, *Licens till patent och företagshemligheter I avtals- och kontraktsrätten* (Stockholm, 2014) deals in depth with some of the related questions.

[97] See, eg, Johansson, *Nials Svensk associationsrätt i huvuddrag,* 8th edn (Stockholm, Norstedts juridik, 2007) 317, Svernlöv, C, *Internationella joint ventures. Samriskföretag* (Stockholm, Norstedts juridik, 1997) and Micheler, *Joint Ventures in English and German Law* (Oxford, Hart Publishing, 2000).

In the area of transport and insurance, there are various co-operation agreements in use, however, not very often of a standard type.[98] They often seem to exist under the heading of 'pool agreements'. Often, the parties draw up their special agreements for their individual contract relations. Competition law aspects often set a certain legal framework for the joint venture.

G. Construction Contracts

The construction industry is one of many important business sectors in international commercial transactions. This is an industry where different areas of law need to be considered in the contract such as property law, environmental law, labour law, competition law etc. It is also an area where there are several examples of joint ventures between private businesses but also involving co-operation between the private sector and the public sector, eg, PPP contracts.[99] Apart from competition rules, public procurement also impacts on this sector.[100]

Construction contracts bring into play a variety of contractual parameters, which emanate from different segments of the law and which the parties need to consider. The types of contract in use may be differently designed depending on their coverage, such as 'plain' construction (the duty to build and construct only), or covering design, construction and functioning etc. In many countries, there is no particular legislation for this type of contract but still several relevant rules may have to be considered in the drafting of the individual contract. It is a business sector which, in many countries, seems to be dominated by particular standard contracts. The parties to a construction contract (sometimes found under the heading engineering contract) are often referred to as the builder and the owner (but the terminology varies).

In international construction, the FIDIC conditions are frequently used.[101] There are several forms of FIDIC conditions designed for specific purposes and related to the particular type of construction involved.[102] These standard contracts have been specially drafted for B2B relations where both

---

[98] In some business areas, such agreements are known as pool agreements, see *Skibsfart of samarbeid. Maritime joint ventures i rettslig belysning,* Oslo 1991 and *Poolsamarbeide, management, åpne register,* Marius, Oslo 1998.

[99] Ie public private procurement contracts.

[100] See the growing importance of EU law as well as of national rules. See, eg, Schmitthoff (n 4) p 643 et seq and p 807 et seq.

[101] Fédération Internationale des Ingénieurs-conseils, founded by Belgian, French and Swiss associations of consulting engineers in 1913. The conditions are now used worldwide but generally more frequently in some parts of the world than in others.

[102] The various books cover different types of building projects: The Green Book—Short Form of Contract; the Red Book—Conditions for Construction; the Gold Book—Conditions of Contract for Design, Build and Operate projects.

parties are regarded as being equally strong financially. The FIDIC terms have gained considerable recognition and use, and may also be used for building projects, as is the case in Sweden. Their use also seems to have increased in a number of countries where there were previously no similar recognized standard conditions in use.

Apart from these international standard conditions, there are also various regional and national building contracts as are found for example, in the Nordic countries or the UK etc. In none of these countries is there immediately applicable legislation on construction but instead the national standard conditions related to construction are in use. In Sweden, for example, the AB conditions (general conditions for the building industry) have been used for almost 100 years. They are amended and updated regularly (although not very frequently), the latest version being from 2002.[103] In this regard, it is also important to mention that the ICC has designed a specific set of rules with respect to turnkey projects.[104]

H. Contracts of Carriage and Charter Parties and Some Other Contracts Related to the Maritime Environment

Another area where there is an extensive use of international standard conditions is maritime law, and for that matter other parts of the transport industry. I shall not delve into the particularities of the various documents which have been developed with respect to transportation and, in particular, the maritime industry, but it is important to bear in mind that shipping involves several segments of business where several different standard terms have developed.[105] Hence, such documentation covers all these various business areas. Among these documents, mention can also be made of charter parties of different kinds (voyage, time, bareboat, contracts of affreightment), other transport documents (such as bills of lading), shipbuilding contracts, second-hand sales agreements (the Norwegian Sale Form), management agreements, salvage contracts etc. There are thus different types of agreements intended to be used in different contexts and for different tasks.

---

[103] Thus, different sets of rules, like the FIDIC conditions, are applicable depending on the type of construction intended. With respect to developments in Sweden see, eg, Samuelsson, P, *Entreprenadavtal. Särskilt om ändrade förhållanden.* (Stockholm, Karnov Group, 2011). There are similar but not identical standard conditions designed for and used in the other Nordic countries intended for their particular markets and purpose.

[104] There is also a Swedish set of rules for the delivery of industrial construction, the present version being the ABA 99 terms, which are also being gradually updated. These terms have been developed by the suppliers' organizations.

[105] In several countries there are traditionally particular codes or law book sections on maritime law such as, eg, in the Nordic countries, but not in the United Kingdom. In spite of particular legislation related to bills of lading and to charter parties, there is in the shipping business, an extensive use of international standard contracts.

As already mentioned above, BIMCO plays a particularly important role with respect to several of the standard contracts which exist in this area, some recognized as recommended forms, others as adopted forms, and others again as agreed forms.[106] Apart from the various BIMCO charter party forms, several charter party documents have been designed as private forms (by individual corporations) or by other trading organizations. In this context, it is also important to mention, eg, the ICC combined transport document. With respect to shipbuilding contracts, most major shipbuilders have their own forms which are often reasonably similar in substance, but this is also an area where BIMCO has for some years now designed a particular form, the Newbuildcon.[107] So far there has been (for good reason) comparatively little EU involvement in this area, except where the maritime carriage of passengers is involved.[108]

Where road, rail and air carriage is involved, Europe and the EU has had considerably more direct involvement. In these transportation segments, more transportation is geared at carriage within the EU and to geographically non-distant countries. From this perspective, it may not be surprising that there has been more direct EU involvement in these transport sectors. This means that the background of various air consignment notes, waybills or similar seem to stem from the relevant conventions.

Also freight forwarders should be mentioned in this connection. Freight forwarders play different roles in the transport chain, sometimes working as a kind of agent, at other times undertaking the transportation in their own name. Particular mention should be made of the freight forwarder conditions in use, based on an international form and also turned into a particular set for Nordic transportation, the NSAB conditions.[109]

I. Payment and Financial Security

Another legal area which has benefited from a global approach is the area of trade finance.[110] The role of standard terms as well as soft law have been mentioned above and, in the field of trade finance, this distinction may not

---

[106] These various forms may have different contractual effects, see Gorton, Hillenius, Ihre and Sandevärn, *Shipbroking and Chartering Practice*, 7th edn (London, 2009) p 105 et seq.

[107] See above under II.B. Among West European shipbuilders, there used to be an AWES shipbuilding contract, more used as a model form agreement. In Norway, there is an agreed form developed by builder and shipowner interests.

[108] There is, however, the growing involvement of the EU with respect to international conventions also in the maritime field. The EU seems to a growing extent to prefer to be a signatory power to international conventions rather than the Member States.

[109] See above under III.C.

[110] Here I disregard payments, where the Bill of Exchange Convention plays a role, and also the Payment Services Directive 2007/64/EC. I also do not take matters which are dealt with in the MIFID into consideration. Nor do I take into consideration the UNCITRAL Convention on Independent Bank Guarantees which so far has not received much acknowledgment.

always be entirely clear. The ICC has designed the Uniform Customs and Practice (UCP) related to letters of credit, the latest version is from 2006 (UCP 600). The use of the concept of customs and practice probably stems from the fact that the first version of the UCP dates back to the 1930s, and that letters of credit can be traced back to principles already laid down in the law merchant.[111]

Different views have been expressed concerning the legal status of the UCP as usual standard contracts or as 'commercial custom' which might apply even without reference being made to them. Since there is little legislation worldwide with respect to trade finance, and in specific documentary letters of credit, it is understandable why the UCP has such a particular legal standing. Since they are used primarily by banks, it is in practice unlikely that reference to the UCP in a letter of credit would be left out, but if that were the case, it would not be unlikely that a court or arbitration tribunal having to determine the rules applicable to the credit would still fall back on the UCP (latest version) failing other reasonably useful rules.[112] It is also generally in the underlying contract, often a sales contract, that there is a specific payment clause calling for payment by letter of credit. If that underlying contract did not set out that the letter of credit shall be issued according to an agreed law, it would still be the case that the bank issuing the letter of credit called for would issue it subject to the UCP. It should also be underlined that there is in the UCP no jurisdiction or choice of law clause.

The situation is somewhat different with respect to demand guarantees, often used as financial undertakings in international transactions.[113] There seems to be very little specific national legislation related to this particular financial undertaking,[114] but gradually some case law related to them has evolved in a number of jurisdictions including inter alia England, Germany and the United States. Failing specific legislation, courts may in this connection choose to fall back on national rules and principles related to suretyship and/or promissory notes and/or some other legal method.[115] The legal

---

[111] The first version was produced failing specific national legislation and when London was still regarded as a centre for international trade finance although fading. The background of letters of credit dates back to at least the medieval use of such documents to create credit in a foreign country for the holder of a letter of credit, see, eg, Gorton, *Rembursrätt* (Lund 1980), but there are, of course, more recent publications dealing with related questions, such as Schmitthoff, (n 4) in particular chapters 10 and 11. With respect to guarantees, see, eg, Kurkela, *Letters of Credit and Bank Guarantees under International Trade Law*, 2nd edn (Oxford, OUP, 2007). See also Adestam, *Den dokumentrelaterade rembursen* (Stockholm, 2014), where the guarantee is analysed against a background of general obligatory law and where there is also a classification of different types of guarantees (accessory and independent) on p 89 et seq.

[112] There are only relatively few national rules on letters of credit, eg, in the US where the Uniform Commercial Code has a chapter on commercial credit.

[113] On demand guarantees are often characterized as independent undertakings in the sense that they shall be deemed to be independent of an underlying contract, eg the sale's agreement.

[114] There is in national legislation frequent examples of specific rules on suretyship.

[115] See Persson, *Borgen—ett rättsinstitut i förändring?* Festskrift till Lars Gorton (Lund, 2007) p 487 et seq, where she deals with suretyship from a European perspective. See also

perception of demand guarantees varies, and a dispute related to such a guarantee may be decided differently depending on the jurisdiction where the dispute is heard and settled.

At the end of the 1970s, the ICC started to discuss a set of rules regarding these instruments. In the early 1990s, the ICC managed to gain acceptance for a set of rules regarding demand guarantees, and the Uniform Demand Guarantees Rules (URDG) 1992/1993 were launched (known as URDG 458), later amended in 2010 (URDG 750). The difference in language between the UCP and the URDG could be noticed in that the URDG are referred to as 'rules' and not as customs and practice. This could be explained by demand guarantees not really emanating from a long developed practice, but they were actually drafted as a set of contractual provisions to which reference should be made in the individual contract in order to make them part of and, thus, applicable to a particular relation. It may also be the case that during the course of the latter part of the twentieth century a large number of standard contracts and rules were designed and launched by the ICC, which did not set out to be anything other than 'contracts'. It is, however, obvious that the draftsmen of the URDG were much influenced by the UCP.

Today, the URDG would certainly not be regarded as customs and practice (and, failing a reference, I believe that they would not apply in an individual relation unless as a consequence of custom between two specific parties, something which under Swedish law is referred to as 'partsbruk').[116] This being said, it should nevertheless be noted that URDG 750 seem to be increasing in use, although there is some reluctance from banks in certain countries.[117]

In this connection, it is also important to mention another difference between the UCP and the URDG, namely that the UCP do not contain any rules on choice of law or dispute settlement, whereas the URDG do.[118]

'Personal Security" prepared by U Drobnig, U, in *Principles of European Law. Study Group on a European Civil Code* (Oxford, OUP, 2007).

[116] Usage between the parties.

[117] Beside the ICC rules concerning demand guarantees UNCITRAL adopted in 1995 a Convention on Independent Guarantees and Standby Letters of Credit, which has, however, gained little success.

[118] The URDG Articles 34 and 35 set out:

'Article 34. Governing law.

a. Unless otherwise provided in the guarantee, its governing law shall be that of the location of the guarantor's branch or office that issued the guarantee.
b. ...'

'Article 35. Jurisdiction.

a. Unless otherwise provided in the guarantee, any dispute between the guarantor and the beneficiary relating to the guarantee shall be settled exclusively by the competent court of the country of the location of the guarantor's branch or office that issued the guarantee.
b. ...'

Possibly the Docdex dispute settlement rules, intended to ensure cheaper and quicker dispute settlement in disputes related to letters of credit, subject to the UCP, will play a more prominent role in the future.[119] Another peculiarity related to the UCP and the URDG is that special opinions may be obtained from the ICC Expert Group on Trade and Finance concerning the understanding and application of the two instruments. These opinions are not binding on courts but they seem to be gradually gaining in importance, and they are referred to more frequently and also taken into consideration in court decisions to an increasing extent.

J. Loans and other Financial Agreements

Something should be said about loan agreements where, at least in certain respects, there has been some development regarding international standard documents. This is a business area where B2B transactions have to an increasing extent been carried out transnationally. Particularly after the end of the Second World War and as a consequence of the free movement of capital, globalization seems to have taken on. Undoubtedly, loan agreements are rather particular, and although contractual in nature they are also often tied to a financial security, ie property questions and the risk of insolvency on the part of the borrower are a very real risk for the lender. When special reference is made to loan agreements here, this is a direct consequence of the development of the Loan Market Association (LMA) agreements, which have evolved gradually over the last 15 years.[120] The use of LMA agreements is connected with the increase of syndicated loans, where several banks appear as lenders in the same loan transaction. The LMA agreement is a model agreement designed to be used as a basis by the parties in their negotiations.[121] The LMA agreement is continuously amended following new legal and practical occurrences.

Another set of documents related to particular financial products are the International Swaps and Derivatives Association (ISDA) agreements.[122]

---

[119] See above 2.2. See Soon, 'Sectoral Dispute Resolutions in International Banking. Documentary Credit Expertise. Docdex', (2013), *Arizona Journal of International and Comparative Law*. There are presently ongoing negotiations for a revision of the Docdex rules.

[120] The Loan Market Association (LMA) is a London-based organization with worldwide range.

[121] See further Mugasha, *The Law of Multibank Financing. Syndicated Loans and the Secondary Loan Market* (Oxford, Oxford University Press, 2007) p 204 et seq and Wood, *International Loans, Bonds, Guarantees, Legal Opinions*, 2nd edn (London, Sweet & Maxwell, 2007) p 35 et seq.

[122] International Swap Dealers Association. See Hudson, *Law of Finance*, 2nd edn (London, Sweet & Maxwell, 2013) 1169 et seq and Wood, *Set-off and Netting, Derivatives, Clearing Systems*, 2nd edn (London, Sweet & Maxwell, 2007) 228 et seq.

These standard contracts are used for various types of derivatives and have worldwide application. These contracts are complex in design and may not be easily interpreted and applied, but they have gained worldwide recognition, and there is also American and English case law which may provide solutions or guidance in individual cases although of course not binding for courts in other countries.[123]

V. IS THERE A NEED FOR MORE EU LEGISLATION IN THE AREA OF INTERNATIONAL BUSINESS?

It is obvious that commercial law is developing in various ways and through different means. It is also obvious that there are forces within the EU which would prefer to promote EU solutions rather than letting the business communities find their own ways. In view of the international character of commerce, my view is that the EU should be cautious with respect to its involvement in legislation where the international commercial community has already set a legal framework, and in particular when the international business community stands out as more efficient in creating useful solutions. This does not mean that the EU should refrain from getting involved in legal matters related to international business. Guidance may be better than prohibitions.

At the start of this chapter, reference was made to national, regional and global regulation. Legal development takes place at all these levels depending on the particular type of rules involved and the contractual relations. My perception is that law is rarely global in character, but the less precise the rules or principles are, the easier it is to apply them globally. The risk is, however, that they may be applied differently.

Nevertheless, if the concept of global commercial law is used, it covers several legal parameters, parameters which have their foundation in different segments of law and which may have different legal characteristics.[124] They also mirror various legal traditions. One of the problems pointed out above concerns the choice of method for dispute settlement and choice of relevant law in the case of a dispute by contracting parties.

As indicated above it is not given that the same considerations should apply for all contractual relations, but there are different legal elements which have to be considered when concluding an agreement. A broad

---

[123] In Swedish case law, the Supreme Court has referred to the practice of foreign courts in a number of cases, and it should also be mentioned that where international conventions are involved, there are currently often provisions setting out that in the interpretation of the convention regard should be had to the international character of the convention and the need of common interpretation, see eg CISG art. 7.

[124] Several legal areas have here apparently not been dealt with.

freedom of contract is beneficial for the contracting parties in that they may find and agree on better solutions with respect to their contractual relations. The downside is that if there is not really any choice for one of the parties then there is of course not much freedom. Similarly, when freedom of contract leads to less competition then business efficiency is reduced to the detriment of the customers. This is where the legislation in both the US and the EU rather prefers competition to freedom of contract, although the practical outcome may not always seem obvious.

Parts of global commercial law have a long tradition and a rather solid legal base, although the particular principles which have evolved are not necessarily identical in all national legal systems. Also, even if they are similar, they may not be understood in exactly the same way in different legal systems. In other parts of the legal system, the relevant principles are much more recent and have evolved over a much shorter period of time. They also often concern other (often regulatory) aspects of the legal system, where specific events and circumstances may have called for a particular, quicker and more precise need for legislative and political action. They frequently cover more limited areas geographically. Questions of administrative law character thus generally seem to require quicker action from the legislative bodies than questions related to traditional private law matters. This seems to be the case not least with respect to financial matters and the regulation of financial markets and financial players, where new regulations have been developed in various ways at the international, the regional (not least the EU) and at the national level following a previous financial meltdown. Such quick reactions may turn out to be not so well reasoned and drafted, and they may, therefore, have to be amended fairly soon.

Globalization has been accused of ruining the happiness of local communities and of local business. Undoubtedly, globalization has had negative side effects, but it has also meant better business efficiency in many respects. In B2B relations, global solutions are probably in many cases and in the long run better than specific legal solutions adopted for commerce in, eg, the EU. One problem is that global business entities tend to be too large for their own good and the good of society. This is, however, where competition rules have proved to be insufficiently effective.

Globalization in the area of business as it developed during the 1990s and the early 2000s has for many reasons come to a halt or at least slowed down considerably. One effect of this is the failure to reach a new general and extended agreement related to the WTO. Even if a limited agreement was reached at the end of December 2013, it remains to be seen how it will develop in the future. Possibly more regional trade agreements, some of them bilateral, will come into effect covering different areas of trade. It may be, however, that bilateral agreements are better than no agreements at all.

In the field of financial law, efforts have been made to reach agreements at the global level, but it seems difficult to arrive at binding conclusions, and for the time being, while there are still ongoing discussions in different worldwide organizations, different steps have been taken in the US and in Europe marking their own ways in this area.

In the field of private law, the CISG is a particular international achievement as is the New York Convention on the Recognition of Arbitral Awards. With respect to matters related to other commercial contracts, no other conventions have gained similar success. There was a long period of preparatory work, before the CISG was concluded, and as of September 2014, 83 states have ratified the CISG. Apart from these two successful conventions, there is also other work which has not led to a binding convention, but where the work carried out in UNCITRAL or UNIDROIT may still prove to be of some importance to legal development.

Maritime law is one area where convention work started early and has been extensive, and where several international conventions have been agreed covering different maritime areas. This is a consequence of the international nature of shipping. Maritime international conventions were introduced during the latter part of the nineteenth century and gradually increased during the twentieth century. These conventions cover specific parts of maritime business and the particular environment of maritime affairs (eg, the law related to ocean carriage, limitation of liability, maritime liens, collision, oil pollution etc). It has, however, to be recognized that these conventions have sometimes been replaced by local and regional legal regimes which have come into being when the international achievements, if any, have proved to be no longer sufficiently far reaching or efficient. To a growing extent several rules on an international level have been introduced to increase maritime safety.

In some areas of commercial law, soft law has been dominant, particularly in relation to trade finance. This is an area where the ICC to a growing extent has played and plays a major role especially with respect to the designing and drafting of standard contracts, but where customs and practices (international, regional or local customs) in some respect have a very long history. There is no clear line between the two. Beside the ICC, there are also a number of other international (and also regional) organizations which have played an important role in the development of new standard contracts.

The PICC merit a mention in this context since these principles were specially designed for international commercial relations. In their particular framework, they have a certain impact and it is not unusual for reference to be made to these principles in some international contracts. Also in several of the ICC standard documents, reference is made to international principles or similar which may imply the use of the PICC.

Commercial law from an international perspective has thus evolved in different ways along the respective roads of hard law and soft law. Businesses are of course different in many ways. There are differences with respect to types of businesses, the commercial area, the size of the business entity, the types of legal documents and instruments used. All these differences may require a variety of rules. I have not brought up consumer relations here (B2C contracts) which in my view should be treated in their own context and, therefore, differently to B2B contracts.[125] There are differences which require international solutions for global (international) business rather than legal solutions at the EU level, but it may prove difficult to achieve global rules of hard law character related to commercial transactions.

Whether and to what extent it will be possible to create and promote globally commercial legal solutions of various types remains to be seen. It seems to be easier to achieve such solutions through standard terms with respect to particular business areas than through global legislation of a more general nature. There are also situations, where it appears to be easier and possibly more practical to reach more narrow geographical solutions.

Different methods may be and have been used with different degrees of success. Obviously, obligatory law matters are more easily dealt with through contractual methods than, eg, property law and insolvency law matters, where mandatory legal rules and principles may set limits to the contractual freedom. The use of electronics has had an impact on the use of certain types of documents and there is a need for legal adaptation to such new technology.

There may be various restrictions regarding the parties' ability to regulate certain legal items. However, contractual solutions can still be reached as long as all the parties involved are prepared to stay with that particular contractual solution. In this sense, it may prove to be more effective to work for contractual solutions, where solutions applied in national law (and by national courts) appear to be less effective. In such situations, it may be better to apply soft law principles or contractual solutions which may be practically acceptable even though they lack the relative power of legislation.

During their negotiations, parties would also do well to consider the relevant choice of law provisions and suitable dispute settlement methods in their contract. As briefly touched upon above, it is still common for standard contracts to set out provisions with reference to national law, but in certain contract types there seems to be a slight increase in the use of references to *lex mercatoria*, international trade law and also to the PICC as applicable law provisions. As can be understood from the observations above, *lex mercatoria* is not the same as it was originally. As it is understood today, it is not a very precise set of rules and the parties should discuss whether it is

---

[125] Having said that, it is, however, also necessary to bear in mind that legislation with respect to B2C relations may also in the long run have an impact on commercial contracts (B2B relations).

sufficiently precise to be suitable for dispute settlement. In individual cases, it may prove to work well as the applicable law as long as the parties are aware of its character.

However, the PICC contain a large number of provisions which the parties may not wish to include as part of the contract. I believe that parties to commercial contracts should be largely allowed to choose the design of those contracts which they want to use between them and also to agree on the particular rules and principles that should apply in the case of a dispute.

EU bodies should be careful not to draft EU rules if there are already satisfactory international rules (this is, in my view the case with, for example, the Directive on a European Sales Law, which seems to be uncalled for at least in B2B relations).

To conclude, in my opinion, international commercial law should develop and be allowed to develop at a global level as far as is reasonably possible. This development should take place at different levels and the various bodies involved should be considered competent in the furthering of global commercial law. Hencethere seems to be little reason for EU bodies to promote particular EU solutions where international commercial transactions are involved, unless this is generally accepted by the international business community. It goes without saying that there may be cases where a particularly unacceptable development is taking place which may require restrictions at the regional or national level. To that extent, there may be specific instances where the involvement of the EU may be called for. In relation to international commercial law, particular legislation at the EU level should, therefore, be limited to specific areas and circumstances, and I believe that measures at the EU level should be restricted to those situations where there is a specific need and where there is little prospect of acceptable international solutions.

Part IV

The Future of European Private Law

8

What Happened to the Harmonisation of Securities Law in the EU?

KARIN WALLIN-NORMAN

I. INTRODUCTION—LEGAL RISK

A. International Securities Markets

SECURITIES MARKETS HAVE been international for decades. However, they are often referred to by their geographical names, like Stockholmsbörsen, the New York Stock Exchange and Deutsche Börse, giving the impression that they are actually local or national. The name conceals the fact that the market in question is not really situated in a 'place' as such since markets are usually virtual (even if the market participants and machinery are physical and solid). Very often owners, members and participants of market places and clearing houses, banks, brokers and other intermediaries and service providers, as well as the issuers and investors of securities and financial instruments do their business in many countries other than their own. These facts lie behind the notion that securities markets are global, borderless and international.

B. Excessive Costs for Legal Uncertainty

Risks and costs for cross-border investments are higher than domestic investments. The legal uncertainty may in turn lead to higher systemic risk and also to market inefficiencies. The cost of these risks for cross-border trade has been estimated to rise by 22.2 % compared to domestic trade.[1]

---

[1] Philipp Paech, 'Market Needs as Paradigm: Breaking Up the Thinking on EU Securities Law' in Conac et al (eds) *Intermediated Securities—The Impact of the Geneva Securities*

The need for action to address these problems through stricter regulation and supervision as well as harmonised legal frameworks has generated much work among regulators and supervisory authorities globally for a long time. Action has also been taken both at the EU and the global level through UNIDROIT. However, and in spite of, international conventions and proposals for legal harmonisation in this area and even in spite of some agreements having been reached, there is still no unified European legislation or international legal instrument in force to guarantee legal certainty regarding the effects of cross-border securities transactions.

C. The Aim of this Chapter

It is remarkable that so much work and time has been devoted by so many highly professional experts without any material result so far. Also after all those investigations, discussions and negotiations with the explicit aim to harmonise the legal treatment of holdings and dispositions of securities on securities accounts, you may ask yourself, what more can be done? What new perspectives and insights regarding the relevant issues can be added? If the global financial crisis after 2008 has not been enough as an argument for harmonised securities laws, what other arguments can be found?

In this chapter, I will dwell on the efforts that have been made—and still need to be made—to tackle the issue of legal certainty and its repercussions on systemic risk and market efficiency.

The chapter concludes that in spite of all the work that has been done in the last decade, much more is still needed. I will first recapture in section II the most important projects in the international arena when it comes to the harmonisation of securities law regarding the holding and dispositions of securities in the past ten years. I will also discuss some of the legal problems that—in my view—have been both the most important issues and the main obstacles to reaching a common understanding and agreement. Those are: (i) the notion of a securities account as a property item in relation to choice of law rules (section III); (ii) the transformation of immaterial rights and claims into paper-backed securities in physical form and then into immaterial book-entry securities (section IV); (iii) the tendency to overestimate intermediation as the prime source of uncertainties while overlooking the importance of the immateriality of the items of property (section V); and (iv) the problems that follow from letting traditional 'ownership' concepts govern the analysis instead of applying a consistent functional approach (section VI). A short concluding remark will follow in section VII.

Convention and the Future European Legislation (Cambridge, Cambridge University Press, 2013) pp 41–45.

II. A BRIEF RECAP—EFFORTS TO HARMONISE SECURITIES
LAW IN THE LAST TEN YEARS*

A. The Hague Securities Convention

The first issue that was dealt with by the international community with the direct aim to affect legal certainty in the international securities markets was the question of the choice of law: which law should govern transactions on securities accounts involving cross-border elements. It is now 11 years since the Convention on the Law Applicable to Certain Rights in Respect of Securities Held with an Intermediary (Hague Securities Convention) was concluded in 2002.[2] The Convention has, however, not yet been approved by a sufficient number of signatories to enter into force.

B. The UNIDROIT Project

After having concluded the Hague Securities Convention, a number of legal experts in securities law gathered again under the auspices of UNIDROIT to start another project in the securities law sector. The project grew and, in 2009, an agreement was finally reached on the UNIDROIT Convention on Substantive Rules for Intermediated Securities, in short referred to as the Geneva Securities Convention (GSC).[3] The purpose of this Convention is to enhance the internal stability of national financial markets and their cross-border compatibility, and to promote capital formation. After four years, only one state has signed the Convention, so there is still a long way to go before it can enter into force.

C. EU Legislation

In 2005, while the UNIRDROIT project was underway, the EU Commission appointed a group of 36 legal experts from 23 Member States with the task of investigating what the actual problems were and to come up with advice as to how to create a viable European legal framework for what is now generally referred to as intermediated securities. In 2008, the Legal Certainty Group delivered their Second Advice on solutions to legal barriers related to post-trading within the EU (LCG Advice). In general,

---

* For readers of Swedish, see my article 'Kontorätt i ett internationellt perspektiv—harmonisering av äganderätt och panträtt till kontoförda värdepapper', 2010 *Ny Juridik* 2:10, pp 7–27. For an updated and thorough survey of this development, I recommend Conac et al (eds), *Intermediated Securities—The Impact of the Geneva Securities Convention and the Future European Legislation* (Cambridge, Cambridge University Press, 2013).

2 See www.hcch.net.index

3 See www.unidroit.org.

it covers the same issues that are dealt with in the Geneva Securities Convention although the latter also includes other issues that lie outside the scope of this article.[4]

The Advice included 15 Recommendations covering in turn: (a) a harmonised legal framework for legal effects of book entries made to securities accounts; (b) the dismantling of obstacles arising in connection with cross-border holdings of securities on securities accounts; and (c) the rights by issuers to have their securities issued and entered in a foreign CSD. The EU Commission had, as of December 2013, not come up with a final proposal regarding legislation on these issues. However, there was a consultation process in 2009 and 2010 and the documentation that was the result of that process, both the Consultation Document and the summary of responses, was (going back to the documentation) published in 2011.

III.   WHAT PROPERTY IS TARGETED BY THE CHOICE OF LAW RULES?

A.   The PRIMA Approach

Private international law (IP law) rules tell us which law is applicable to a certain problem. In relation to the holding and disposition of securities, IP law has traditionally adopted what is known as the *lex rei sitae* approach, meaning that the law where the securities are located will apply. This causes a problem for the modern markets where securities are often not situated in a particular place at all, but rather 'exist' in immaterial form through registrations in securities accounts. The approach which was substituted for *lex rei sitae* is called PRIMA (meaning 'place of relevant intermediary approach').[5] PRIMA comes in one basic form, pointing to the law of the place where the account is maintained, which is the approach taken in EU legislation (Settlement Finality Directive and Winding Up Directive). There is also a more 'extended' variant/version of PRIMA, adopted by the above-mentioned Hague Securities Convention, where the parties to the account agreement may agree on the law which is applicable on the condition that—generally speaking—the relevant intermediary is established in that jurisdiction.

---

[4] Reference is made to Chapter V of the GSC with Special Provisions in Relation to Collateral Transactions. According to Articles 38 and 36 (2), a Contracting State has the opportunity to make an opt-out declaration of Chapter V, either in part or entirely.

[5] This approach is laid down both in Article 9 (2) of Directive 98/26/EC (Settlement Finality Directive) [1998] OJ L166/45 and in Directive 2002/47/EC (Collateral Directive) [2002] OJ L168/43.

B. Criticism of the PRIMA Rules

Both variants of PRIMA use the same basic factor to determine which law is applicable, namely the securities account. A securities account can be described as constituting a particular relationship between an account holder and an account provider. The holding pattern in today's international securities markets, therefore, involves securities held cross-border through two or more 'tiers' of account providers, established in different countries, often other countries than the issuer or investor of a certain issue of securities. Therefore, the PRIMA approach in both variants has been criticised for resulting in two or more jurisdictions governing the 'same' securities held in one 'chain' of intermediaries through different accounts in different countries.[6]

In my view, this criticism is inherently contradictive in that it both assumes (correctly) that the property items for the application of the PRIMA rule are the securities accounts (being governed by different national laws) and at the same time declares (incorrectly) that the PRIMA rule applies to 'the same securities' which are quite different items of property. In section IV of this article, I take a closer look at what should generally be regarded as the item of property in a property law context when securities are held and disposed of in securities accounts.

C. What Property is Targeted by PRIMA?

For the application of any choice of law rule, it is essential to decide precisely which property is concerned. The PRIMA rule in the Hague Securities Convention deals with 'securities held with an intermediary' and this is further described in Article 2 (1) a) as 'the rights resulting from a credit of securities to a securities account'. It seems evident that this must mean that the property to which the rules apply can be nothing but the 'securities credited to an account'—in contrast to securities being stored in a vault or securities registered in the books of the issuer or something like similar. If this is the property, it means that each account holder in a chain who holds an account to which securities are credited holds an item of property. The legal effects that may be deduced from this fact shall—so says the PRIMA rule—be decided and interpreted according to the law of the place of the account (provider).

---

[6] For a thorough analysis of the convention and criticism thereof see Maisie Ooi, *The Choice of a Choice of Law Rule* in L Gullifer et al (eds), *Intermediated Securities—Legal problems and Practical Issues*, 17th edn (Oxford, Hart Publishing, 2010) pp 219–244.

D. Harmonised IP Law is Not Enough

The criticism thus emanates from the false—and in my view inconsistent—perception of what a 'security' and a 'securities account' are. No doubt when book-entry securities are held in a multi-tiered 'chain' of intermediaries, the result of PRIMA is bound to be multiple jurisdictions being applicable on the holdings on different tiers of accounts.[7] This should, however, not be seen as an anomaly or a problem; it is, on the contrary, the result of the recognition of each account holder's rights related to its securities account in the holding chain. The holding chain itself is not the problem for the choice of law. The problem is that national laws attribute different legal effects to the credits on securities accounts. This is why it is so important not just to harmonise IP law, as it deals only with choice of law rules, but also to promote sound and efficient rules regarding the legal effects of credits on securities accounts. Without the latter, the former lacks real importance in securities markets. A global acceptance of the Hague Securities Convention through a formal act of ratification, therefore, can make a difference as a harmonising instrument only if there exists at the same time in the relevant jurisdictions a minimum degree of sound and efficient regime for legal effects of credits on securities accounts applicable in cross-border situations.

IV. WHY THE FORM OF SECURITIES MATTER

A. The Propertification of Debt and Obligation

The development of securities as objects of relevance for legal rights and obligations has followed different paths in different jurisdictions. It would be going too far to go into the historical details in this article and my knowledge is fairly basic since it is mainly limited to the Swedish situation. Generally, however, you can assume that the transformation of mere claims and rights of participation (in corporations) into items of property has at some point in most jurisdictions manifested itself in paper form.[8] Thus, the claim and the rights have been manifested in a piece of paper. The 'invention' of simple paper documents carrying within them the material value of not just a piece of paper but the value of the claim/partnership written on it, its 'face value', has been an important commercial and legal development in many

---

[7] Theoretically, the same would be the case if one certificated security was being held through a multi-tiered 'chain' of depositaries.

[8] See also Luc Thévenoz, 'The Geneva Securities Convention: objectives, history and guiding principles' in Conac et al (eds) *Intermediated Securities* (Cambridge, Cambrige University Press, 2013) pp 3–9.

jurisdictions.[9] It happened centuries ago but was—just like many other developments in private law—the result of market demands for safe and efficient ways of transferring value. Thus, the 'materialisation' of securities in paper documents seems to have been a universal method of transforming mere rights or claims into items of property, thereby subjecting them to the regular and traditional legal regime for tangible property in each jurisdiction.

B. Computerisation

There is no doubt that the materialisation of securities has made a profound contribution to the development of the financial markets over the past hundred years.[10] During the second half of the twentieth century, however, computers made their entry into the financial world and made a great difference in almost all areas of the market. We know that the techniques of issuing, acquiring and holding securities through entering information in computer systems and passing it on through electronic communications have made the physical holding and handling of paper securities unnecessary. In practical terms, the physical securities were replaced by securities accounts. The exact way in which this happened may be similar or vary considerably between jurisdictions according to legal tradition and culture. The general result, however, has been the same in all financial markets: the persons generally regarded as the owners of securities have become 'account holders' with their holdings of securities recorded on 'securities accounts' operated and maintained by banks, brokers and other securities intermediaries acting as 'account providers'.[11] In the first phase of this change, the actual physical securities still existed and were often kept in safe custody (and) in vaults guarded by the relevant banks and brokers as valuable property belonging to clients.

C. Immobilisation

In due course the relevant securities laws adapted to the new practice of using computers and electronic communication. In many jurisdictions,

---

[9] The 'invention' has by no means been a singular act or decision but rather a process which can only be detected in retrospective and judged by its result. For the process in US commercial law, see JS Rogers, *Negotiability, Property and Identification*, 1990, available at www.ssrn.com.

[10] At least, this is true for the Swedish securities markets that grew considerably after the passing of the Promissory Notes Act (1936:81). This law is still in force and explicitly sets out the rules for negotiability and good faith acquisitions of debt instruments. It is also interpreted and regarded as generally applicable to all debts.

[11] I use the terms 'account holder' and 'account provider' here as technical terms indicating the general and not legal position of the investor and its intermediary in relation to the securities account.

various forms of collective papers were allowed to facilitate efficient holding practices for intermediaries with a multitude of customers owning and trading in securities. Likewise, company law was adjusted to accommodate 'collective' exercise against issuers by intermediaries on the account of the many customers/investors with the same kind of security. In some jurisdictions, the practice of holdings of collective securities documents was accepted and underpinned by written law while in others, it was supported by case law or other rules. The practice of letting one or a few paper documents represent the whole issue of a certain security is called immobilisation and is still practised in some jurisdictions. However, the 'global' shares or bond certificates are not items of property; no one 'owns' these papers, they are just kept safely in a bank vault. Instead, the relevant jurisdictions have construed legal rules according to which ownership and other rights in the relevant securities are acquired through recordings on securities accounts held by investors. The legal construction of an immobilised regime involves theories regarding trust, co-ownership and similar more or less elaborate legal concepts depending on the relevant jurisdiction. The actual situation for investors and others who are involved in the holding and dispositions of securities is, however, very similar to the one that would exist if the 'underlying' paper securities were totally abolished, since no one is supposed to ever touch them.

D. Dematerialisation

Dematerialisation in this context refers to the process by which holdings of securities accounts have literally replaced holdings of physical securities documents. Securities are no longer issued in paper form and for those that were in the past, the documents have been maculated. Ownership and other rights in dematerialised securities are evidenced solely through registrations by account providers on securities accounts. The dematerialisation process has taken some decades to become a general phenomenon in many of the world's financial markets. As mentioned above the actual situation for the investor is the same as in jurisdictions where immobilisation is practised. The legal underpinnings of dematerialised securities are, however, usually more straightforward and specifically designed to guarantee legal certainty for the account holders' holdings and transactions as well as for the duties and responsibilities of the account providers.

E. Preserving Propertification in spite of Dematerialisation

Thus, materialised securities had to go through another transformation process in order to become 'paperless' without losing their quality as items of property. The immaterial claims and co-ownership rights were packaged into securities accounts; the network required to operate these accounts was formed by banks and brokers and other financial intermediaries who became account providers. Those market players made both the transformation process and the transactions and handling of this new form of property possible in a controlled and orderly way. This is why I think that it is important to realise that dematerialised and immobilised securities are primarily characterised by their immateriality, while still being items of property, ie not mere claims or co-ownership rights. It is a fact that they are also intermediated by account providers but this is not an accidental side effect but a deliberate choice. Neither immateriality nor intermediation should, therefore, be treated as problems but as universal solutions to a common problem: the insupportable multitude of paper documents.

V. INTERMEDIATION AND IMMATERIALITY

A. Shift in Perspective

In practical terms, there are many similarities between immobilisation and dematerialisation. In both cases, there is a need for intermediation. The markets have become dependent on the existence of securities accounts and these are in essence a certain kind of relationship between investors and account providers. That is why these securities are called 'intermediated securities'. Yet it is clearly not the intermediation that makes the securities accounts different from certificated securities; it is their immateriality. Before computers were invented, certificated securities were very often held and transferred by intermediaries on behalf of their customers. The intermediaries were at that time just depositaries. But after dematerialisation or immobilisation, the property item took a completely different form which required that someone opened and administrated an account for the relevant holder. Otherwise those securities could not be held, owned or disposed of.

Both issuers, investors and intermediaries in today's securities markets expect and intend that buyers of securities receive them with the same protection against sellers' creditors and other third parties as they would have had, had the securities been incorporated in individual bond or share certificates. Since it is now a worldwide and long-since established practice to deal with securities being recorded on securities accounts, it must now be a task for legal experts and not for the market players collectively to find and create the legal underpinning for this practice. In my view, intermediation as the key factor for the analysis of this modern form of securities is overestimated. We should shift perspective and be struck by the fact that these securities have now returned to their original essence of being immaterial. What does this mean? In my experience, it is important to take a step back from the unconscious and everyday acceptance of 'securities in securities accounts' to fully understand what it means that an item of property has dissolved into thin air.[12]

B. The 'Same' Securities

Immateriality means in particular that the traditional principle of specificity, which requires the identification of a specific object in order for 'ownership' to be recognised, can no longer be applied in its traditional sense. In my opinion, the full consequences of this change are not properly reflected in any of the aforementioned conventions or legislative proposals. An example where this is apparent is in connection with a good-faith acquisition rule for securities credited to securities accounts. It is no longer appropriate to talk about the 'same securities'. An acquirer cannot logically have the 'same' securities credited to its account as was earlier credited to another account. The 'sameness' is truly impossible. The only link between a particular credit on one account and a debit on another account that can possibly be observed is a matter of mathematic calculation and causality.

C. The 'Securities Themselves'

An expression that has been mentioned in many working documents, reports, proposals, legislative acts, regulations, comments, books etc on book-entry securities and securities markets that have been published in the EU or elsewhere is the term 'securities themselves'. The general idea when this term is used seems to be, on the one hand, that there are securities and, on the other hand, that (book-entries on) securities accounts and the relationship between the two is described in a number of more or less fantastic terms—or not at all.

Credits or book-entries are said to 'reflect', 'represent', 'mirror', 'substitute' or in similar ways be related to securities. Very rarely are the credits or book-entries said to be or constitute the securities 'themselves'. It does not seem possible to refer to the mere debt or obligation created by the issuer in relation to its creditors and participants as the 'security itself'. Before this debt or obligation became a security, it must have gone through the process of propertification referred to in section IV and become a 'security'. So what is meant by 'securities themselves'? Also book-entries on securities accounts are sometimes said to be related to the 'underlying securities'. Maybe 'underlying securities' are the same as the 'securities themselves'?

---

[12] I have discussed and thoroughly analysed this in Karin Wallin-Norman, *Kontorätt—rätt till kontoförda värdepapper* (Stockholm, Jure förlag, 2009).

In jurisdictions where immobilisation is the rule and physical securities documents actually exist, these documents may of course be referred to as the 'securities themselves' or the 'underlying securities'. The link between the securities credited to a buyer's securities account and the global share or bond certificate held in a central vault, often in a foreign country, is, however, pure fantasy, a legal construction without any clear unambiguous evidence. Therefore, any reference to the 'security itself' is quite illusory unless you are speaking about the global security certificate itself and this is very rarely the case, since no one actually deals with that document.

But when securities are dematerialised, what is a 'security itself' and which security is lying under what and where? Dematerialised securities do not by definition exist at all except as an imaginary content of what is registered 'in' the account. Thus, anything that could be referred to as 'the security itself', 'the real security' or the 'underlying security' does not really exist. In my view, this language is confusing and I am afraid that sometimes those who use it may be doing so on purpose.

VI. THE IDENTIFICATION OF OWNERS AND THEIR PROPERTY

A. Owners and Ownership

A functional approach was established from the outset for both the UNIDROIT and the LCG projects.[13] Even if there has been some disagreement as to what this means, there should be more consensus over what it does not mean. It surely is not the harmonisation of property law concepts in general or a definition of terms like 'owner' and 'ownership'.[14] The aim was 'simply' a harmonised legal framework for holdings and dispositions of securities over securities accounts. Therefore, there did not need to be an answer to the question: who is the owner? Unfortunately, however, this limited scope of the task in both projects has been effectively buried by legal scholars from a number of jurisdictions who have eloquently embroidered on issues of legal ownership, beneficial ownership, legal title, root of title and other terminology from the realm of traditional property law in many—but far from all—jurisdictions. A great number of papers, articles and books have now been published on the subject of 'intermediated securities'. Unfortunately—at least from an international perspective—many of them deal with the subject of ownership and the question of who is or should be regarded as the 'owner of intermediated securities' and also proposes answers to this question.

It would certainly be a miracle if legal experts in securities law from all UNIDROIT and EU Member States were now finally able to 'solve' the issue

---

[13] See the 6th Recital of the Preamble to the GSC.
[14] See also Paech, 'Market Needs as Paradigm' (n 1) p 46.

and come up with a common view and a comprehensive agreed definition of 'ownership' to be applied in relation to 'securities' or 'securities accounts'. This will of course not happen. Neither the GSC nor the future European legislation can or should give an answer to the question. They should only set out what can be described as minimum rights that should be granted to an account holder with securities credited to its account. Therefore, the harmonisation of the legal effects of credits and debits on securities accounts will have to be separated and kept apart from the ownership concept.

B. The Specification of the Property Item

The principle of specificity—meaning that in order for property rights to arise the object of property has to be identified and specified (as the 'asset')—lies at the core of property law in many jurisdictions. The principle of specificity is based on—to summarise—the age-old legal conception of ownership as a right that requires an 'object', which must be specified, in such a way that the owner can identify its own property among other objects. But how can an immaterial object be specified? The evident answer for securities credited to an account seems to be: through the entering of information about the security in the account. This answer is, however, not satisfactory because it gives rise to further questions such as: What is an account? Is the securities account the same object as the securities? How can an account be specified? Can an account be transferred? How is it at all possible to ascertain that an account actually exists?

One common view, at least in common law jurisdictions, seems to be that intermediated securities are fungible intangibles and that the doctrine of specificity cannot easily apply to this reality. The 'solution' to the problem of fungible intangibles is—according to some authors—to uphold the fiction that securities can be separated and distinguished and to apply the legal construct that the securities actually do exist in the securities account.[15] In my view, this solution has a considerable drawback in that it requires the workings of legal fiction and that legal fiction varies between jurisdictions in the exact same way as other legal concepts and language as such. Therefore, it is probably not a proper solution at all.

C. A New Interpretation of Specificity

I propose a new interpretation of the doctrine of specificity based on the acceptance that nothing but bits of information exist 'in' securities

---

[15] See Erica Johansson, *Property Rights in Investment Securities and the Doctrine of Specificity* (Springer-Verlag Berlin and Heidelberg GmbH & Co, 2008).

accounts.[16] The securities credited to an account cannot be identified or distinguished in any other way than through the specification of a number or amount of a certain kind of securities. In order for the principle of specificity to be applicable on securities credited to securities accounts, the principle must be 're-constructed' for this kind of property. A re-construction requires that the 'object' can be identified as a property item of an account holder. For decades now, the rule in practice in all securities markets has been to accept the idea that: (i) a securities account operated by (ii) a specific account provider, identifying (iii) a specific account holder and (iv) a certain amount or number of securities (v) of a certain kind constitutes an item of property, ie an 'object'. This market practice needs to be supported by legal rules, as those which can be found in both the GSC and LCG Second Advice.

D. Rights and Claims Against the Issuer

In the materialisation process the question regarding how the owner of a documented security would be able to assert its claim on the issuer must have been common for all jurisdictions (just like many other issues like, for example, the negotiability issue). In principle, it seems that the physical security was often regarded as a 'manifestation of' the relationship between the issuer and investor as well as the object of the owners' general right of disposal. In general, the means of legitimising the investor to assert its rights against the issuer have thus centred on a paper document—either in a bearer form or in the books of the issuer. But when it comes to details regarding how and when—and sometimes by whom—the right or claim must or can be presented to the issuer, there are still many variations in the legal rules and practices. Often they are related to other company law issues and to the question of ownership, since mostly—on certain conditions—an 'owner' is generally entitled against the issuer. Now, if the question regarding who the owner is forbidden—according to the functional approach for intermediated securities—the question asked must instead be: who is entitled to the rights emanating from the issuer?

E. The Inevitable Interference with Company Law

The answer to this question does not necessarily have to do with either book-entry securities being immaterial or with intermediation. Indeed both the UNIDROIT and the LCG projects have tried to seek agreement on a common solution to this problem but failed. The real reason for that—in my

---

[16] See Wallin-Norman, *Kontorätt* (n 12) p 159.

view—is that both projects were very careful not to deal with or intervene with company law and that the question is inseparable from company law. In this matter, I believe that company law—when it deals with entitlement against the issuer for rights embedded in securities—must be harmonised. As mentioned above, it has nothing to do with intermediation but more to do with the fact that all relevant persons, ie all account holders in a holding chain, are identifiable through their accounts—and only through their accounts. Of course not all account holders in a holding chain for a certain securities holding can be entitled to receive dividends or to vote. So the trick is to design a rule which: (i) entitles only one account holder in a chain; and (ii) at the same time is not based on ownership concepts; and also (iii) that interference with company law is kept to a minimum. There seem to be a few examples of how this can be achieved, the Swedish law rules for legitimising rights and claims against an issuer of intermediated securities perhaps being one.

F. 'Harmonised' IT Systems for Securities Accounts

Clearly, in those jurisdictions where physical securities have been abolished—often through legislation and sometimes through market practice only—this is seen as a positive and desired development and there will be no interest to revert to the earlier practice with paper documents. Also, in jurisdictions where immobilisation is the rule, this is due to legal considerations that dematerialisation cannot be accommodated. This means that, for the time being, the overall international securities markets will have to accept both methods like they have already done for so many years. Securities market players have developed a common and practical means of accommodating different legal concepts: securities accounts maintained for their customers/investors. It is true that there is considerable homogeneity and resemblance between how IT systems all over the world create 'securities accounts' as a tool for securities intermediaries to service their clients. The technical systems (both hardware and software) used by banks and brokers all over the world, therefore, seem to be 'harmonised' to a much greater extent than the legal systems of jurisdictions governing these banks and brokers.

VII. CONCLUSION

Many conclusions may be drawn from this—one being important to the issue discussed in this article: if legal systems could be 'harmonised' in the treatment of securities accounts to a sufficient degree, many of today's uncertainties in the international securities markets would disappear. For the legal treatment of securities accounts and book entries in such accounts, it is not necessary to also harmonise property law concepts like ownership, or to deal with the legal treatment of the 'security itself'. Legal harmonisation should only focus on the securities accounts and the legal treatment of the accounts and the rights and obligations of account providers and holders in relation to the securities accounts. The totality of these legal effects— some of them consisting of rights for the account holder, some rights for the account provider and some rules for administrators of insolvency estates— may of course for practical reasons be given a name but the name in itself is not necessary for the effects to be harmonised throughout the EU or globally.

For anyone who has taken part in or followed the harmonisation projects of the past ten years, it is not easy to be optimistic about the outcome. The main reason for the failure so far does not seem to be a lack of expert knowledge or insufficient insight into the present situation.[17] In my view, what is needed more than anything is a common political will. It seems, however, that much work still remains to be done. It is, therefore, important to realise that harmonisation can be achieved through other means than mandatory legislation. During the past decade, many EU countries have implemented new legislation 'on their own' and it seems evident that these national laws are more or less influenced by both the Geneva Securities Convention and the LCG project or at least the thinking that lies behind some of these articles and recommendations. Also, harmonisation can be achieved through business consolidations in the market as well as new technical standards and common IT solutions. Therefore, perhaps there is no need to be too pessimistic about the achievement of a common legal framework for securities accounts in the EU.

---

[17] Paech (n 1) pp 24–27 including notes.

9

E Pluribus Unum?

A Constitutional Perspective on the Pluralism and the Unity of European Private Law

OLA ZETTERQUIST

Private Law relates to the interests of individuals. Thus Private Law is said to be threefold in its nature, for it is composed of precepts of Natural Law, of those of the Law of Nations, and of those of the Civil Law (*Corpus Iuris Civilis, Digesta, Institutiones, I:IV*).

I. INTRODUCTION

A S EUROPEAN INTEGRATION, and with it European law (as well), has expanded over the past decades, the European legal landscape has changed dramatically. What started out as a legal order for a common market for coal and steel in six European states has over time turned into a constitutional legal order and a common market comprising 28 states and 550,000,000 people—the European Union. The common market now encompasses perhaps all the economic sectors in all of the Member States. Indeed the EU does not stop at market (commercial) regulation. The EU currently has powers to legislate in such former bastions of state sovereignty such as the areas of criminal and family law and is also a major player on the international stage by virtue of its common foreign and security policy. Seen against this background, it may seem slightly odd that the EU does not already boast a proper civil code of its own or, in other words, that it has not proceeded to harmonise the central areas of contract and tort law. The question of whether to harmonise this area or not is consequently one of the most important questions in current legal debate. The purpose of this chapter is to examine, from a legal philosophical and constitutional point of view, whether such harmonisation is desirable or not. More precisely, I aim to analyse the question through the lens of the idea of constitutional pluralism which has been a central component of the constitutional theory of the EU ever since the ECJ stated that the European legal order was a new, separate and independent order from the legal orders of the Member States.[1] The thrust of the argument of constitutional pluralism is that relations between legal systems are pluralistic rather than monistic and interactive rather than hierarchical.[2]

II. THE PROPOSED ALTERNATIVES

Admittedly, the idea of a European civil code has existed for a long time, particularly among legal scholars. The more recent starting point of the modern debate on the possible harmonisation of European contract law dates back to the 11th July 2001 when the Commission put forward four possible paths for the future development of European contract law:[3]

1. To leave the solution of any problems identified to the market.
2. To promote the development of non-binding, common contract law principles. These principles could be useful for contracting parties in drafting their contracts, for national courts and arbitrators in their decisions and for national legislators in drawing up legislative initiatives.
3. To review and improve existing Community legislation in the area of contract law so as to make it more coherent or to adapt it to cover situations not foreseen at the time of adoption.
4. To adopt a new instrument at Community level, combining rules on general aspects of contract law and on specific questions.

The first alternative is basically a minimalist 'do nothing' proposal. The second alternative argues for a looser form of promoting some sort of 'cross fertilisation' (or, to use a classical EU law concept, 'spill over') across Europe but without resorting to legislative measures at the EU level. The third alternative amounts to a clean-up and revision of the existing legislation but stops short of harmonisation. The fourth proposal is the maximalist proposal of the adoption of a European body of contract law by means of European legislation.

---

[1] As first laid down in Case 26/62 *van Gend en Loos v Nederlandse Administratie der Belastigen* [1963] CMLR 105.

[2] The origin of this idea is usually ascribed to the British Professor Neil MacCormick and his landmark article 'The Maastricht Urteil: Sovereignty Now', (1965) *European Law Journal* p 259. For a general overview of the topic see Matej Avbelj and Jan Komarek (eds), *Constitutional Pluralism in the European Union and Beyond* (Oxford, Hart Publishing, 2012).

[3] Commission Communication on European Contract Law, COM/2001/0398.

The somewhat ill-disguised preference of the Commission was, and seems to remain, the fourth alternative for the adoption of European contract law.[4] The gist of the Commission's argument is that the internal market does not function as well as it might as long as there are discrepancies in contract law between the Member States since this discourages parties from entering into contracts with parties under different jurisdictions.

Unsurprisingly, the argument for harmonisation has not gone unchallenged. Broadly speaking, the opposition can be grouped into two different categories; firstly, those who believe that such harmonisation lies outside the scope of EU competence and, secondly, those who allege that such harmonisation is undesirable.

The argument that European contract law would lie outside the scope of the competencies of the EU may be interesting in principle. Nevertheless, it would be reasonable to assume that if the political institutions by common agreement were to adopt such a body of law (having duly taken the principle of subsidiarity into consideration), stating that such a body of law is necessary for the proper functioning of the internal market, it is highly unlikely that the ECJ would strike it down as ultra vires.[5]

The argument that harmonisation is undesirable is perhaps more interesting from the point of view of constitutional theory. One of the most forceful expressions of this view is to be found in the Finnish Professor, Thomas Wilhelmsson's famous article *Europeiseringen av privaträtten: För ett fragmenterat utbyte av erfarenheter* (loosely translated as 'The Europeanisation of private law: In favour of a fragmented exchange of experiences').[6] The thrust of Wilhelmsson's criticism against the harmonisation of European private law is twofold: firstly, that European contract law would not be rooted in a legal culture of its own and, secondly, that such a body of law would be static and morally biased towards economic liberalism with insufficient scope for social values. With regard to the second point, Wilhelmsson holds that a fragmented approach is more in line with the core of European identity, notably the pluralism of languages and cultures.

The argument that European contract law would not be rooted in a legal culture of its own sounds intuitively credible. All lawyers are well aware of the fact that contract law, in general, often displays several national characteristics even though, as any comparative lawyer of elementary skills can tell

---

[4] See, inter alia, 'The Commission Communication on a Common European Sales Law to Facilitate Cross-border Transactions in the Single Market', 11 October 2011, COM/2011/0636.

[5] The possibility still remains that a national court could come to the conclusion that European contract law would lie outside the scope of EU competencies duly conferred by that particular Member State. I will not dwell further on this question since it is not a question of EU constitutional law.

[6] *Tidskrift for Rettsvitenskap*, vol 114 [2001], pp 1–32.

us, the vast amount of rules and principles in the European national legal orders are rather similar to one another.[7] Seen from a longer historical perspective, however, the picture of distinct national legal cultures is less clear. As stated in the *Corpus Iuris Civilis*, the Romans took an explicitly pluralist approach to the nature of private law, holding it to contain significant elements of natural and international law. The Roman pluralist attitude to private law was also in tune with the Constitution of the Roman Republic which was pluralist to a fault, there being no sole source of public power or any political institution designated as superior to the others. The constitutional concept of (internal) sovereignty was accordingly utterly incompatible with the constitutional principle of the Roman Republic.[8] The Romans also had little problem in handling a legal pluralism where Roman, international and local law co-existed (in the same place). In short, as argued by the Roman Republic's most forceful later advocate Niccolo Machiavelli, the ideal republic was characterised by healthy friction between the different forces in the republic.[9] Conflict, not unity, drove the development of society, an idea which would later appear in the philosophies of both Hegel and Marx.

The Romans, at least in theory, thought that there was a core of private law which was 'fixed', ie beyond the reach of the magistrate or legislative assembly. On the contrary, part of the private law was common to all jurisdictions of the (then) known world. This idea was to outlast the Roman Republic. In combination with the legal practice of the (likewise Roman) ecclesiastical canon law, the old Roman private law survived well into the Middle Ages known as the *jus commune* which formed the basis of a common system of legal thought in most of Europe. A common body of (Roman) law, a common system of legal education and a common body of literature bound European lawyers together in a single intellectual system.[10] This common frame of reference among European lawyers would not disappear until

[7] This is particularly so in Member States that share the same contract law, as in the Nordic countries, or that once upon a time had the same contract law such as the countries sharing the French Code Civil or the German BGB even though subsequent developments may have altered the original.

[8] As reflected in the official motto of the Roman Republic *Senatus Populusque Romanus* (SPQR), meaning 'the Senate and people of Rome', expressing the idea that Roman power was shared between the Senate and the people.

[9] Niccolo Machiavelli, *Discourses on Livy*, (Oxford, Oxford University Press, 1997) p 26. See also Ola Zetterquist, 'Out with the New, in with the Old', in Jan Komárek and Matej Avbelj (eds) *Constitutional Pluralism in the European Union and Beyond*, (Oxford, Hart Publishing, 2011) pp 213–230 at p 220.

[10] See Kenneth. Pennington, *The Prince and the Law* (University of California Press, 1993) pp 6–7. With the terminology of Tuori, to which Wilhelmsson explicitly refers, this could be expressed as the medieval lawyers sharing a common *legal culture* and perhaps even a legal *deep-structure*, *cf* Kaarlo Tuori, 'Law Beyond Law', in Ann Numhauser-Hennning (ed), *Normative Patterns and Legal Developments in the Social Dimension of the EU* (Oxford, Hart Publishing, 2012) pp 58–59.

the emergence of the sovereign state, the mighty *Leviathan*, in the seventeenth century. The sovereign state also led to the creation of national legal systems and, in particular, national private law. The nationalisation of private law is thus closely connected to the constitutional transformation from the medieval pluralist constitutional landscape, with multiple legal sources, to the mono-lithic and unitary order of the sovereign state where all law is, ultimately, state law.[11] Private law was, accordingly, exorcised from two of its original Roman components, natural and international law leaving only national law. In short, *Leviathan* loves national civil codes because they prevent the danger of competing legal authorities.

The argument that the EU does not have a proper legal culture of its own is thus very much a consequence of the constitutional revolution of the early modern period of the seventeenth and eighteenth centuries. As such, this does not invalidate Wilhelmsson's point that there may currently be more of a, say, Swedish legal culture than an EU legal culture. It is, however, an argu-ment that is ultimately dependent on the sovereign state and the correspond-ing constitutional monism that emanates from such a state. Adherence to the cultural argument would consequently preclude, or at least seriously undermine, the position that Europe of today is characterised by a con-stitutional pluralism encompassing both the EU and its Member States as separate and independent legal orders.

Wilhelmsson's second argument that a European body of private law would be static and insufficiently open to different values seems much more promising from a pluralist point of view. In this regard, Wilhelmsson has held that it is a strength, not a liability, that European private law is frag-mented into several different legal orders since it allows legal experimenta-tion and the 'free movement' of inspiring ideas between the participating legal orders to be more in line with the core of European identity which is pluralism (of languages and cultures). These arguments are as such quite similar to those advanced by the scholars of constitutional pluralism who criticise the sovereign state as an insufficient basis for understanding the transnational legal landscape of contemporary Europe. Instead, they stress legal cross fertilisation and judicial dialogue as cornerstones of a heterar-chic constitutional system encompassing individuals, states and European institutions.

Looking at contemporary Europe through a slightly Roman lens, a pic-ture of interacting and overlapping legal orders emerges. In this contem-porary world, there is a constant dialogue between the European courts (whether national or European). This pluralism seems paradoxical at first sight but it may be more easily understood through reference to the distinc-tion, made by the Finnish Professor Kaarlo Tuori, that the broad concept

---

[11] The canonical work on the nature of the sovereign state and the relation between law and state is to be found in Thomas Hobbes' masterpiece, *Leviathan*, from 1651.

of law or a legal system is composed of a legal order—understood as law as a symbolic-normative phenomenon—and the legal practices (law making, adjudication and legal scholarship) whereby the legal order is produced and reproduced.[12] These two aspects of the law constantly interact with each other—indeed one cannot exist without the other. The distinction makes it possible to imagine the European and national legal orders as being autonomous and distinct and yet, by virtue of the legal practices, as being part of the same European legal system.[13] This also implies that those practising law in Europe are committed to both legal orders and under a corresponding duty to accommodate and integrate their respective claims.[14]

The notion of constitutional pluralism can of course be used in a purely descriptive sense, ie that national and European courts seem to rub along without any major difficulties and that none of these courts have made an all-out claim of supremacy over the other legal order(s). Constitutional pluralism could, however, also be construed as a normative idea meaning that there is, from the constitutional point of view, an added value of having European constitutions alongside the constitutions of the European states. To paraphrase the former Advocate General, Miguel Maduro, heterarchy is superior to hierarchy as a normative ideal in circumstances of competing constitutional claims of final authority when those competing constitutional claims are of equal legitimacy or, at least, cannot be balanced against each other in general terms.[15] Heterarchy logically entails that arguments of substance and principle are to be preferred to arguments of authority and form—a constitutional rule of reason if you like. Recognising heterarchy as a normative ideal also means recognising that all the courts involved have important contributions to make, the occasional disagreement more often leading to dialogue between the courts than an all-out conflict. A heterarchic system will also in all likeliness have a more open approach to legal cross fertilisation than a rigid hierarchical system (will have).

Constitutional pluralism may have worked in mysterious ways but there can be no doubt that it has had a profound effect on both legal order and legal practice in the Member States. The fundamental values expressed in general terms in Article 2 of the TEU, and particularly, in the European

---

[12] See Kaarlo Tuori and Suvi Sankari, 'Transnational law: on legal hybrids and legal perspectivism', in Kaarlo Tuori, Miguel Maduro and Suvi Sankari (eds), *Transnational Law—Rethinking European Law and Legal Thinking*, (Cambridge, Cambridge University Press, 2014) pp 11–58.

[13] In fact, this is what is happening every time a national court decides on European legal matters within the framework of the national procedural rules, thereby applying both national and European legal principles to the case.

[14] See Miguel Poiares Maduro, 'Three Claims of Constitutional Pluralism', in Matej Avbelj and Jan Komarek (eds), *Constitutional Pluralism in the European Union and Beyond* (Oxford, Hart Publishing, 2012) p 70.

[15] See Maduro (n 14) p 75.

Convention on Human Rights (ECHR), have already been the object of considerable adjudication and have thus, to a large degree, slowly morphed from principles to rules familiar to any lawyer practising in, say, Portugal or Finland alike.[16] In more recent years, there has also been a gradual change of many national constitutions whereby the rule of law and judicial review for safeguarding individual rights have become more prominent. The Swedish constitution was amended in 2011 to give room for a more extensive scope of judicial review and the courts were finally separated from the administration in the Instrument of Government. Notably, the Swedish constitution, like many other national constitutions, now explicitly recognises that Sweden is an active member of the European Union and that Swedish law may not be in conflict with the ECHR. In this sense, Sweden has become a bit more like other European states (where similar changes have occurred as well). At the same time, the Swedish constitution still retains many of the special characteristics from before and some of these, for example, transparency and the parliamentary ombudsman, have served as sources of inspiration for both Member States and EU institutions alike. This is not the place to further onreflect on the merits of European constitutionalism but I believe that there have been ample examples of this added value over the past half-century or so that Europe has been experiencing constitutional pluralism. Given this development, I am inclined to believe that there is actually a slow but steady surge of a common constitutional legal culture (if not yet a deep structure) in Europe. I am, consequently, not as sceptical as Wilhelmsson on the question of whether there could, eventually, be a proper European legal culture or a European *ius commune* based on the common legal principles and fundamental values of Europe[17]

On the other hand, I fully agree with Wilhelmsson that a harmonisation of European private law runs the risk of becoming static and that such a development would indeed be at odds with the ideal of pluralism that lies at the heart of the European project. Constitutional pluralism may in this regard have shown a positive way for private law pluralism. A harmonised body of European private law would run the risk of destroying the emerging *ius commune* much in the same way as the national civil codes destroyed the medieval Roman *ius commune*. The fragmented approach favoured by Wilhelmsson, and similar to that of constitutional pluralism, would also restore private law to its more original Roman form after a 300-year long monogamous affair with *Leviathan*. Constitutional pluralism has served us well; private law pluralism will serve us equally well.

---

[16] This is particularly true of the rights of access to justice laid down in Articles 6 and 13 of the Convention where there is now a considerable degree of similarity in virtually all contracting states.

[17] For an in-depth study of this question see Xavier Groussot, *Creation, Development and Impact of the General Principles of Community Law—Towards a jus commune europaeum* (Faculty of Law, Lund University, 2005).

Index

www.ingramcontent.com/pod-product-compliance
Lightning Source LLC
Chambersburg PA
CBHW061214220326
41599CB00025B/4634